AF540521

FINANCIAL ADMINISTRATION IN INDIA

Changing Contours and Emerging Challenges

FINANCIAL ADMINISTRATION IN INDIA

Changing Contours and Emerging Challenges

Edited by

R.K. GUPTA
Professor of Finance
Panjab University, Chandigarh

and

P.K. SAINI
Director
ICSSR North-Western Regional Centre
Panjab University, Chandigarh

Foreword by

SWAMI (DR.) PARTHASARATHY
D.Litt., Ph.D. (Chicago), MBA (Chicago)
Management Exponent &
Sir Johan Alex Stuart Chair Professor
of International Business, UB., USA

DEEP & DEEP PUBLICATIONS PVT. LTD.
F-159, Rajouri Garden, New Delhi - 110 027

FINANCIAL ADMINISTRATION IN INDIA
Changing Contours and Emerging Challenges

Indian Council of Social Science Research
North Western Regional Centre, Chandigarh
Senior Citizens' Council for Human Resource Development,
Chandigarh

ISBN 978-81-8450-040-0

Typeset by RAHUL COMPOSERS
358, Pocket-B, Phase-II, Sector-16B, Dwarka, New Delhi - 110 075

Printed in India at MAYUR ENTERPRISES
WZ Plot No. 3, Gujjar Market, Tihar Village, New Delhi - 110 018

Published by DEEP & DEEP PUBLICATIONS PVT. LTD.,
F-159, Rajouri Garden, New Delhi - 110 027 • Phone : 25435369, 25440916
E-mail : ddpubs@gmail.com • ddpbooks@yahoo.co.in
Showroom :
2/13, Ansari Road, Daryaganj, New Delhi - 110 002 • Telefax : 23245122

Contents

Foreword

Till the onset of reforms in the early 1990s, India was a relatively closed economy, being largely insulated from the vicissitudes of global markets. It was not, of course, totally insulated from exogenous shocks. The severe drought of 1965 to 1967, the oil shocks of 1973, 1979 and 1989, and wars all had significant effects including the emergence of external payments crises. However, the financial system was effectively controlled, particularly in the 1970s and 1980s and the risk of financial contagion were therefore not high.

The gradual opening up of the economy since the 1990s raised several important challenges. The opening of the external sector meant that developments in India came to be increasingly influenced by developments abroad. As the Finance Minister observed in a lecture at Yale University, whereas India's GDP in 2004-05 was roughly US $ 700 billion, the gross flows on the current account and the capital account, put together, came to US $ 500 billion. This is despite the fact that trade tariffs are still higher than in most other countries in the world, and that capital account controls still exist. The large capital inflows, despite the cautious approach to liberalization, meant that such flows can endanger volatility in exchange rate movements. Exchange rate instability arising from external events can give rise to domestic instability in the operation of the stock market, government securities markets and the money markets along with their attendant effects. For emerging economies such as India, it therefore becomes necessary to institute special defenses for ensuring financial stability.

More broadly however, the period since the 1990s has been testimony to several shocks impinging on the economy. Illustratively, nuclear sanctions and the border tensions in the late 1990s, the monsoon vagaries in the recent past, most recently in 2003, the crises in East Asia in 1997 and 1998, the upheaval in domestic stock markets in May 2004 coupled with the recurrent oil price fluctuations, has meant that the economy has been susceptible to intermittent shocks. And unlike the shocks of earlier decades, the economy has been able to withstand these disruptions with limited impact on the financial sector.

The seminar papers included in procedure, system, sanction, legislation and appropriation of financial resources as per the pre determined priorities of the government, which include the direction of development recommended by the Planning Commission and approved by the National Development Council. The readers can get information of the Financial Administration and Procedure from the papers. Analysis of the past three budgets and the requirements of globalisation process has also been presented. Few others criticize the mismanagement of public finances. The present volume consists of papers presented timely by various experts, professionals, students and faculty.

The compilation—"*Financial Administration in India : Changing Contours and Emerging Challenges*" will do a great service to the people of India to create public opinion in favour of public welfare and not allowing the Government to make investments in wasteful activities. This will serve the purpose of collecting different views and suggestions for proper spending of public money in the changed environment of International Competence and Competition. I convey my wholehearted appreciation to Prof. R.K. Gupta and Prof. P.K. Saini for their excellent task which they have performed and express my strong feeling. This contribution will bring a new dimension to the financial administration in India.

SWAMI (DR.) PARTHASARATHY
D.Litt., Ph.D. (Chicago), MBA (Chicago)
Management Exponent &
Sir Johan Alex Stuart Chair Professor
of International Business, UB., USA

Preface

India today is looked upon as a future super power and the developing world is viewing it with ever growing admiration. For our own good, it is imperative that the country becomes also economically strong in keeping with her enhanced international status. The financial managers of the government coffers can contribute their expertise to realize this cherished dream of a strong and a vibrant India. Historically speaking, the British handed down to us a Mai-Baap government, where the ruled looked up to the largesse of the government for all kinds of benefits. However, the course of economic thinking of the government changed in the early '90s when, learning from the experience of other countries, India and its policy-makers chose to follow market-oriented economic policies. The Planning Commission, since its inception, successive Finance Commissions appointed as necessity arose, and initiation of liberalization of Economy in 1991, have changed the whole spectrum of the concepts and their practice in conducting public finance in India.

With this change in thinking, direction and approach, change also must now be made in the way the government garners and deploys its financial resources. It is in this area that the theme of the book makes a significant contribution by bringing together the rich experience and thoughts of the contributors to this volume.

This volume has taken shape as a result of the National Seminar organized under the title "Changing Contours of

Financial Administration in India: Emerging Challenges". The ICSSR North-Western Regional Centre, and Senior Citizens' Council for Human Resource Development, Chandigarh, organized the seminar from January 27-28, 2005.

In the key note address, Dr. B.P. Mathur, IAAS (Retd.), President of the Senior Citizens' Council was of the view that financial administrators need to come out of legacy of British colonialism which had a peculiar way of conducting the economic affairs of the Country. The Government, in the earlier times, worked on the principle of shortages whereas the private sector functioned on the abundance of resources. He emphasized on cutting deficit in the budget and to have surplus budget like position obtaining in some western countries. He suggested if the country is to progress fast then the financial administrators should be leading the change in the way the Government now seeks to manage its financial resources.

Professor D.D. Narula, former Member-Secretary, ICSSR, New Delhi, in his inaugural address, said that change is the most important aspect in all walks of life but the question is that change should lead us through pre-determined direction and for specified targets of that change. Tracing the economic development of the country since independence, Professor Narula said that at the time of independence, the country had two development models to choose from, the Soviet Model and the British Fabian Socialist Model. Our leaders followed the Soviet Model for economic development and Fabian Socialist Model for Political development. Today, the country has numerous profitable public sector units which are the result of consciously choosing the Soviet Model of import substitution and selfreliance. He was of the opinion that it was because of these policies that the private sector found the right kind of environment to grow and flourish. However, from the 5th Plan onwards, the efficiency of the public sector undertakings came to be questioned; they were fast becoming a source of creating deficits rather than surplus for the State. Therefore, from the 80s onwards, our economic policy-makers moved towards economic liberalization, greater participation of the private sector, withdrawing gradually from the public sector. This process is not yet complete and may take some time but the direction, nevertheless, is unmistakable, i.e. creating climate where private sector grows and flourishes, and in consonance with that progress, the Government also changes the way in which it manages its financial resources.

Professor K.N. Kabra, in his paper on "Some Ideas for a People-Friendly Budget—2005-06" declared that in common parlance, 'administration' and 'management' are polymeric but analytically both have some similarities and also differences. Both share reliance on instrumental rationality but substantive rationality remains largely a function of social relations, institutions, historical and global context. Hence, the fact that financial administration and financial management can not be differentiated so sharply—hence the continuity. The elements of change are, however, unmistakable at many levels—e.g. research, pedagogy. Both financial administration and management came to acquire pedestrian character among the excessive, if not exclusive, pre-occupation with descriptive accounts of constitutional—legal provisions, rules, etc. This tendency is not confined to academia alone—it also serves the forces of *status quo*.

Some of the important changes in post-liberalization phase have been fiscal crises of the States, state failure leading to loss of ownership of fiscal policy, administration and management. There is a need for a consistent policy framework to build state's capacity to extract financial resources by using effective means which do not stifle the normal operations of the economy.

Shri S.C. Pandey, IAAS, Officer on Special Duty, Department of Economic Affairs and Dr. J.S. Mathur presented a paper on "Budgetary System in the Government". Their major concern in the presentation was the proportion of tax to GDP which was being divided amongst the Centre and the States. He highlighted the fact that 80% of the GDP is used to service debt. There is an asset-liability mismatch. They spoke in great detail on the major planks of budget reforms like zero-based budgeting, convergence/consolidation of public expenditure portfolio and minimizing Central Government's role as financial intermediary. Another major area of presentation in their paper was devoted to the Expenditure Reforms Commission which was established for appraisal of Centre's and State Governments' expenditure. Measures for increasing the tax base and simultaneously reducing the tax rates also formed an important part of their presentation. The Economic Reforms in the light of the fiscal responsibility and budget management Act 2003 was also discussed at length.

Professor Manoj K. Sharma from the University Business School, Panjab University, Chandigarh, in his paper on "Tax Reforms in India", discussed at length the annual budgets of the Union Government for the last five years, the change in life style, change in socio-cultural environment of the society and causes of change in the market pattern, managerial issues and problems of fiscal consolidation and the contribution of Budget towards fiscal consolidation.

Professor R.K. Gupta from DCS, Panjab University, in his paper on "Taxes and Public Finance" suggested that rates of corporate tax should be reduced. The slabs on personal tax should be rationalized. A tax rebate for rearing of two children (treating it as social responsibility) should be introduced in the hands of parents. He also suggested that the scope of tax deduction at source should be increased. He emphasized on some changes in VAT and service tax.

Professor Som Deo, Deptt. of EAFM, University of Rajasthan, Jaipur presented a paper on "Fiscal Management in India: Walking on a Tight Rope". He discussed in detail the fiscal deficit. His main concern was centred around the component, configuration and proportions of fiscal deficit. He elaborately discussed how to reduce the policy rigidities. His overriding concern was how to achieve the set targets of FRDM Act. His main recommendation was that, instead of the FRDM Act, there should be a Political Responsibility and Budget Management Act.

Professor Pawan Kumar Taneja discussed in detail about "Agricultural Income Tax : A Blame Game" in his paper. He discussed the need of Agricultural Income Tax and brought into focus the problems that would crop up in imposing the Agricultural Income Tax. He suggested various measures to regulate taxation on Agricultural Income.

Praneet Rangi and Swarnjit Kaur, in their paper on "New Dimensions of Budgeting Process in India" discussed that Government is seen reshaping the future of our country. It is more of a facilitator than a provider of services. The paper covers two major developments, the move from traditional budgeting to outcome budgeting and the incorporation of fiscal responsibilities in the budgeting exercise.

Dr. B.P. Mathur discussed, in his paper on "Expenditure Management—A New Paradigm", about Expenditure Management and Budgetary Reforms in this session. He emphasized that money is powerful source but a very bad master. He emphasized on performance and reduction of size of debt, i.e. 5 to 8% of budget may be planned to be surrendered every year. There is need of strengthening of control mechanism in State Governments in regard to spending of excess over grants.

A paper titled "Management of Public Expenditure—A Performance Orientation" was presented by Dr. Anjali Anand Srivastava, Professor of Finance, National Institute of Financial Management, Faridabad. Her main thrust was on finding whether inefficiencies exist in the system and what the quantum of inefficiencies, lack of planning, etc. are there. She was of the opinion that lack of planning as well as delays in decision-making is the cause of loss of substantial public funds. There are deficiencies in identification of beneficiaries of public support, she said. She further said that the objectives are not clearly stated nor are these observed meticulously. She pointed out that there is deficiency in the system of delivery of funds and there is mismatch between receipts of funds and need in terms of adequacy as well as timeliness. She further discussed methods to improve performance of public expenditure. She said that there is need of "private-public conscious partnership" in delivering better services to the target sector. She emphasized upon the need of stronger civil society. She showed her concern over the aspects of efficiency and control, means versus ends and direct involvement versus regulation. She discussed how operational efficiency could be achieved. Overall emphasis by her was on Result-based system, Flexibility in Rules, Empowerment of Agents of change and Accountability of Results.

Mr. Rajan Kashyap, IAS (Retd.) formerly Chief Secretary to the Government of Punjab, reflected on "Private Sector Participation in Economic and Social Infrastructure". He said that traditionally governments have accepted direct responsibility for building up infrastructure in regard to railways, roads, power, air-ports, water supply etc. However, if the country is to break free from the projected growth rate of 6% and 7%, then it would require investments of the order of 7,500 billion rupees for the plan period 2001-06. He was of the view that in order to make social infrastructure strong, the responsibility of day-to-day functioning of the same had to be passed on to local elected bodies such as Panchayats. He said that decentralization in the Government tends to strengthen service delivery in the shape of better health service, better education service and need-based development at the local level.

Mr. Jagbans Singh, IAAS, Financial Adviser and Chief Accounts Officer, Bhakra Beas Management Board, in his paper on "Public-Private Partnerships in Economic and Social Infrastructure", said that the public sector had done good service during the early years but it has now failed to deliver the promised services as expected of it. Also, the experience of some states to deliver these promises through the route of privatization has also not been happy either. He was of the opinion that we need to tread a middle path where the responsibility of the Government is utilized to deliver the services with the efficiency of private entrepreneurs, that is to introduce professionalism in the public sector.

Professor (Ms.) Perminder Khanna, in her paper "Development of Economic Infrastructure: Public and Private Participation", highlighted that, in the market-oriented system, achieving a target of 8 per cent growth of Gross Domestic Product against a backdrop of slow growing Agriculture and Infrastructure sectors is highly skeptical. Hence, the reforms process is a pre-requisite for attaining the desired targets, thus stressing the urgent need of a 'change' from inefficiency under the present system to efficiency by way of private participation in development, of the economic infrastructure particularly relating to the exploitation/exploration of coal, oil and electricity. Persistent energy shortages clearly reflect inadequate investment. Demand Management of Energy takes a backseat in the domestic consumption and requirement as well as in sectors like agriculture, manufacturing, commercial and transport. The entire gamut of management of energy supply *vis-a-vis* its demand through a country-wide network under the governmental nodal agency as also with the co-operation of the private sector can go a long way to help India to become self-reliant in energy in the near future.

Professor Janak Raj Gupta presented a paper on "Pricing of Public Services and Return on Investment". He said that there could be no uniform formula whereby costs incurred by the Government could be recovered from the users. The decision to price public services had to be made keeping in view the utility and social use of a service.

Professor B.S. Ghuman presented a paper on "Major Sources of Revenue of the Central Government : The Indian Experience". He said that over the years, the income sources of the Government have been shifting from custom duties to service tax. The indirect taxes have contributed a major share to the tax revenues of the Government. However, in the post-reform period, the share of direct taxes is on the rise.

Dr. P.K. Vasudeva and Ms. Monika Aggarwal, in their paper on "Capital Account Convertibility in India", discussed Prime Minister Manmohan Singh's suggestion to revisit the issue of convertibility. The RBI had constituted an Expert Group under the Chairmanship of S.S. Tarapore, the ex-Dy. Governor of RBI and an Economist of Standing. The issue of convertibility of the rupee is back to Centre stage with the Reserve Bank of India releasing the Tarapore Committee's report in March 2006. The more recent report advocates a three-phased approach, the first phase beginning this year (2006-07), the second during 2007-09 and the last ending 2011. Even before the rather lengthy report of the Tarapora II Committee could have been assimilated, there have been strong reactions to it. At this stage, full capital account liberalization promises large benefits while it increases the risk of the liberalization of short-term loans. The step may enhance costs that outweigh the benefits. Venations in the flow of short-term capital, like bank loans, give rise to recycling of the capital account, which provides the main mechanism (velocity of money) by which free capital flows create problems (expansion of money supply in the economy, setting in inflationary trends). For the next 10 years at least, they said, many other liberalizing reforms need to take priority for bringing about growth and stability of economy over capital account liberalization.

Mr. D.P.S. Rathore in his article on "Corporate Governance and Policy Framework in Indian Banking Sector—A Bird's Eyeview" emphasized that there is divergence in the understanding and practice of Corporate Governance in general and in respect of banks in particular across the World.

At the outset, Professor Shital Parkash, Former Professor of Public Administration and Managing Director, Senior Citizens' Council for Human Resource Development, Chandigarh, welcomed the participants and gave brief introductions of the paper presenters.

Shri P.K. Saini, Director (In-charge) ICSSR North-Western Regional Centre, Chandigarh, presented a paper on "Reforms with Human Face". He has discussed the economic reforms and the growth rate of economy. He has evaluated the Budget of 2004-05 and the effects of the various welfare schemes on the common man.

Shri S.C. Pandey, IAAS, Officer-on-Special-Duty, Department of Economic Affairs presented a paper on "Sustainability of Public Debt". He discussed in detail fiscal and revenue crisis both at the Centre and the State level. He suggested various measures and how we can bring down the fiscal deficit, cost of debt and achieve the sustainable growth.

Shri G.I. Diwan, Consultant and Faculty, International Trade and Finance, Chandigarh, in his paper on 'Management of Forex Reserves : Innovations and Opportunities' has emphasized on various sources of Foreign Exchange Reserve. He has identified the various sources of reserve accumulation and put forward some innovative ideas for using the reserve. He discussed the degree of comfort at various levels of reserve and the opportunities linked with the degree of comfort.

R.K. GUPTA
P.K. SAINI

List of Contributors

Dr. B.P. Mathur, IAAS (Retd.), Formerly Deputy Comptroller and Auditor General of India and Director, National Institute of Financial Management, Faridabad. # 1621, Brahmputra Apartments, Sector-29, Noida.

Jagbans Singh, IAAS, Financial Adviser and Chief Accounts Officer, Bhakra Beas Management Board, Madhya Marg, Sector 19-B, Chandigarh.

Professor Janak Raj Gupta, UGC Emeritus Fellow, Department of Economics, Punjabi University, Patiala.

Professor Som Deo, Professor of Economic Administration and Financial Management, University of Rajasthan, Jaipur.

S.C. Pandey, IAAS, Officer on Special Duty, Department of Economic Affairs, Ministry of Finance, Government of India, New Delhi.

J.S. Mathur, IAAS (Retd.), Formerly Additional Secretary (Budget), Ministry of Finance, Government of India and Member Secretary Expenditure Reforms, #7485, Sector 10-B, Vasant Vihar, New Delhi.

Professor B.S. Ghuman, Chairman, Department of Public Administration, P.U., Chandigarh.

Prof. (Ms.) Anjali A. Srivastava, IAAS Professor and Financial Advisor, National Institute of Financial Management, Faridabad.

Mr. Rajan Kashyap, IAS (Retd.), Formerly Chief Secretary, Government of Punjab, Chandigarh, 131, Sector 10-A, Chandigarh.

Professor Kamal Nayan Kabra, Formerly Professor of Economic Administration, Indian Institute of Public Administration, New Delhi, B-202, Purvasha-Anand Lok, Mayur Vihar, Phase-I, New Delhi.

Dr. Praneet Rangi, Lecturer in Commerce, DAV College, Sector-10, Chandigarh.

Ms. Swarnjit Kaur, Lecturer, Department of Correspondence Studies, P.U., Chandigarh.

Dr. P.K. Vasudeva, Professor, (International Trade), ICFAI Business School, Chandigarh and Principal, College of Communication and Management, Bharatiya Vidya Bhavan, Chandigarh.

Ms. Monika Aggarwal, Research Scholar, University Business School, P.U., Chandigarh.

Dr. (Ms) Perminder Khanna, Professor of Economics, Department of Correspondence Studies, P.U., Chandigarh.

Professor R.K. Gupta, Professor of Financial Management, DCS, Panjab University, Chandigarh.

Dr. Manoj K. Sharma, Professor of Business Management, University Business School, Panjab University, Chandigarh.

Dr. Pawan Kumar Taneja, Asstt. Professor, IIMT-OBU, 336, Udyog Vihar, Phase-IV, Gurgaon.

Dr. G.I. Dewan, Consultant and Faculty, International Trade and Finance, Chandigarh.

Mr. P.K. Saini, Director (In-charge), ICSSR N.W. Regional Centre, P.U., Chandigarh.

D.P.S. Rathore, Regional Director, Reserve Bank of India, Chandigarh.

PART I

Budgeting Challenges Including Budgetary Reforms

Some Ideas for a "People-Friendly" Budget

KAMAL NAYAN KABRA

While various rounds of open lobbying for the budget 2005-06 are over and the Finance Ministry presumably is at an advanced stage of making its the budget, one would never know when and if the real, effective round of clandestine and subtle lobbying would ever come to an end. After all, many roll backs follow the budget and some are carried out with an extra-ordinary alacrity, like, for instance, the adjustment in the turnover tax on the stock market transactions following the last budget. The whole package, one may recall, was recast according to the wishes of the share market operators, especially sensitively according to the needs of the day traders who impart depth, road casino character, to the share markets. Coming to think of the budget, 2005-06 and the likely announcement of a slew of non-fiscal policy initiatives which now routinely lace the budget speech—a major media event of the year—one may factor in a number of influences that will leave their mark on the exercise. Loudly reiterating commitment to carry forward the so called reforms will have to be married to the main human face imparting features of the National Common Minimum Programme (NCMP).

The near nullification of the Employment Guarantee Programme (EGP) in the law placed before the Parliament clearly shows the clout of the financial pundits, supported by the army of pink press commentators, practitioners of Carlyle's dismal science who want that if the programme can not be fully jettisoned, it should be substantially watered down to become another name for the discredited and ineffective rural public works programmes and at as low a wage rate as the market of livelihoodless labour, with voice until the next general election, may be made to accept. As against this, choice of the components of the 'reform' agenda clearly shows close behind the scene confabulations with their beneficiaries. In addition, the commitments flowing from the FRMB Act will surely be an overriding influence. Anyone familiar with the supply-side, anti-statist fiscal orthodoxy advocated by the World bank-IMF duo for the borrowing-dependent, fiscally-impotent poor countries would know who the owners of this piece of legislation with its different avatars reigning over the annual budgetary exercise of dozens of countries are. It is ironical indeed that none of the fiscal responsibility provisions would apply to the US with its ballooning fiscal deficit of nearly 6 per cent, as rest of the world, including India, bends over backwards to finance it at very low of interest and of their own apparent volition! One need not refer to the shared domination of the fiscal processes by a tiny domestic minority. This formidable combine seems to overpower the present fragility of the ruling coalition at the Centre; otherwise it is difficult to understand the ineffectiveness of the Left in the determination of the policies of the UPA government. Apparently, the danger of communal back-lash has many uses for the hegemonic classes! What comes out clear and sharp is that the two presently effective alternative political formations competing for power at the Union level have tacit understanding to stand by the same policy package, sans its packaging and labeling. In this context, the value of any alternative set of budget proposals is basically restricted to popular mobilization and intellectual sphere lest hopelessness and despondency takes over.

Howsoever dim their prospects of acceptance, one must state the basic concerns which actuate the alternative proposed in the following. Given the major casualties of the present economic policies in general and fiscal policies in particular, one can unhesitatingly vote for equity, employment and environmental improvement as the major national goals which any real democratic processes and structures would like to address. With almost doubling of the annual rate of growth of GDP after the 'reforms', the rate of growth of employment has come down to one-third of its earlier none-too-healthy level. Similarly, there is clinching evidence of the sharp deterioration of distributive justice. This can be seen in sharp decline in the share of farm output to as low a level as nearly one-tenth of the incremental GDP recorded during the Ninth Plan. Massive increase in the market capitalization of the listed companies has fortuitously enriched a few lakh shareholders and with only negative effects on the rest of society. This is related to the rising share of non-mass consumption luxury goods and rich man's services in our GDP. With nearly 75 per cent of the population without purchasing power large enough to permit the purchase of food, satisfying minimum calories needed for survival, relying on the NSS figure of people below poverty line is simply perverse. Let alone reckonable positive steps for environmental improvement, even the degradation inherent in our present system, has not been addressed. The dismal picture of education and health, in so far as the common citizens are concerned, further adds strength to any set of proposals assigning the highest priority to the triple objectives of equity, employment and environment. One wonders when evaluating the budget on the evening of 28th February, how many commentators would remember these national goals.

As for employment, acceptance of the improvement suggested by the National Advisory Council and allocating adequate funds for guaranteed 100 days of work to everyone who opts for working at the regional minimum wage is not just an instance of political honesty, but a major corrective of the development strategy seen so far. It would generate a steady flow of widely dispersed demand for food and other goods originating from local and small scale production to generate large and regular addition of employment opportunities in a dynamic manner over time. These programmes have to be used for creating productivity-enhancing assets for the small and marginal farmers, obviously under the aegis of self-help groups and Panchayats, keeping our parasitic bureaucracy at an arm's length. Other strong candidates for selection under the EGP are local level environmental protection and social and economic infrastructure works leading to better sanitation, equipping of schools and all-weather link roads and paving of the intra-village pathways (just to mention a few), diversification of the sources of work and income generation. This measure thus could lead to substantial improvement in the quality of life and initial empowerment of the socially and economically deprived population. Equity thrust in the tax policy has found no place in dozens of tax reform proposals making the rounds. If there ever was time for going full steam ahead with the NCMP item of raising the tax ratio, it is now when the first full budget of the UPA is going to be unfolded. Equity can be attained by curbing the incessant growth of non-work, rentier incomes and inherited wealth, especially held in unproductive and asocial forms, like the huge packages granted to themselves by the CEOs of the corporate sector or the tax-free dividends in the hands of the controlling interests of the companies. How can one justify thousands of times higher than per capita income tax-free dividend for any one individual, let alone the non-comparable magnitude of such private income flows compared to the poverty-line income which also is decades away for majority of the Indians? Re-introduction of inheritance tax and giving some real meaning to wealth tax can not weaken any body's incentives for work enterprise and innovation, while, to an extent, weakening the pull of inordinately huge incomes on the allocation of resources especially foreign exchange in the form of import of bullion, luxury goods with rather high import-intensity and a growing penchant for foreign travel and its use as a means for import of consumer goods.

One has to bid good-bye to an unscientific notion that the goals of a real break-through in favour of massive livelihood security and pro-poor policies and against runaway concentration of income and wealth can go on merrily hand in hand, and even that the latter may by means of trickle-down processes, help the poor in an elusive long-run.

An equally unambiguous decision has to be made that one can not at the same time tax a commodity heavily and subsidise it as well. The reference is to the petroleum products, mainly kerosene and cooking gas, which are claimed to be heavily subsidized, but are, in fact, heavily taxed. Similar contradiction is involved in adopting user charges for public and quasi-public services like health and education which have strong elements being merit services as well.

One hopes that the coming budget lives up to the spirit of the NCMP and avoids the trap of so called fiscal 'reforms' sponsored and supported by some multilateral financial institutions.

Fiscal decisions which are motivated by the largest good of the largest number over a long enough time horizon are difficult decisions. In our country lately, it has become fashionable to term anti-people, especially anti-poor decisions as 'hard decisions'. Overly sensitive attitude to the stock market equity price response in the wake of the budget is a sure indicator of anti-democratic credentials of any regime. The manner in which unproductive casinofication of the economy has been encouraged by such speculator-friendly policies has led to hyper growth of futures trading of about Rs. 2 lakh crore annually in many essential commodities in recently started commodity exchanges. In these exchanges, actual physical deliveries are generally under 2 to 3 per cent of the total turnover, indicating not only the dominance of speculators but also virtual absence of the victims of price volatility, that is, the farmers, stockists and exporters or processors who are genuinely interested in hedging against wayward price behaviour. In addition to extending regulatory controls over these exchanges and elimination of sensitive essential commodities from futures speculation, it is also imperative that this unproductive, speculative trade is brought under the tax net on par with the share market.

The obligations under the FR an BM Act must be met by an increase in the tax effort and curtailing of wasteful revenue expenditure, including that on providing unconscionable ostentation at the cost of public exchequer. A powerful attack on both hoarded black wealth and massive generation of black incomes, including their smashing away in various tax havens, facilitated by the reigning liberal external openness, have to avoid the folly, seen so often in the past, of rewarding dishonesty by going for varieties of amnesty schemes. One general principle of considerable relevance in our kind of highly inequality-ridden society, especially for framing budget proposals, is to avoid uniform treatment to various highly unequal entities, whether on the expenditure side or resource mobilization side. Such uniformity conceals and fosters tremendous perverse differentiation repugnant to our national ethos. Even if one is unlikely to see hardly anything of the foregoing in the coming budget, their merits or demerits need debate and discussion.

Budgetary System in the Government

J.S. MATHUR AND S.C. PANDEY

INTRODUCTION

Under Article 112(1) of the Constitution, Government (Ministry of Finance) is required to present to the Parliament, every year, an *Annual Financial Statement* giving details of its estimated receipts and expenditure during the ensuring financial year. In common parlance, this Statement is known as Budget. The Budget requires the approval of the Legislature to enable the Government to raise revenues through taxation and incur expenditure from the Consolidated Fund. The Budget is not merely a statement of receipts and expenditure. Over the years, the Budget has become an important instrument of policy pronouncement by the Government, both in the areas of taxation and important schemes and programmes of Government. It has also become an important occasion for performance evaluation and assessment of the direction in which the policies of the Government are oriented.

SALIENT FEATURES OF THE INDIAN BUDGETARY SYSTEM

- Financial Year is from 1st April to 31st March and the budget is generally presented on the last working day of February every year.
- Constitution mandates legislative control on taxation and government expenditure.
- Constitution enables legislative control on government borrowings. "Fiscal Responsibility and Budget Management Act, 2003" was passed by Parliament in August 2003 but the date of its enforcement was left to the discretion of the Government. The Act and the Rules made under the Act have been brought into force on 5th July 2004.
- Constitution mandates annual reporting to Parliament of estimates of receipts and expenditure in the ensuring year.
- Expenditure is distinguished between Revenue (recurring) and Capital (non-recurring, asset creating); Plan (generally developmental in nature) and non-Plan (generally non-developmental in nature); Voted (the expenditure for which the demand can be accepted, rejected or reduced by the Lower House of Parliament) and Charged (special items of expenditure in respect of which Parliament's control is limited to debate and discussion).
- Under a standing legislative arrangement, indirect tax proposals contained in a budget come into effect immediately and are required to be considered by Parliament within 75 days. The period is utilized in a general discussion on budget in both the Houses of Parliament, examination of individual Ministries' budgets by the Standing Parliamentary Committee and full House discussion on expenditure and taxation proposals before its approval.
- No demand of funds for any expenditure can be brought before Parliament unless recommended by the President. Power of the Lower House is limited to accepting, rejecting or reducing any demand in respect

of "Voted" expenditure. Parliament does not have the power to modify the demands put forth by the Executive.

- Parliament's approval to government expenditure is in terms of statutory ceilings on expenditure. The expenditure need not necessarily be funded.
- Government of India has a single account with the Reserve Bank of India. Individual Ministries/ Departments are not authorized to maintain separate bank accounts. However, designated officers are authorized to maintain imprests, which are recouped from time to time after rendering account.
- Pending approval of expenditure demands, Parliament gives the government temporary authorization to spend moneys from the Consolidated Fund on ongoing activities through a "Vote on Account". In exceptional circumstances where compliance with normal legislative requirements of presenting and passing the budget is not expedient and these need to be short-circuited, Parliament can approve "Vote on Credit" or "Exceptional Vote".
- Certain re-appropriations require prior Parliamentary approval, while certain others require ex-post reporting to Parliament. Re-appropriation from Revenue to Capital and *vice versa* and from Voted to Charged and *vice versa* requires Parliament's approval.
- There is a Contingency Fund created out of the Consolidated Fund under an Act of Parliament, which can be used by the President to meet unforeseen requirements of expenditure pending *ex-post facto* approval of Parliament.
- Government budget and accounts are on cash basis. Gradual shift towards simultaneous reporting on accrual aspects of public finance is contemplated in the fiscal transparency aspects of the FRBM Act.
- Ministry of Railways presents its Demands for Grants separately as the "Railway Budget" but the General Budget presented by the Minister of Finance is the Budget mandated under the Constitution for the Government of India as a whole including Railways.

Hence, it includes the receipts and expenditure of the Railways on aggregate basis.

Consolidated Fund

It consists of all revenues received by Government, loans raised by it and the receipts from recoveries of loans given by the Government. All expenditure of Government is incurred from the Consolidated Fund. However, no expenditure from the Consolidated Fund can be incurred without authorization from Parliament.

Contingency Fund

It is in the nature of an imprest placed at the disposal of the President to incur urgent and unforeseen expenditure pending authorization from Parliament. At a subsequent date, the Government obtains the approval of the Parliament for incurring such expenditure and for withdrawal of an equivalent amount from the Consolidated Fund to recoup the amount to the Contingency Fund. At present, the corpus of the Contingency Fund is Rs. 50 crore.

Public Account

This part of the Government accounts records the transactions in respect of which Government acts more as a banker. Examples are: transactions relating to provident funds, small savings collections, other deposits, etc. Since the funds kept in the Public Account do not belong to the Government, which acts only as banker in relation to these funds, approval of Parliament for payments from the Public Account is not required. The Public Account also contains certain earmarked funds created by debit to the Consolidated Fund to meet the expenditure on specific objects like sugar development, replacement of depreciated assets of commercial undertakings, etc. The transfer of the funds is done with the approval of Parliament and subsequently the details of the actual expenditure are submitted for vote of Parliament.

THE BUDGET DOCUMENTS

The Budget documents presented to the Parliament consist of the following:

1. Annual Financial Statement.
2. Demands for Grants.
3. The Finance Bill.
4. Speech of the Minister of Finance (Part A and B).
5. Key to the Budget Documents.
6. Budget at a Glance.
7. Receipts Budget.
8. Expenditure Budget—Volume I.
9. Expenditure Budget—Volume II.
10. Memorandum explaining the provisions in the Finance Bill.
11. Macroeconomic Framework Statement, Fiscal Policy Strategy Statement and Medium-term Fiscal Policy Statement presented for the first time with Budget 2004-05 (July 2004) as required under the Fiscal Responsibility and Budget Management Act, 2003 effective from 5th July 2004.

Annual Financial Statement

This is the main Budget document. The Annual Financial Statement shows the receipts and payments of Government under the three parts in which Government accounts are kept: (i) Consolidated Fund, (ii) Contingency Fund, and (iii) Public Account.

Demands for Grants

The estimates of expenditure from the Consolidated Fund included in the Annual Financial Statement are submitted in the form of Demands for Grants in pursuance of Article 113 of the Constitution. These are required to be voted by the Lok Sabha to enable the Government to incur expenditure. Generally, one Demand for Grant is presented in respect of each Ministry or Department. However, in respect of large Ministries or

Departments more than one Demand is presented. Each Demand normally includes the total provisions required for a service, that is, provisions on account of revenue expenditure, capital expenditure, grants to State and Union Territory Governments and also loans and advances relating to the service. In regard to Union territories without Legislature, a separate Demand is presented for each of the Union Territories, where the provision for a service is entirely for expenditure charged on the Consolidated Fund, for example, interest payments, a separate Appropriation is presented. Appropriation refers to an expenditure that is not required to be voted by Parliament whereas an expenditure proposed as a Demand is required to be voted by the Parliament. In case the expenditure on a service includes both voted and charged items of expenditure, the latter are also included in the Demand presented for the service but the voted and charged provisions are shown separately in the Demand.

The Demands for Grants are presented to the Lok Sabha along with the Annual Financial Statement. Each Demand first gives the totals of voted and charged expenditure as also the revenue and capital expenditure included in the Demand separately and also the grand total of the amount of expenditure for which Demand is presented. This is followed by the estimates of expenditure under different major heads of account. The break up of the expenditure under each major head between Plan and Non-Plan is also given. The amounts of recoveries taken in reduction of expenditure in the accounts are also shown. A summary of Demands for Grants is given at the beginning of this document, while details of New Service or New Instrument of Service such as formation of a new company, undertaking a new scheme etc., if any, are indicated at the end of the document.

FINANCE BILL

The Finance Bill contains the proposals of Government for levy of new taxes, modification of the existing tax structure or continuance of the existing tax structure beyond the period approved by Parliament. To facilitate understanding of the taxation proposals made in the Finance Bill, the provisions of the Bill are explained in the *Memorandum explaining the provisions in the Finance Bill.*

Other Budgetary Documents

The Budget documents presented in terms of the Constitution have to fulfil certain legal and procedural requirements and hence may not by themselves give a clear indication of the major features of the Budget. To facilitate an easy understanding of the Budget, certain explanatory documents are presented along with the Budget. These are described below.

Key to the Budget Document

This gives an overview of the Budget documents presented.

Speech of the Minister of Finance

Part A of the Speech sets out the economic context and the Budget strategy. It dwells on the various sector of the economy and spells out the policy parameters proposed by the Government to address the sector specific issues. Part B of the Speech pertains to the tax proposals in respect of both the indirect and direct taxes.

Budget at a Glance

It shows in brief the receipts and disbursements along with broad details of tax revenues and other receipts. It also exhibits broad break-up of Plan and Non-plan expenditure, allocation of Plan outlays by sectors as well as by Ministries/Departments and details of resources transferred by the Central Government to State and Union Territory Governments. This document also shows the revenue deficit, the gross primary deficit, the budgetary deficit and the gross fiscal deficit of the Central Government. These concepts have been explained in the chapter on the deficits. In the budget documents, gross fiscal deficit and gross primary deficit are, in short, referred to as fiscal deficit and primary deficit, respectively.

Receipts Budget

Estimates of receipts included in the Annual Financial Statements are further analyzed in the Receipts Budget. The document consists of two parts: Part A gives details of revenue receipts and Part B gives details of the capital receipts and explains the estimates. Trend of receipts over the years and details of External Assistance received are also included.

Expenditure Budget—Vol. I

It deals with revenue and capital disbursements of various Ministries/Departments and gives the estimates in respect of each under Plan and Non-Plan categories. These also give analysis of various types of expenditure and broad reasons for the variations in estimates. It serves as an explanatory memorandum to the expenditure part of the Budget of the Central Government. It is divided into three parts: Part I—General, Part II—Non-Plan Expenditure and Part III—Plan Outlay. Under the present accounting and budgetary procedures, certain classes of receipts, like payments made by one department to another and receipts of capital projects or schemes are taken in reduction of the expenditure of the receiving department. *The estimates of expenditure included in the Demands for Grants are for the Gross amounts while the estimates of expenditure concluded in the Annual Financial Statement are for the net expenditure as will be reflected in the accounts, that is after taking into account the recoveries.* The Expenditure Budget makes certain other refinements like netting expenditure of related receipts so that inflation of receipts and expenditure figures are avoided. In separate Annexures, guarantees given by Central Government and outstanding as at the end of March of the preceding financial year and contributions to International bodies are shown. A statement showing the estimates of strength of the establishments of various Government Departments and provision made for it is also included.

Expenditure Budget—Vol. 2

The provisions made for a scheme or a programme may spread over a number of major heads in the Revenue and Capital sections in a Demand for Grants. In the Expenditure Budget—Vol. 2, the estimates made for a scheme/programme are brought together and shown on a net basis at one place by major heads. To understand the objectives underlying the expenditure proposed for various schemes, programmes, etc., in the Demand for Grants suitable explanatory notes are included in this volume in which, wherever necessary, brief reasons for variations in the estimates are also given.

Detailed Demands for Grants

The Demands for Grants are followed by the Detailed Demands for Grants laid on the table of the Lok Sabha some time after the presentation of the budget, but before the discussion on Demands for Grants commences. These detailed Demands for Grants show further details of the provisions included in the Demands for Grants as also of actual expenditure during the previous year. A breakup of the estimates relating to each programme/organization, wherever the amount involved is not less than Rs. 10 lakhs, is given under a number of object heads which indicate the categories and nature of expenditure incurred on that programme, like salaries, wages, travel expenses, material and equipment, grants-in-aid, etc. At the end of these Detailed Demands are shown the details of recoveries taken in reduction of expenditure in the accounts. Physical and financial aspects of major programmes and schemes are included in the performance Budgets presented to Parliament separately by the Ministries/Departments.

The Statements Required to be laid under the FRBM Act

These include *Macroeconomic Framework Statement* detailing the underlying assessment of growth prospects and the macro-economic considerations that guided the Budget making. It defines the macroeconomic backdrop under which the fiscal policies and projections are being made. *The Medium-term Fiscal*

Policy Statement specifies three-year rolling targets for prescribed fiscal indicators, and the underlying assumptions. *The Fiscal Policy Strategy Statement* specifies the policy measures pertaining to taxation, expenditure, subsidies, administered prices and borrowing.

Performance Budget

Performance Budgets are prepared and circulated to Members of Parliament by all Ministries/Departments dealing with developmental activities. The Performance Budget presents the budget of the Ministry/Department in terms of functions, programmes and activities and gives appraisal reports separately in respect of major central sector projects/programmes estimated to cost Rs. 100 crores or more. It also includes a statement on the programmes and performance of the various public sector undertakings or autonomous bodies under the Ministry/Department indicating, among other things, the capacity installed and utilized, physical targets and achievements, results of operation, return on capital, etc. Performance Budget serves as a tool of administrative and financial control in the implementation of development programmes.

Public Sector Enterprises Survey

A large part of the Plan expenditure incurred by the Central Government is through public sector enterprises. Budgetary support for financing outlays of these enterprises is provided by Government either through investment in share capital or through loans. Expenditure Budget—Vol. 1 shows the estimates of capital and loans disbursements to public sector enterprises for Plan and Non-Plan purposes and also the extra-budgetary resources available for financing their plans. A detailed report on the working of public sector enterprises is given in the document titled Public Enterprises Survey brought out separately by the Department of Public Enterprises. A report on the working of the enterprises under the control of the various administrative Ministries is also given in the Annual

Reports of the various Ministries circulated to Members of Parliament separately. The annual reports along with the audited accounts of each of the Government companies are also separately laid before Parliament. Besides, the reports of the Comptroller and Auditor General of India on the working of various public sector enterprises are also laid before Parliament.

Annual Report

A descriptive account of the activities of each Ministry/ Department during the previous year is given in the document "Annual Report" which is brought out separately by each Ministry/Department and circulated to Members of Parliament at the time of discussion on the Demands for Grants.

Economic and Functional Classification of the Central Government Budget

The Budget of the Government has an impact on the economy as a whole. For a better appreciation of the impact of governmental receipts and expenditure on the other sectors of the economy, it is necessary to group them in terms of economic magnitudes, for example, how much is set aside for capital formation, how much is spent directly by the Government and how much is transferred by Government to the sectors of the economy by way of grants, loans, etc. This analysis is contained in the document, "Economic and Functional Classification of the Central Government Budget" which is brought out by the Ministry of Finance separately.

Appropriation Bill

Under Article 114(3) of the Constitution, no amount can be withdrawn from the Consolidated fund without the enactment of such a law by Parliament. After the Demands for Grants are voted by the Lok Sabha, Parliament's approval to the withdrawal from the Consolidated Fund of the amounts so voted and of the amounts required to meet the expenditure charged on the Consolidated Fund is sought through the Appropriation Bill.

Vote on Account

The whole process beginning with the presentation of the Budget and ending with discussions and voting on the Demands for Grants requires sufficiently long time. The Lok Sabha is, therefore, empowered by the Constitution to make any grant in advance in respect of the estimated expenditure for a part of the financial year pending completion of procedure for the voting of the Demands. The purpose of the vote on account is to keep the Government functioning pending voting of final supply. The vote on account is obtained from Parliament through an Appropriation (vote on Account) Bill.

Statement of Action Taken on Budget Announcements

This contains status of initiatives announced by the Finance Minister earlier.

Tax Reforms in India

MANOJ K. SHARMA

I. POST-INDEPENDENCE ERA

After attaining Independence in 1947 and on declaration of India as a Democratic Republic Welfare State, ways and means were thought and sought to levy and collect additional revenues to enabling the Government to meet the cost of governance, internal security, defence and for welfare measures of teeming millions grinding in abject poverty. On the recommendation of Prof. Kaldor, wealth-tax, gift-tax, expenditure tax and estate duty were levied. In early sixtees, an humble citizen was required to pay tax on income—maximum rate being 97.5%; tax rate on wealth being 2-3%; tax on expenditure, tax on gift, tax on death by way of estate-duty—as direct taxes apart from sales-tax, central sales-tax, excise duty, customs duty, and other indirect taxes. India earned the name of a highly taxed country. Much of the Indian funds started flowing to Swiss Banks. Menace of evasion of tax and proliferation of black money started. Paying high taxes, in some cases more than 100% by way of tax became unproductive with no incentive to work.

On the assassination of our beloved Prime Minister, Smt. Indira Gandhi, Shri Rajeev Gandhi took over as Prime Minister in the year 1984. It was found that over-all impact of direct taxes and indirect taxes had been substantial, confiscatory and agonizing. To set right the mistakes, to create an atmosphere as well as climate where an honest tax-payer may dare to declare true, correct and full income, a number of remedial measures were taken. The Finance Act, 1985 substantially reduced the maximum rate of income-tax and wealth tax; estate duty and interest tax were abolished and certain provisions against concept of real income were withdrawn. The paper on Long Term Fiscal Policy was placed before the parliament. Long Term Fiscal Policy was formulated.

Prof. Madhu Dandavate, Minister of Finance, Government of India, placed the maiden budget of the National Front Government before the Parliament on 19th March, 1990, practically three weeks after the normal date. A sensible step taken was to abolish the Gold Control Act. Shri Yashwant Sinha took over as the Union Finance Minister. He could not place the Union Budget before the Parliament on 28.2.1991. The economic condition of the country was in a very bad shape. Balance of Payment position became precarious. Our country was likely to be declared as "defaulter" in meeting International liabilities. Letters of credit opened by Indian Banks were not being readily accepted by the foreign banks. To meet the situation, the Union Government had to disposed of 22 tonnes of gold which was sent outside India in the month of July, 1991. The fiscal deficit in the year 1989-90 was Rs. 35,630 crores, which increased to 43,331 crores in 1990-91. Overall deficit was at an alarming figure of 11,347 crores in the year 1990-91. The foreign exchange reserves dipped down to equivalent of merely Rs. 2600 crores.

With the advent of Congress rule in the centre under the leadership of Shri P.V. Narasimha Rao, Dr. Man Mohan Singh, a noted economist, was inducted as Union Finance Minister. He placed his maiden budget before the Parliament on 24.7.1991. He had to take very hard decisions. Union government proceeded on the path of liberalization with speed. Dr. Man Mohan Singh continued to carry forward the path of liberalization. Wealth-tax was reduced on commercial assets by enhancing threshold limit to Rs. 15 lacs, reducing the number of tax payers falling in the net to less than 10%. Maximum rate of income was reduced to 40% in 1994. It has now been reduced to 30%. Gift Tax has been abolished. A number of Commissions and Committees for reforms were constituted. Suggestions were implemented in part thus distorting the form and substance of economy.

Tax on agricultural income remained in State list. Such tax existing in certain States was abolished. States could not dare to levy tax on agricultural income in spite of recommendations and suggestions of economists. Agricultural rich became richer. New levies by way of house-tax, land and building tax, professional tax, entry tax, service-tax, interest-tax, luxury tax and many more taxes were levied. There was a race in the Union and States to invent, evolve and coin new names for levy by way of tax, cess, duty, fee, charge, etc. It became necessary to meet the cost of establishment, salaries, interest, payment of debts and to bear with scams, scandals, wasteful expenditure and unaccountability, negligence and arrogance at all levels. An honest and humble citizen felt victimised and considered it as extortion and price for civilization.

2. THE INCOME TAX ACT

The Indian Income-tax Act, 1922 was repealed and replaced by the Income-tax Act, 1961. The objective was to make it more effective; to eliminate the menace of evasion of tax; to levy and collect due taxes as envisaged in Article 265 of the Constitution of India. "Nothing more and Nothing less"; to give due honour, recognition, dignity, and samman to the tax payers and to enrich the national exchequer for providing drinking water, food, cloth and shelter to the weaker sections of society. Numerous amendments, modifications, additions, deletions, insertions have been made to the Act and Rules during the last 41 years. The length and width of the Act has been extended and expanded more than 50 times with numerous Circulars, Instructions, Notifications, and Press releases. The Income Tax Rules, 1962 contains forms, Rules and Regulations, such rules are tinkered with in less than a few months. Every Finance Act contains several amendments followed by changes in rules and forms. In less than five years Amending Act was enacted. It is a formidable task to keep a track of such plethora of legislation. Even jurists, judges and experts have to keep every year's edition handy, while giving and formulating opinion, what to think of the plight of a normal and an ordinary humble law abiding tax payer.

3. THE TAX LAWS

The Tax Laws are complicated, complex and highly technical. Interpretation of tax laws is very much painful and difficult. An honest effort has been made during the past ten years to simplify and rationalise the tax laws. However, it is too difficult a task particularly when tax laws are interpreted and construed by a fairly large number of intelligentsia but are made by a very few persons in number. Lately, there has developed a tendency to amend tax laws frequently and retrospectively on a slight provocation as to misuse by ignorable few. Amendments are made, very often retrospectively, to nullify the view expressed by the Hon'ble Supreme Court. Such amendments are made on the pretext that view expressed by the Apex Court is against the intention of the legislatures but it is more tainted with the wishes of the bureaucrats. It may be legal but surely immoral and unethical. It does not very much affect the national exchequer but puts a greater injury to a citizen of this great democracy. It shakes faith of the tax payers in tax laws, puts hurdles to voluntary compliance and drags the tax payers to adopt unethical means. Making way simpler towards such dirty path is not in public interest.

4. EXPANSION AND RESTRUCTURING

Till early seventies, the Great Income Tax Officer had to issue notice for advance tax, call for returns, examine, scrutinise, verify and on satisfaction frame an assessment, collect tax, give appeal effect, issue refund vouchers, rectify orders and make recoveries. Every assessment was a scrutiny assessment. Assessment Orders used to be well knit and well discussed. The tax professionals used to derive pleasure. Atmosphere was homely, calm and quiet with mutual respect and trust. It was difficult to identify the perverse tax authority with malafides and bad motives of personal gain. If such qualities were found in an Appellate Authority, it used to carry a stigma and persons used to disassociate.

First Appeal lay to Appellate Assistant Commissioner and there was no post of Commissioner of Income-tax (Appeals). In mid-sixtees, for the first time, post of Commissioner of Income-tax. (Administration) for whole of the State of Rajasthan was sanctioned. Concept of Commissioner of Income-tax (Appeals) came into existence in 1978. Direct Tax Laws (Amendment) Act, 1987 inserted the posts of Chief Commissioner, Deputy Commissioner in the list of Income-tax Authorities. Additional Commissioner, Joint Commissioner were added from 1.6.1994 and 1.10.1998, respectively. Thus, presently, ten classes of income-tax authorities exist in Section 116 of the Act, against less than one-third in late sixties. There has been further restructuring last year (2004), under the regime of former Union Finance Minister, Hon'ble Shri Yashwant Sinha, a bureaucrat turned politician, expanding the tax administration and giving whole-sale promotions to the existing authorities. Now, the State of Rajashtan alone has three Chief Commissioners of Income-tax, apart from Director General of Income tax (Administration). Commissioners of Income-tax (Appeals) are 23. Number of Joint Commissioners, Additional Commissioners, Deputy Commissioners and Assistant Commissioners is in abundance. The same is the position in other States of India, particularly every city with a population above 5 lacs is having a Commissioner of Income-tax and other tax authorities below him.

To reduce the workload on an Assessing Authority, the philosophy of doing away with issue of notices for advance-tax and furnishing of return, provisions for tax audit by technically qualified Chartered Accountants, self-assessment, payment of tax and interest, scrutiny in less than 3% cases and that too only in survey, search and other specified category of cases, was introduced. Powers of assessment were conferred on Assistant Commissioners, Deputy Commissioners, Joint Commissioners and higher authorities, and upon lower authorities on approval from the higher authorities. In spite of restructuring, entailing heavy cost on establishment like salaries, etc., tax collections last year were short by about Rs. 20,000 crores and collection cost increased to about 3.6%.

5. PRESENT SCENARIO

With unprecedented re-structuring bringing about extension in tax net, a tax payer is unable to find out in which Ward his/her case falls. Records are in a mess. Old records are untraceable. Even PAN Numbers are not issued on time. Refunds are abnormally delayed. Those concerned with rectifications and appeal effects, have to be reminded again and again. Some of the Officers do not have proper place to hold office peacefully. Staff for administrative work is in plenty but very little number to assist an assessing Officer for assessment. The 'Great Income Tax Officer' cannot frame special assessment in search cases and his jurisdiction in other cases has been substantially curtailed. With what result—Fall in collection ? It is apparent and patent that there is no accountability. Transparency is absent. Work culture is wanting. Discipline has reached the lowest ebb. Right hand does not know what the left hand is doing. Corruption is at its peak. Many officials possess in tons and lead aristocratic life, accountable to none, not even to oneself. Image of the tax administration has been irreparably tarnished. A respected tax collector is under shadow of suspicion. Honest officers are sufferers. Their number is negligibly low. However, I salute such bold, duty conscientious, disciplined sons of the soil who are still, though few in number but holding their ground according desired standard of discipline, integrity and honesty.

Corruption is a cancer eating into the roots of the society. It is difficult to fight against corruption because the chances of success are bleak but this is no reason for despondency. Nobody is born corrupt, it is the vitiated atmosphere in the society and the system of governance which converts the clean into the corrupt. An honest person resists corruption but allurements and temptations at times prevail upon him and once corrupt, even an honest person prefers and finds it convenient to stay corrupt. The seeds of corruption are sown in the mind of the man and the cure, if any, lies in eradicating the seeds of corruption from his mind. An honest revenue official says, "The honest are hounded; they are humiliated; they are ignored; they are manipulated: they are used, they are punished; they become the laughing stock in society and in their families: even their very honesty is suspected". In spite of that, there are many many honest officers in the department who remain honest against all odds. They are a special species; they have to be preserved and protected.

Efficiency and expeditious disposal of cases are absent. Papers do not move. Petitions remain unacknowledged. No decision is taken in spite of repeated reminders. It is required of a tax-payer to make petition again and again and to forward it to the Vigilance Cell, Unending time, energy and money is required, simply to be wasted by a tax-payer. Though it is unlikely that the tax collector shall collect only such tax which is legitimately leviable and due and it is equally unlikely that the taxpayers would pay the tax which is legally due. But there is always a need for the above said authorities to resolve the disputes of the tax collectors and tax-payers in orderly manner. It is for the tax administration to evolve ways and means whereby an honest, upright and clean tax-payer is provided atmosphere to remain honest and clean and is not dragged to the path of corruption. The tax-payers are not basically corrupt but are corrupted on account of ill-treatment received at the hands of the tax administration.

Reforms by Recent Finance Ministers

Manmohan Singh

Dr. Manmohan Singh, the chief architect of India's economic reforms, reduced the top income-tax rate further to 40 per cent in his Budget for 1992-93 and compressed the slabs to just three. He also acted on Chelliah Committee recommendations and scaled down the corporate tax rate to 40 per cent in 1994-95 and reduced the number of exemptions. In his 1994-95 Budget, Dr. Manmohan Singh extended the reforms to indirect taxes by chopping the number of excise duty rates by half and making a major transition to *ad valorem* rates and reducing substantially the myriad end-use specific concessions.

He also brought down the Customs duty rates drastically between 1991 and 1995, the peak tariff rate falling from over 200 per cent to 50 per cent.

P. Chidambaram

Thereafter, Mr. P. Chidambaram took the bold step of reducing the marginal rate of personal income-tax to 30 per cent in his "dream Budget" of 1997-98. He also reduced the rate of company taxation to 35 per cent for Indian firms, and to 48 per cent for foreign outfits from 55 per cent. He also announced a rationalisation of excise duties, lowered the peak Customs duty rate from 50 per cent to 40 per cent.

Yashwant Sinha

Mr. Yashwant Sinha carried forward the process of tax reforms by reducing the number of excise duty rates from 11 to one—that is, 16 per cent Cenvat. However, because of the introduction of a number of exceptions and special rates, there remained a wide gap from the goal of a single-rated retail stage VAT.

The objectives of tax reforms were to simplify the rules and procedures, lower the tax rates and widen the tax net so as to ensure better compliance and raise the tax-GDP ratio. However, despite lowering the tax rates and doing away with many of the rigidities, the successive governments have not been able to widen the tax net and strengthen the tax administration. Agricultural income is totally out of the tax net, and services, which today account for a little over 50 per cent of GDP, are also largely out of the tax net. The recent efforts to extend the tax net to services have met with little success. The Centre's tax-GDP ratio has, in fact, fallen from 10.10 in 1989-90 to 9.10 in 2001-02.

Available evidence suggests that there is large-scale evasion of both direct and indirect taxes. In the case of personal income-tax, almost the entire burden falls on the salaried class, as the tax is deducted at source. Traders, businessmen, transport operators and professionals hardly pay any income-tax and a majority of them remain out of the tax net. According to data compiled by the Finance Ministry, of the 28.2 million income-tax assesses, not more than 6.2 million, or 22 per cent, had an income of Rs. 1-4 lakh, and not more than 3 per cent above Rs. 4 lakh. And this in a country where the sales of cars and other luxury goods have been booming.

In the case of indirect taxes, there is evidence of large-scale evasion of excise duties, particularly by small-scale units, and of Customs duties by way of duty drawback benefits based on manipulated invoices. Consequently, while there has been a small improvement in direct tax collections following a little widening of the base, indirect tax collections actually declined over the past 12 years. The Kelkar panel proposals need to be evaluated against this backdrop of declining tax-GDP ratio over the past decade and the urgent need to increase the gross-saving-to-GDP ratio to set-up the growth rate of the economy during the Tenth Plan. In respect of direct taxes, the panel's proposal to raise the exemption limit on personal income tax to Rs. 1 lakh will not provide any relief to taxpayers, particularly the salaried, as it is to be accompanied by abolition of standard deduction and all tax exemptions on specified investments.

Doing away with standard deduction is unfair and would amount to discrimination against salary earners, as it is intended to provide relief against expenses incurred for earning salary such as travel, purchase of books, and so on. When professionals and those in business are allowed all kinds of expenses, why should the salary earner be denied the same?

By not providing any real relief to taxpayers, the proposals would result in some 75 per cent of assesses going out of the tax net. In other words, the number of persons coming under the tax net will come down drastically to around seven million compared to 12 million in 1990-91. Since India's income-tax base is as yet too small, it would be imprudent to leave 75 per cent of the assessees out of the net, after all the efforts made to widen the net over the past decade.

A better course would be to keep the current 10 per cent slab for the lower income group by raising the exemption limit to, say, Rs. 60,000 from the present Rs. 50,000 without disturbing the tax exemption regime. In fact, some experts have suggested an additional slab of 5 per cent at the entry level in order to reduce the tax burden on those in the Rs. 1-1.5 lakh income category.

The Kelkar panel proposals also include other unfavourable provisions, such as phasing out the deduction for mortgage interest in respect of loans for acquiring a owner occupied dwelling by 2006-07; eliminating income-based deduction under Section 80L for interest income and dividend; and removing Section 88C rebate for women taxpayers below the age of 65. The unkindest cut is proposed for senior citizens, by doing away with the Section 88B rebate. They will also be denied rebate on medical expenses.

The proposal to withdraw tax breaks on housing loans is retrograde, as it would deny the salaried middle-class the opportunity to have a house of their own. This would also hit the housing sector hard.

Known for its employment-generation potential, this is one sector that has started looking up despite the prevailing recessionary conditions in the economy. Even in the West, where housing is not as acute a problem, exemptions are provided for housing mortgage and servicing payments.

The unjust and retrograde proposals prompted the Finance Minister, Mr. Jaswant Singh, to state that the Government cannot renege on commitments made to the taxpayers and that the exemptions given to promote employment and investment in the infrastructure sector, particularly housing, will not be rolled back.

If the existing tax incentives on specified savings are abolished, there is a real danger of the savings rate in the economy falling and affecting the investment rate. The need of the hour is to make all-out efforts to raise the savings and investment rates and push up the growth rate of the economy as proposed in the Tenth Plan.

One should not blindly follow the developed country models and abolish the incentives for savings. Rather, we should be guided by the policies pursued by the newly industrialising economies (NIEs) of Asia to actively promote savings.

For instance, the average gross savings rate in the 1990s was 47.6 per cent of GDP in Singapore, 40.6 per cent in Malaysia, 40.7 per cent in China and 35.4 per cent in the Republic of Korea compared to 23 per cent in India. Incidentally, East Asia has relatively low rates of taxation, which are applied to high rates of incomes. According to some tax experts, if the prevailing tax incentives are abolished, the savings rate in India could fall to below 20 per cent. Unfortunately, because of a number of retrograde and controversial proposals, even some of the more sensible and pragmatic suggestions are likely to be ignored. These include the proposal to set-up a national Tax Information Network (TIN) on a build, operate and transfer (BOT) basis; implement a State-level VAT by April 2003 and move to a two-slab Customs duty structure by 2005 (20 per cent on finished goods and 10 per cent on raw materials); reduce the peak Customs tariff to 25 per cent from 30 per cent by 2003-04; and abolish dividend tax, minimum alternative tax (MAT), wealth tax and long-term capital gains tax.

Notwithstanding the many shortcomings, it is a matter of some satisfaction that the two consultation papers of the Kelkar Committee may not be a futile exercise after all. They have generated widespread debate on the desired roadmap for further reforms in the tax system and helped in moving towards greater transparency in the Budget-making exercise, which continues to be shrouded in too much secrecy.

"The maximum revenue collection with the minimum expenditure in transaction costs is the chief goal of indirect taxation, and reallocating such resources is an important objective. But taxation reforms have to keep in mind the macro-problems of unemployment, casualisation of labour, uncertain and unexpected conditions of production, and their human aspects", points out P.R. Brahmananda.

Revenue collection with the minimum of expenditure by the government in the transaction costs of collection is one of the goals of indirect taxation. There is also the important objective of reallocating the direction of expenditure on commodities, (goods and services) and, hence, of resources. The allocative function of indirect taxation is also important.

Import duties can primarily be for revenue purposes or also for protecting domestic industry. Normally, export duties are not generally levied, but when they are, the object is to take for the government a portion of the benefits of booming exports. The revenue goal is equally important here as in the case of import duties. Indirect taxation also helps keep down inflationary pressures.

In recent years, there has been a worldwide process of reductions of the levels of import duties. This process has been pushed forward by the World Trade Organisation (WTO). The fundamental idea is that high import duties in any country disturb the allocation of resources from the global angle and also distort domestic allocations of resources. The reallocative goal in regard to resource flow directions is now gaining dominance in discussions on the subject.

The developing countries that had high import duties, both from the angle of revenues and as a protective device, are being asked or being forced to reduce the levels of their duties, so that ultimately these levels must be uniform on similar imports and that is probably the distant objective. It is believed that the efficient use of the world's resources will thus be considerably improved. Consequently, it is expected that the growth rate of world trade will be higher than otherwise and this, in itself, is supposed to help production and growth in all countries, including developing ones.

Recent Suggestions on Tax Reforms

Kelkar Report on Tax Reforms

Highlights

- Income tax exemption limit should be hiked to Rs. 1 lakh from Rs. 50,000.
- Two slabs of 20 per cent for income Rs. 1-4 lakh and 30 per cent beyond Rs. 4 lakh proposed.
- Additional tax reliefs for senior citizens and widows and doubling of exemption under 80CCC.
- Standard deduction should be eliminated.
- Surcharge should be removed.
- Interest payment upto Rs. 50,000 on home loans should be exempted and interest subsidy offered.
- Income tax on agriculture.
- Corporate tax should be 30 per cent.
- Elimination of tax incentives under section 10A, 10B of I-T Act.

- Lifting of dividend tax and capital gains tax.
- Depreciation rate should be reduced to 15 per cent from 25 per cent.
- Customs duties should be reduced to 10 per cent for raw materials, inputs and intermediate goods and to 20 per cent for consumer durables by 2004-05.
- Custom duty for coal, ores and other raw material should be reduced to five per cent, capital goods, basic chemicals to eight per cent by 2006-07.
- Custom duty on crude oil should be reduced to eight per cent and 15 per cent for petroleum products by 2003-04 and further to five and 10 per cent, respectively, by 2004-05.
- Higher duty of 150 per cent for specified agri-products and demerit goods.
- Complete exemption of customs on life saving drugs, equipments, Defence-related goods and imports by RBI.
- All exemptions should be removed except for life saving goods, security items, relief and charitable goods and international obligations.
- Excise duty should be 14 per cent for most items, 20 per cent for motor vehicles, air-conditioners and aerated water.
- Excise on processed food products should be reduced to 6 per cent while exempting life saving drugs, security items, and agri-products.
- Excise on petroleum products should be fixed after quarterly reviews.
- Central excise duty on kerosene should be raised by Rs. one per liter.
- Uniform duty of 16 per cent for textile fibre and yarn, which should be reduced to 14 per cent by 2004-05, 12 per cent duty on all fabrics till 2004-05.
- Duty exemption for SSIs with turnover upto Rs. 50 lakh.
- Nationwide value-added tax and a comprehensive service tax from April 2003.

Reactions

The reactions to the recommendations of the two high-level task forces headed by Dr. Vijay Kelkar, Economic Advisor to the Finance Ministry, on reform of direct and indirect taxes have been mixed. While some have hailed them as sweeping and "big bang", others have termed them half-baked prescriptions that are too harsh on the honest tax-payer and not in conformity with the basic objectives of tax reforms.

Considering the time given to the panels to frame their recommendations, they had to do a rush job, drawing heavily on some of the earlier committees. Even so, it is rather surprising that they have failed to address some of the crucial issues and challenges that have already been discussed threadbare by some of the earlier committees, more recently by the Planning Commission Advisory Group on Tax Policy and Tax Administration.

In this context, it would be worthwhile to briefly review the efforts by different governments in recent years to reform the country's tax system and see if the reforms introduced thus far have had the desired effect. Serious efforts in this direction were made for the first time in the second half of the 1980s, when Mr. V.P. Singh's Budget for 1985-86 introduced the concept of long-term fiscal policy (LTFP) and committed the government to implementing a modified system of value-added tax (Modvat). The LTFP had stated : "A broader base taxation . . . combined with moderate rates of taxes and stricter enforcement can yield better revenue results." Mr. Singh also acted swiftly to implement Modvat for the first set of industries in his 1986-87 Budget. The system of Modvat was gradually extended to cover virtually the whole of industry. The 1985-86 Budget reduced the personal income-tax slabs from eight to four and cut the top marginal rate to 50 per cent from the absurdly high levels prevailing earlier.

6. THE TASK FORCE

Task force on Direct Taxes had been constituted by the Ministry of Finance, Department of Revenue, under the Chairmanship of Dr. V.L. Kelkar to make suggestions to simplify the system of the direct taxes. All India Federation of Tax Practitioners organised National Tax Conference at Indore on September 7-8, 2002 with the theme: *"Tax Scenario—Performance And Expectations"*. It is conducting survey of more than 5000 professionals asking their view on the various administrative issues. It is conducted seminar on 12th of December, 2002 with the theme subject in Mumbai from 24th to 26th of December, 2002 with the theme subject of "From Tax Evolution to Economic Revolution—Role of the Tax Professionals". One of the topics, kept for discussion, was 'Model Tax Law and Tax Administration'. It submitted a memorandum for the consideration of the task force dealing with : (1) Conceptual framework; (2) Specific changes; and (3) increasing monetary limits; to assist in preparing draft consultation paper. I hope effective steps must have been taken to bring back the mutual trust and mutual respect in between the tax administration, tax payers and the tax professionals.

7. EXPECTATIONS

The Assessing Officers should be courteous, well behaved and should give respect to the tax-payers. They should repose confidence in and should trust the tax-payers and the tax consultants. They should understand the problems and difficulties of the tax-payers, their approach should be humane. The tax-payer should be treated as a friend. Adequate and proper opportunity of explanation, representation and adducing of evidence should be afforded. After complete scrutiny, verification, satisfaction and application of mind, detailed and speaking orders should be passed.

8. THE TAX PAYERS

Larger section of the tax-payers is not upright, honest, straight-forward and does not pay taxes fully and correctly. The tax-payers should have a desire and will to understand and comply with the legal obligations—One should seek advice, help and guidance of the tax Department; should keep to the right side of the thin line dividing tax avoidance and tax evasion; and should refrain from concealing income or resorting to colourable devices to circumvent the law. It should be noted that tax evasion is never a paying proposition, the fear of penalty and prosecution, harassment and inconvenience and cost of litigation shall be much more than the savings on tax. It is humble duty of every citizen to pay taxes voluntarily, promptly and fully. One should adopt such ways and means whereby he may live peacefully and honourably, should feel pleasure and pride in payment of due and legitimate taxes, should not carry any fear from the authorities, and should not hesitate in expressing grievances and inconveniences before the tax administration. Those who evade taxes, lead a precarious life and live on mercy of the tax authorities. It is not dignified living and should not be the aim of a proud citizen of India.

9. THE EVIL OF TAX EVASION

There is no denial of the facts : evasion of tax is rampant, proliferation of black money is vast, parallel economy is creating havoc, there lay ample provisions of tax laws to check evasion but the collecting administration machinery has utterly failed in putting a check on tax evasion. When I analyse the reasons, I believe—(a) there is constant erosion of human values; (b) there is no education of tax laws; (c) no social stigma is attached, on the contrary tax evaders having money power and vast resources get respect in the society; (d) disclosure schemes are frequently announced practically every fifth year during the last 45 years; the latest is the Voluntary Disclosure of Income Scheme, 1997, surpassing all the past Schemes by giving a golden opportunity to tax evaders to convert black money into white on nominal and substantially reduced tax; (e) there lay provisions conferring discretion and power to reduce, waive or not to levy interest, penalty nor prosecute, etc.; (f) innumerable deductions, reliefs, incentives and exemptions providing a tool to reduce effective rate of tax; (g) wasteful expenditure at Government level; and (h) no accountability for the tax administration. It is high time that ways and means to stop evasion of tax are evolved and effective measures taken.

10. TAX MANAGEMENT

A rupee of tax saved is much more than the rupee of income earned. After understanding the tax laws, availing of various exemptions, deductions and incentives provided under the tax laws and resorting to tax planning, many tax-payers could promote their resources and prosper. Some could earn the status of zero tax Companies. Brunt of taxation can be substantially reduced by adopting proper tax planning. Reduction in taxes improves cash flow. Tax planning is sound moral law and certainly not bad morality to so arrange one's affairs as to reduce the brunt of taxation to a minimum arranging commercial affairs in such a manner that charge of tax is minimized. Availing various recognised methods of tax planning is lawful and has the sanctity of the courts. Avoidance of tax is not tax evasion. End effect of tax planning, tax avoidance and tax evasion is one and the same but tax evasion alone deserves to be depreciated and need not be resorted to. Adopt Tax Planning, Not Evasion. Tax Management is inherent right and not bad morality.

11. SUGGESTIONS

Existing Tax Laws contain powerful armoury in the hands of the tax authorities to eliminate and eradicate menace of tax evasion. However, tax evasion is rampant, there is no fear of the tax administration. The tax payers consider that tax authorities are manageable. Tax net has loose ends and big holes to escape taxation. Following suggestions need to be discussed, deliberated and necessary resolutions need be passed and forwarded to the Union and State Finance Minister(s) for consideration and appropriate action:

(1) Levy of tax on Agricultural Rich;
(2) Deductions and Exemptions;
(3) Work Culture;
(4) Work Conditions;
(5) Accountability and Transparency;
(6) Treatment with the Tax Payers;

(7) Abolition of Amnesty, Voluntary Disclosures, Samadhan and such other Schemes.
(8) Utilisation of Revenue Collections; and
(9) Education of Tax payers and Social stigma on tax evaders and corrupt tax collectors.

12. CONCLUSIONS

It is heartening to find that the Hon'ble Supreme Court and various High Courts are taking cognisance of high-handedness on the part of the tax authorities and levying cost and damages. It deserves to be charged from the wrong-doer and a black mark put on his Character Report. It is opportune time to handle the endemic menace with strong measures and bold decisions. I would like to conclude by reproducing the loud and significant observations of the Hon'ble Supreme Court in the case of Panna Lal Brijraj as early as in 1957: "A human and considerate administration of the relevant provisions of the I.T.-Act would go a long way in allaying the apprehensions of the assessee and if that is done in the true spirit, no assessee will be in a position to charge the Revenue with administering the provisions of the Act with an evil eye and unequal hand". In my humble view, what is needed is an introspection by the tax authorities and to evolve ways and means whereby to change work culture for public good and in public interest.

References

Tax Reforms in India, N.M. Ranka, Senior Advocate.
http://www.financialexpress.com/about/feedback.html
http://fecolumnists.expressindia.com/fullcolumn.php
Tinkering with Tax Reforms, by S.D. Naik.
The Radical Path to Tax Reforms, by Udayan Ray.
India's Economic Reforms, by Tanweer Akaram.
Economic Times.
Macro-economics, by Johnson and Mathew Adms.

Taxes and Public Finance

R.K. Gupta

INTRODUCTION

The notification of Fiscal Responsibility and Budget Management (FRBM) Act in August 2003 and its rules framed under it in July 2004 streamlined the process of the presentation of the Union Budget. Government finances witnessed some improvement in 2003-04, reflecting the robust macroeconomic performance and the commitment towards sustainable fiscal conditions. All the key deficit indicators, viz., gross fiscal deficit, revenue deficit, and primary deficit of the centre in the revised estimates as well as in the provisional account for 2003-04 turned out to be lower than their budgeted levels, facilitated by higher revenue realization and containment of non-plan expenditure.

An overview of the combined finances of the centre and the states shows an improvement in 2003-04 on account of a lower growth in aggregate expenditure *vis-a-vis* non-debt receipts. Some of the Fiscal Management Achievements during 2003-04 are as follows:

- Borrowings declined by 27% from Rs. 459 crore in 2002-03 to Rs. 334 crore in 2003-04.
- Interest outflow significantly reduced by 40% from Rs. 64.43 crore to Rs. 58.48 crore.
- Debt equity ratio strengthened from 1.6 to 1.0.

The publication of Task Force Report (TFR) in July 2004 on Fiscal Responsibility and Budget Management has thrown up a number of issues that need further reflection. In India, there is an urgent need for improved management of "national finances"—specially the public finance—which includes budgetary problems, resource mobilization, allocation and financial services.

Since the subject is very vast and complex, in this paper, I will be concentrating only on resource mobilization, i.e. through direct and indirect taxes.

WHAT IS A TAX?

Tax is an involuntary fee or, more precisely, "unrequited payment", made by individuals or businesses to a government (central or local).

PURPOSES AND EFFECTS OF TAXATION

Governments Collect Taxes

- to support the operation of that government itself;
- to influence the macroeconomic performance of the economy (the government's strategy for doing this is called its fiscal policy);
- to carry out the functions of the government, such as national defence, and providing government services;
- To redistribute resources between individuals or classes in the population; and
- To modify patterns of consumption or employment within an economy, by making some classes of transactions more or less attractive.

Types of Taxes

There are two types of taxes.

(i) *Direct Tax*: That are paid by the people or organizations on whom they are imposed, e.g. income tax, wealth tax, corporation tax etc.
(ii) *Indirect Tax*: It is borne by someone other than the person responsible for paying them, e.g. excise duty, custom duty, service tax.

- Contribution of taxes to gross national product in India is 9.2% whereas it is 35% in UK, 23% in USA, 23% in Japan and 19% in Canada. Keeping in view the low disposable income in India, tax burden is not low. Table 4.1 shows the break-up of tax structure in India as compared to other countries.

TABLE 4.1

		Direct	Indirect
(a)	India	*Direct*	*Indirect*
	During 1950-51	36.8	63.2
	During 2002-03	28.3	71.7
	During 2003-04	40.3	59.7
	During 2004-05	44.0	56.0
	During 2005-06	46.0	54.0
(b)	England	55%	45%
(c)	Japan	70%	30%
(d)	Australia	70%	30%
(e)	U.S.A.	67%	33%

The table shows that the contribution of direct taxes is more in other countries as compared to indirect taxes, whereas in India, it is totally reverse. The contribution of indirect taxes is more.

Of late, the Government has taken diverse steps to increase the share of direct taxes and to reduce the burden of indirect taxes over a period of the last or few years.

Fiscal Projections in India

Table 4.2 shows the fiscal projections in India from 2003-04 to 2008-09. It depicts that revenue receipts which were Rs. 263027 crore in 2003-04 are expected to increase to Rs. 404021 crore in 2007-08. Simultaneously, total receipts, which were Rs. 427653 crore are expected to grow to Rs. 607151 crore in the same period. At the same time, total expenditure which was Rs. 427653 crore in 2003-04 is expected to increase to Rs. 607151 crore in 2007-08. Table depicts that fiscal deficit of Rs. 132103 crore in 2003-04 will increase to Rs. 187041 crore in 2007-08.

Table 4.3 shows the share of Gross Tax revenues to the GDP from 2003-04 to 2007-08. It has increased from 9.19% to 10.32% in the same period. During the same period, percentage to revenue receipts increased from 71.30% to 81.87%.

Tax Projections in India

Table 4.4 shows the Tax projections in India. It depicts that the share of Direct Taxes which was 40% in 2003-04 is expected to increase to 54% up to the 2008-09. Simultaneously, the share of indirect taxes will decrease from 60% to 40% during the same period, which is in consonance with Government objectives. The share of service tax in indirect taxes is expected increase from Rs. 8300 crore to 21244 crore during 2008-09. It is the service area where Government is concentrating more in the present environment. The total gross taxes, which were Rs. 254923 crore in 2003-04, are expected to increase to Rs. 515052 crore during 2008-09. It can be concluded that there is good growth in the increase of tax revenues both in Direct and Indirect Taxes.

Table 4.5 shows number of tax assessees in India. Total number of new assessees are increasing over the last ten years. During the year 1998-99, 1/6 scheme was introduced by which the number of assessees increased to 41.68 lakh as compared to previous year's 23.32 lakh. The Finance Minister, in his budget speech 2005, pointed out that in India 3.4 crore persons are filing Income Tax Returns, out of which only 2.7 crore assessees are tax payees. It means there is need to strengthen the tax structure to extend the base further.

Further, Table 4.6 shows the rank and number of individual assessees with income of Rupees ten lakh and more in India as

TABLE 4.2
Fiscal Projections in India

(*Rupees in Crores*)

Sr. No.	*Particulars*	*2003-04 (RE)*	*2004-05 (BE)*	*2005-06*	*2006-07*	*2007-08*
(1)	*(2)*	*(3)*	*(4)*	*(5)*	*(6)*	*(7)*
1.	GDP	2772194	3104857	3477440	3886039	4332934
2.	Gross Tax Revenue	254923	317733	338155	388479	447463
3.	Revenue Receipts 4+5	263027	309322	323538	360480	404021
4.	Tax Revenue, Net to Centre	187539	233906	248990	286659	330787
5.	Non-tax Revenue	75488	75416	74548	73821	73234
6.	Capital Receipts	164626	168507	189891	199719	203130
7.	Recoveries of Loans	18023	27100	13395	12725	12089
8.	Other Receipts	14500	4000	4000	4000	4000
9.	Borrowings and other Liabilities	132103	137407	172496	182994	187041
10.	Total Receipts	427653	477829	513430	560198	607151
11.	Non-plan Expenditure	306146	332239	349175	374886	398082
12.	Interest, Debt Servicing	124555	129500	143970	158659	173427
13.	Defence	60300	77000	71762	78027	84839
14.	Susidies	44707	43516	44497	43924	39883

(*Contd.*)

TABLE 4.2 (Contd.)

(1)	(2)	(3)	(4)	(5)	(6)	(7)
15.	Grants, Loans to States, UTs	15850	19576	21181	22450	23797
16.	Other Non-plan Expenditure	60734	62647	67765	71827	76136
17.	Plan Expenditure	121507	145590	164255	185312	209069
18.	Total Expenditure	427653	477829	513340	560198	607151
19.	Revenue Expenditure	362887	385493	414214	451945	489825
20.	Capital Expenditure	64766	92335	99214	108252	117325
21.	Revenue Deficit	99860	76171	90676	91466	85804
22.	Fiscal Deficit	132103	137407	172498	182994	187041

Abbr. GDP : Gross Domestic Product.
BE : Budget Estimates.
RE : Revised Estimated.
Source : Report of the Task Force, July 2004, Ministry of Finance, Govt. of India.
Year : Period of fiscal year in India is April to March, e.g. year shown as 1990-91 relates to April 1990 to March 1991.
Units : (a) 1 Lakh (or lacs)= 100000.
(b) 1 Crore (or Cr.) = 10000000.

TABLE 4.3

Fiscal Projections in India
(2003-04 to 2008-09)

(Rs. in Crores)

Year	*GDP*	*Gross Tax Revenue*	*% GDP*	*Revenue Receipts*	*Tax Revenue net to centre*	*% to revenue receipts*	*Fiscal deficit*
	(1)	*(2)*	*(3)*	*(4)*	*(5)*	*(6)*	*(7)*
2003-04 (RE)	27,72,194	2,54,923	9.19	2,63,027	1,87,539	71.30	1,32,103
2004-05 (BE)	31,04,857	3,17,733	10.23	3,09,322	2,33,906	75.62	1,37,407
2005-06	34,77,440	3,38,155	9.72	3,23,538	2,48,990	76.96	1,72,496
2006-07	38,86,039	3,88,479	9.96	3,60,480	2,86,659	79.52	1,82,994
2007-08	43,32,934	4,47,463	10.32	4,04,021	3,30,787	81.87	1,87,041

B.E.—Budget Estimate, R.E.—Revised Estimate.

Source: Compiled from report of the Task Force, July 2004, GOI.

TABLE 4.4
Tax Projections In India

(Rupees in Crores)

Particulars	2003-04 (RE)	2004-05 (BE) (BE)	2005-06	2006-07	2007-08	2008-09	Growth 04-05-08-09
(1)	(2)	(3)	(4)	(5)	(6)	(7)	(8)
Direct Taxes	103400	137000	154258	188283	229066	277667	21.8
Income Taxes	40269	50009	58458	69842	83299	99000	19.7
Corporation Tax	62986	86846	95800	118441	145767	178667	23.1
Indirect Taxes	151523	175823	178298	193764	210988	229743	8.6
Excise	92379	107699	107897	117791	128733	140691	8.7
Customs	49350	53500	55281	59039	63288	67843	6.5
Service Tax	8300	14000	15120	16934	18967	21244	20.6
Gross Tax Collection	254923	312823	332556	382047	440054	507410	14.7
Education Cess	0	4910	5599	6432	7408	8542	
Total Gross Taxes	254923	317733	338155	388479	447463	515952	15.0
GDP at Market Prices	2772194	3104857	3477440	3886039	4332934	4820389	11.0

Abbr. GDP : Gross Domestic Product.
BE : Budget Estimates.
RE : Revised Estimates.
Source : Report of the Task Force, July 2004, Ministry of Finance, Govt. of India.
Year : Period of fiscal year in India is April to March, e.g. year shown as 1990-91 relates to April 1990 to March 1991.
Units : (a) 1 Lakh (or lacs) = 100000.
(b) 1 Crore (or Cr.) = 10000000.

TABLE 4.5
Number of Income Tax Assessees in India (1995-96 to 2003-04)

Financial Year	*Total No. of Assessees as on 31st March of FY (in lakhs)*	*Total No. of new Assessees added during the FY*
1995-96	116.58	10.90
1996-97	125.15	15.04
1997-98	143.23	23.32
1998-99	182.26	41.68
1999-2000	211.81	32.99
2000-01	248.00	36.29
2001-02	300.02	NA
2002-03	331.49	NA
2003-04 (Upto Jan. 2004)	297.76	NA

Notes : (1) One by six scheme became operative w.e.f. 1st August 1998.

(2) In Budget speech, FM said –3.4 Crore persons are filing Income Tax Returns in time. Only 2.7 crore assessees are tax payees.

Source : Economic Editors' Conference, 2001 and Annual Report 2003-04, Ministry of Finance and Company Affairs, Govt. of India.

TABLE 4.6
Number of Individual Assessees with Income of Rupees Ten Lakhs and more in India (1995-96 to 2003-04)

CCIT/DGIT Charge	*Rank*	*No. of Assessees*
(1)	*(2)*	*(3)*
Ahmedabad	8	1168
Allahabad	35	76
Amritsar	23	251
Bangalore, Hubli & Panaji	2	13130
Baroda	11	665
Bareilly	38	46
Bhopal	31	146
Bhubaneshwar	10	694

(Contd.)

TABLE 4.6 (Contd.)

(1)	(2)	(3)
Chandigarh	15	489
Chennai	7	2716
Cochin	18	411
Coimbatore	15	512
Dehradun	27	199
Delhi	3	12450
Guwahati	30	165
Hyderabad and Visakhapatanam	5	3835
Indore	21	298
Jaipur	131	531
Jodhpur	29	187
Kanpur	14	498
Kolkata	6	3492
Lucknow	26	217
Ludhiana	14	515
Madurai	39	40
Meerut	22	254
Mumbai	1	18939
Nagpur	19	397
Nashik	25	225
Panchkula	16	431
Patna	24	230
Pune	4	4198
Raipur	36	64
Rajkot	33	110
Ranchi	32	138
Shillong	37	50
Shimla	34	80
Surat	12	587
Thane	9	821
Trichy	28	192
Trivandrum	17	429
Udaipur	20	341
Grand Total		70217

Abbr. : CCIT : Chief Commissioner of Income Tax.
DGIT : Directorate General of Income Tax.

Source : Rajya Sabha, Unstarred Question No. 1357, Dated 17.08.2004.

on 30th September, 2003. The highest number of tax assessees were in Mumbai followed by Bangalore, Delhi, Pune, Hyderabad and Visakhapatanam, etc., whereas the lowest was in Madurai, Bareilly, Shillong, Raipur and Allahabad, etc. There is need to speed up the recovery system of tax in these districts.

Recent Direct Tax Reforms

I. *Introduction of 1/6 Scheme U/S 139.*

w.e.f. 1.4.1998 (amended w.e.f. 1.4.2001), every person has to file a return if he fulfils any one of the following 6 conditions.
(a) Owner of a house, (b) Owner of motor vehicle, (c) Telephone, (d) Travel to foreign country other than the neighbouring country or notified place of pilgrimage (e) Holder of credit card, and (f) Member of club where entrance fee charged is Rs. 25000 or more.
Under Fin. Act 2002—Telephone changed to cellular or WLL connections.
U/S 139 (1A)—Filing of return by employee with his employer.
U/S 139 (1B) Electronic furnishing of return of income scheme 2003. Now the scheme is discontinued.

II. *Introduction of Depositories Act 1996*

III. *Securities Transactions Tax U/S 48.*

IV. Maintenance of accounts U/S 44AA and Audits of accounts of certain persons carrying on business or profession U/S 44 AB—w.e.f. 1/4/1976 and w.e.f. 1/4/85, respectively.

V. Annual Information Return U/S 285 BA and amended by notification No. 238/2004 dated 1.12.2004. From A.Y 2005-06.
W.e.f. 1/4/2004—Incase any financial transaction is more than Rs. 50000 the person has is required to give his PAN number.
U/S 285 BA (1) Any person, being:

(a) an assessee or,
(b) the prescribed person in the case of an office of Government or,

(c) the Registrar under Registration Act, 1908.
(d) the registering authority,
(e) the post master general,
(f) the collector,
(g) the recognized stock exchanges,
(h) officer of RBI, and
(i) a depository under depositories Act, 1996 will be covered under the Acts/Rules.

A person who is responsible for registering, maintaining books of accounts or other document, shall furnish an annual information return in respect of such specified financial transaction which is registered or recorded by him during any Financial Year beginning on or after 1/4/2004 to the prescribed Income Tax authority in form No. 60 under rule 114B.

TABLE 4.7

S.No.	Class of Person	Nature and Value of Transaction
(1)	(2)	(3)
1.	A Banking company to which the banking Regulation Act, 1949 (10 of 1949) applies (including any bank or banking institution referred to in section 51 of that Act).	Cash deposits aggregating to ten lakh rupees or more in a year in any savings account of a person maintained in that bank.
2.	A banking company to which the Banking Regulation Act, 1949 (10 of 1949), applies (including any bank or banking institution referred to in section 51 of that Act) or any other company or institution issuing credit card.	Payments made by any person against bills raised in respect of a credit card issued to that person, aggregating to two lakh rupees or more in the year.
3.	A trustee of a Mutual Fund or such other person managing the affairs of the mutual fund as may be duly authorized by the trustee in this behalf.	Receipt from any person of an amount of two lakh rupees or more for acquiring units of that Fund.

(Contd.)

TABLE 4.7 (*Contd.*)

(1)	*(2)*	*(3)*
4.	A company or institution issuing bonds or debentures.	Receipt from any person of an amount of five lakh rupees or more for acquiring bonds or debentures issued by the company or institution.
5.	A company issuing shares through a public or rights issue.	Receipt from any person of an amount of one lakh rupees or more for acquiring shares issued by the company.
6.	Registrar or Sub-Registrar appointed under section 6 of the Registration Act, 1908.	Purchase or sale by any person of immovable property valued at thirty lakh rupees or more.
7.	A person being an officer of the Reserve Bank of India, constituted under section 3 of the Reserve Bank of India Act, 1934, who is duly authorized by the Reserve Bank of India in this behalf.	Receipt from any person of an amount or amounts aggregating to five lakh rupees, or more in a year for bonds issued by the Reserve Bank of India.

VI. *Implementation of On Line Tax Accounting System*: w.e.f. 1/6/2004.

(a) One challan form for payment of taxes instead of four.
(b) Allotment of CIN (challan identification number) which indicates the Bank branch code, date of presentation, challan serial number of that branch for that day.
(c) Collecting branch enters the data given in the challan and transmits it on line to Income Tax Department through tax information network.

It is evidence that challan is correct and it leads to dematerialisation of challans.

➢ Corruption is reduced and direct credit afforded in your account.

In this system the fault is as follows (Dec. 2004):

(a) PAN is not quoted 10.59%
(b) TAN is not quoted 29%

PAN (Permanent Account Number), TAN (Tax at Source Number).

- By the end of Dec. 2004, PAN/TAN has been allotted in 3.56 crore cases as against 3.01 crore tax payers.
- Procedure has been simplified through appointment of Two services providers, i.e. M/s. UTIISL and M/s. NSDL
- On line facility is applicable.

VII. *National Tax Tribunal Bill :*
(Introduced in Lok Sabha on 6.12.2004)

Government is planning to estabalish Tax Tribunal to be known as the National Tax Tribunal to exercise the jurisdiction, process and authority conferred on such Tribunal under this Act.

It means all disputes with respect to levy, assessment, collection and enforcement of direct taxes and also to provide for the adjudication by that Tribunal of disputes with respect to the determination of the rates of duties of customs and central excise on goods and the valuation of goods for the purpose of assessment of such duties as well as in matters relating to levy of tax on service in pursuance of Article 323B of the constitution.

(It means now there is no need to refer the cases to the High Court. The appeals against Appellate Tribunal will be referred to National Tax Tribunal who will be expert in Tax matters).

VIII. *Voluntary Disclosure Schemes :*

Rs. 10,500 crore was collected and honest regular tax payers have to think. Rs. 33,000 crore in the last disclosure scheme. It is suggested that Government should not follow this type of practices.

IX. *Tax Deduction at Source u/s 190 to 296.*

Revenue can be collected by the Government by :

(a) Advance Tax, (b) Self-assessment Tax, (c) Demand Notice, and (d) TDS.

The purposes of TDS are, *inter alia* :

(a) easy collection before the recipient receives income,
(b) timely collection over a period of time of the previous year,
(c) improving taxpayers' base,
(d) a check on tax evasion, and
(e) exploiting human psychology—tax payment by way of TDS pinches less than direct payment of tax, etc.

Payment of TDS is a payment of tax on behalf of the person from whom income-tax is deducted and it is deemed to be paid on account of person from whose income tax was deducted and, accordingly, credited against advance tax payable and the self-assessment tax payable by the recipient.

- During the last 15 years, effective tax rates have been lowered, whereas the rates for TDS have remained more or less stagnant.
- It should be more broad-based.

X. *Taxation of Dividends : U/S10/34)*

W.e.f. 1.4.2004—any income by way of dividends referred to in section 115-0 is exempted. Income Tax at 12.5 percent was levied on dividend distributed by domestic companies and tax free in the hands of shareholders.

XI. *Computation of Capital Gains Tax:*

- The definition of capital asset u/s 2(14) was amended w.e.f. 1/4/1973 (Gold is added as capital asset).

- Introduction of cost inflation index (1981-82).
- Separate rate of tax—20%.
- Capital gain for securities w.e.f. 2000-01.

  (a) 10% on LTCG without indexing.
  (b) 20% tax on LTCG with indexing.

  > Finance Act, 2004, income arising from transfer of eligible equity shares in a company listed on any recognized stock exchange and purchased between March 2003 and March 2004 are exempted from Tax.
  > Introduction of Transaction Tax @ 0.15% on the buyer.

XII. Frequents amendments in section 16(i) and u/s 88, 88B, 88C & 88D. From the A.Y. 2006-07, these sections stand deleted and deduction is available only under section 80 C up to Rs. 1.00 lakh.

Tax Reforms in Indirect Taxes

I. Introduction of Service Tax (1994)

- The other statutes' application in service tax are the Service Tax Rules, 1994, the CENVAT Credit Rules, 2004 and specific provisions of the Central Excise Act, 1944.
- Earlier, the rate was 5% then increased to 8% and now 10% + 2% education cess.
- Earlier, three items were introduced now it covers 76 services.
- It includes even coaching centers it is run from commercial place.
- In total taxes collected from this sector are more as compared to other taxes.
- Even Practising CA, Cost Accountant and Company Secretaries, Stock Broking services, etc. are included.
- Sept. 2004, Persons who are registered as Service Tax

Providers can get benefit of service tax credit against tax paid on input of services. It is made mutually adjustable and convertable.

II. Introduction of VAT

To cope with Global market, Indian Government has geared to introduce VAT w.e.f. April 2005, the latest buzz in the business community.

In this system, tax will be levied at multiple points. A mechanism has been provided to grant credit for tax paid on purchase of goods.

VAT is a form of sales tax collected by the Government of destination state (i.e. state in which final consumer is located) on consumer expenditure. It is collected through business transactions involving sale of goods within the state. It is a tax at the final or retail point of sale, which is collected at each stage of sale, when there is a value addition to the goods.

It means that inter-state transactions of purchases and sales will continue to be governed by CST till it is phased out.

VAT is levied on the value addition at every point of sale by a registered dealer with the provision of credit for input tax paid at the previous point of purchase thereof.

Value-added in manufacturing activity is the difference between the price at which commodity is sold and the cost of inputs and in case of trading the difference between value of sales and purchases.

Suggestions

The various procedural actions undertaken at the end by the tax officials, including assessment, refunds, rectification, appeals, effect, etc. should be made within a specified time frame.

It is important to build a sense of faith between government and the assessee and the number of scrutiny assessments has to be reduced.

The incidents of suveys, searches and raids are to be marginalized.

Direct Taxes

- Corporate Tax rate to be reduced to 1.30%
- Personal Tax slabs to be rationalized.
- Partnership firms to be taxed as corporates.
- Voluntary disclosure schemes to be introduced.
- Women and senior citizens have an additional rebate of Income Tax. Children are country's future; a reasonable tax rebate upto two children may be introduced in the hands of parents.
- Standard Deduction U/s 24, i.e. 30% of Annual value or interest on loan may be allowed. It can be linked to certain number of years.

VAT : Vat in lieu of sales tax is a good concept subject to—

- Similar legislation on national basis in all states.
- VAT tax rate to be kept low 2% - 4% - 8% in three slabs.
- CST to be completely and immediately withdrawn.
- VAT credit to be allowed for service tax paid also.
- Small traders upto Rs. 10 lacs turnover to be completely exempted with an option for a lower VAT rate.

Service Tax

- The tax rate of 10.2% is very high and needs downward revision. It is creating backdrop for a parallel black money economy.
- A minimum receipt upto Rs. 10 lakh to be exempted.
- In one speech—FM jokingly avoided service tax on advocates by saying that "they do not provide any service". Actually, lawyers provide justice, doctors save life. The CAs help in wealth generation, bring financial discipline and manage economy. All are equally entitled for complete exemption.

Miscellaneous

- Scope of TDS u/s 190 to 206 should be increased.

- There is need of vision, consistency, uniformity and clarity by long-term view. But these often change with changes in political parties/coalitions in power.
- It is not correct to close all the doors for the honest tax payers simply because some persons are misusing it. Some people will always misuse the laws, but it does not mean that to stop misuse, you amend the basic objective of that section.

In the current technologically developed scenario, there is need of effective implementation of e-refiling, e-refunds, e-rectification and introduction of e-scrutiny of cases.

Fiscal Management in India : Walking on a Tight Rope

Som Deo

One of the most daunting tasks before the planners of the country, after liberalization, is the fiscal management. Fiscal management is no more concentrating, as it traditionally did, on collection of tax and spending it alone, but a broader need on maintaining and managing macro-stability variables without sacrificing the micro-interests of the economy. At times, the macro and micro-variables are in conflict, and rightly so, in a mixed economy like ours. Raising of revenue and its proper use is an economic necessity but how to raise (if not rising) is a political compulsion. This dialectism has proved to be one of the most challenging tasks and requires a serious and logical thinking rather than rhetorics or trivializing an issue. All issues of Fiscal management must be calibrated before their implementation. At times, it seems that fiscal crunch has made the reforms necessary in favour of liberalization and privatization.

Not so rising growth rate of tax and non-tax revenue; burgeoning fiscal deficit; falling share of social sector expenditure as a percentage to total expenditure; rising debt GDP ratio; handling of inflation; re-distribution of income; creation of employment; rationalization of tax structure—direct and indirect; pruning of subsidies; reduction of government's interference in the areas which were hitherto considered essential for state, etc. are the issues which have become central to the fiscal management under the present context.

PRESENT SCENARIO

All states are under fiscal stress though the extent varies. Number crunching is boring till the numbers are important. Fiscal deficit was 4.7% of GDP in 1991-92 which went up to 5.3% in 2002-03. At the same time, the revenue deficit as a percentage of fiscal deficits which was only 2.7% in 1991-92 went up to 82.2% in 2002-03. This trend is not only unhealthy but also undesirable for the economy. It tells more about tax administration, tax buoyancy and lackadaisical approach to whole management. Tax revenue (net of states' share) as a percentage of GDP was 9.7 in 1990-91 could reach /to 9.5% in 2003 (prov.) and was decelerated to 9.4 per cent in 2003-04. Non-tax revenue has increased from 2.1 to 2.9% in the same period. There are two important things to note. One, efforts to increase the share of non-tax revenue has been a complete failure, repeated emphasis of various finance commissions and committees notwithstanding. Two, Tax revenue too has not shown any appreciable increase as a proportion to the GDP. The compounded average growth rate has not been encouraging. Direct tax as a proportion to GDP was only 3.4 in 2002-03 and this ratio in terms of indirect tax is only 5.3%. This turns to be 8.7% as tax-GDP ratio. This may not be out of context that tax-GDP ratio in 1990-91 was even higher at 10.1% (see Economic Survey, 2003-04). VAT still seems to be luding on one or the other protext.

EXPENDITURE TRENDS

Total expenditure of the central government after

witnessing compression in the first half of the nineties started rising in 1997-98. Total expenditure as proportion to GDP declined from 17.3% in 1990-91 to 13.9% in 1996-97. Thereafter, it has been rising to reach a level of 16.2% of GDP in 2002-03. The quality of expenditure has also been witnessing a deterioration over the years. Capital expenditure has declined from 4.4 of GDP in 1990-91 to 2% of GDP in 2002-03, clearly indicating that such expenditure has borne the major burden of fiscal adjustments. More so, the level of expenditure, by international standards, is not very high. It is the deterioration in the quality of expenditure that is a matter of serious concern.

INTEREST PAYMENTS

Interest payments, subsidies, pay and allowance and revenue expenditure on defense accounted for 99.2% of net revenue receipts, 68.8% of revenue expenditure and 57.4% of the total expenditure of the central Government in 2003-04 (BE). Such high percentage of these expenses is beyond the prudence of fiscal management, if not a fiscal prodigality due the committed nature of such expenditure. This, however, needs a fresh thinking and calls for a greater political will to contain it. Interest payments alone account for about 30% of total expenditure and 3% of revenue expenditure. Interest payments pre-empt nearly half of revenue receipts. Following deregulation of interest rates on borrowings, the average cost of borrowing had increased from 11.4% in 1990-91 to 13.7% in 1996-97 despite reduction in the weighted average maturity from 18.4 years to 5.5 years in this period. With the softening of interest rate in the recent years, this has started declining. The excess liquidity in the banking system and lower off-take of credit also contributed to keeping the cost of market borrowing low. This has resulted in excessive holding of government papers by the banking sector, much higher than 25% as statutory minimum requirement. The government too was on a borrowing binge. Although the average cost of total internal liabilities has been witnessing a declining trend since 2000-01 yet the effect of lower interest rates on the total interest burden of the government in not distinctly visible because of the growth in the outstanding debt. There has been a trend in various states that they are using borrowing as off-budget item through public enterprises and massive increase in payment arrears to the central corporations. Limits fixed on contingent liabilities are frequently breached.

SUBSIDIES

In India, subsidies have acquired political overtones. Subsidies in our society are hydra headed. Announcement of popular schemes, without their logical implementation has increased the burden of subsidies on Government In the name of rationalization of subsidies, there are areas where subsidies need to be withdrawn but not being done so. Free lunches are still offered by states to many politically potential groups in terms of free power, etc. Highly inefficient mode of subsidization, cross-subsidization and hidden-subsidies are very common features in India. Off-budget or non-voted expenditures are very common in Indian budgets. Food subsidies continue increasing unabated. The entire question of subsidy should be given a fresh look and on priority basis. Subsidy in the petroleum sector needs an immediate attention. Kerosene and LPG should no more be treated as the eligible items for subsidies. The whole argument of social externality should be given a fresh thought. Not charging for scarce power or subsidizing fertiliser use or cross subsidy of passenger transport by Railways, etc. and even a large part of public distribution system for foodgrains cannot possibly be rationalized on grounds of social externality. Elimination of such subsidies would release funds for some better purposes such as recently announced employment guarantee programme. Rationalization of subsidies is the most important pre-requisite of fiscal consolidation.

FISCAL RESPONSIBILITY AND BUDGET MANAGEMENT (FRBM)

The FRBM Act, 2003 has streamlined the budget presentation process. It has to progressively reduce the revenue deficit to zero by the year 2008-09 (amended from the year 2007-08). Under the FRBM, the central government has to lay in each financial year before both houses of parliament three statements, namely, Medium Term Fiscal Policy Statement, Fiscal Policy Strategy Statement and Macro Economic Framework Statement along with the Budget. In India, being a large and diversified nation, the operation of FRBM is not beyond question. All states must introduce such legislation in order to ensure better fiscal consolidation. However, the political will might come out with one or other exceptions to save themselves from inconveniences such as national security and national calamity or some other pretext. In fact, India needs something like Political Responsibility Management Act in addition to FRBM.

VAT implementation too is facing a bumpy road. Diagonal views are coming from various political parties, and coalition polity has made it more complex, theoretical unanimity notwithstanding. Rising salaries and pension bills of centre and states have made the system bleeding and the governments have to divert their resources from developmental and social sector. Fiscal crunch has driven reforms haywire which has worst affected the social sector which is highly important where more than one-fourth population is below poverty line. Federal fiscal relationships too have undergone a stress and autonomies are being asserted in its own manner which may not be suitable for the federal character of the nation in the long-run. Announcing of packages have made the situation from bad to worse. Fiscal reforms are badly needed but neglecting larger section of population does not angur well.

In this debate, certain issues may be raised as the following ones:

- Over the years, the budgeting process has remained as a ritual, Pre-budget and post-budget hikes or concessions have become more and more important part of entire fiscal management.
- A very large part of revenue deficit is being financed by capital receipts which has resulted in low capital formation and smaller resources available for development projects.
- There has been a rising trend in creating off-budget items in borrowings by the states which is not only increasing contingent liabilities but also violating the

democratic process of development which is more serious issue.

- Incremental budgeting, rather than budgeting, has resulted in upward pressure on expenditure. This has become more of a routine rather than episodic.
- Continuous pressure on states has resulted in compression of capital expenditures that are crucial for the growth and maintenance of public sector.
- It has become fashionable to 'privatize' and unbundled and make things 'cost effective' but their long time consequences are sacrificed for short-term gains.
- A long-term fiscal perspective is still lacking. Political suitability of short-term planning has taken over economic viability over long-term.
- Implementation of fiscal reforms, like the recommendation of various committees has been absolutely tardy. Time stretching in such implementations make the things either irrelevant or politically unconvincing.
- Leakages in the revenue collection, legal rigmaroles have blocked hundreds and thousands of crores of rupees revenue in tax arrears. There has to be a ruthless and concerted effort to recover the tax arrears.
- Rising expenditure on salaries and pension has to be looked into keeping in view the state finances.
- Any fiscal reform sans employment creation is of no use. Ambitious plans like EGP should be given a serious thought before jumping on the bandwagon.
- A sense of trustworthiness has to be infused in all such reforms. The policy statements have to be clear and stable. Clarity and stability are by far the most important elements in any reform process.
- More and more transparency in the system is the need of the hour, whether it is administration of tax or policy.
- The government borrowings have to be capped. Compared to tax and borrowing, the latter option is considered to be softer and less noticed. But the long-term subtleties have to be well appreciated.
- The question of subsidies needs an immediate concern,

particularly food subsidies and petroleum products subsidies. Cross-subsidization has to be tackled as priority.

- Tax base needs to be widened. Legal and institutional reforms (like constitutional amendments) are overdue.
- Along with the fiscal responsibility, a thought should be given to political responsibility too. Let there be debate as to how the political responsibility may be assured. Politics cannot be allowed to ride endlessly on economics.

Agricultural Income Tax : A Blame Game

PAWAN KUMAR TANEJA

INTRODUCTION

During the process of development, agriculture has obviously to continue to supply the rest of the economy with larger food surplus and raw-materials. Production and marketed surplus of agricultural goods have to increase to meet the requirement of the Non-Agricultural sector and also to supply an increasing proportion of the community's manpower. Higher price alone may not always bring about increase in production and larger marketable surplus. According to Ved Gandhi, "Imposing heavier taxation on Agricultural population would force the farmers to bring forth increased market supplies."[2] Professor Kaldor argued, "The taxation of the agriculture has critical role to play in the acceleration of the economic development since it is only the imposition of the compulsory levies in the Agricultural sector itself which enlarges the supply of saving for economic development."[1]

But, once again, the Government of India, under the rule of reformist Prime Minister, Manmohan Singh and tax structure reformist, Finance Minister P. Chidambaram, ignores the recommendation of the Kelkar Committee report on Direct and indirect taxes about imposition of Agriculture Income Tax. While delivering his budget speech on 28th February 2005, Finance Minister never named agriculture income tax and even it is not a part of UPA government agenda.[3] None of the political parties in power is interested in imposing tax on agriculture as it has to save its loyal vote bank. As it is from the Statement made by the then Finance Minister, Mr. Jaswant Singh, in the previous year's budget proposals that Agricultural Income Tax is the matter of State Government, the Government of India is not willing to interfere in this matter. One of the Central Government ministers has even reacted on this recommendation that he would resign from his post if it would be implemented. Similar kind of reactions of various political parties depict that even in this year's budget proposals, the new Congress-led coalition Government with reformist Prime Minister, Mr. Manmohan Singh, does not have any plan to impose Agricultural Income Tax. It has also been seen that most of the States are reluctant to tax Agricultural income.

WHY SHOULD THERE BE AGRICULTURAL INCOME TAX?

Equity and Distributive Justice

In this context, the Wanchoo Committee pointed out: "There is also a great inequality between incidence of tax on Agricultural income and that on non-Agricultural income." The basic objective of imposition of Income Tax is to bring about economic equality in the country. Another objective is to use it as one of the tools to achieve balanced socio-economic growth by providing incentives and concessions in Income Tax for various development purposes. This kind of inequality can be studied with the help of the following Table 6.1.

TABLE 6.1

Total Tax Incidence on Agricultural and Non-Agricultural Sectors for Selected Years

(*Rs. in Crores*)

Year	*Agricultural Sector*	*Non-Agricultural Sector*
1951-52	200	450
1961-62	400	990
1968-69	910	2700
1997-98	46100	177900
2003-04	64400	224500

Sources : (1) Ved P. Gandhi, Tax Burden on Indian Agriculture, p. 35.[2]

(2) Economic Times Research Bureau, "Taxable capacity of farm sectors."[4]

The Table shows in general, that the Agriculture sector bears relatively less taxation over the years than non-Agricultural sector. In 1951-52, Agriculture contributes Rs. 200, crores by way of direct and indirect tax, whereas Non-Agricultural sector contributed Rs. 450 crores, thus the ratio between the two sectors was 44:56. With the passage of time, in 1997-98, Agricultural and non-Agricultural sectors, contribution to revenue is reduced to 20:80 ratios.[3]

Insignificant Collection of Land Revenue and Agricultural Income Tax by the State Governments

At present, only six States, which have plantation Agriculture, levy such tax. Maharashtra decided to levy Income Tax on Agricultural Income in the 1970's but it remained on paper and was never implemented. Finally, it was repealed in the late 1980's. Some States have abolished land revenue while some others have not revised the rate thereof for years together. As a result, the combined yield of land revenue and Agricultural Income Tax was only Rs. 1780 crores in 2000-01. This was a mere 0.6% of the total national tax revenue aggregating across the Centre and the States and just 1.5% of tax revenue collected by States (see Table 6.2). So, land revenue could hardly even make a proxy for Agriculture Income Tax.

TABLE 6.2
Direct Agricultural Taxes

Year	*Land Revenue (Rs. Crore)*	*Agricultural Income Tax (Rs. Crore)*	*Total Direct Agricultural Taxes*	*%age of State Tax Revenue*
1951-52	48	4	52	18.6
1970-71	113	11	124	5.4
1997-78	1400	210	1610	1.3
2000-01	1623	157	1780	1.5
2003-04	1965	210	2175	1.7

Source : RBI Report on Currency and Finance, 1997-98, 2003-04 and previous issues.

Indira Raja Raman, "Adding punch to Panchayats", *The Economic Times*, Oct. 10, 2002, p. 4.

Since the time land settlement was done decades ago, the Agricultural sector has undergone such structural transformation in terms of land holding, cropping pattern and practices, agricultural productivity and so on that levy of a scientifically based revised land revenue will not be possible without recource to a fresh land settlement. This will be far too time consuming and a slow and expensive process. The present rate of land revenue is so low that its collection cost itself is exorbitant. Giving the powers of recovery of land revenue to Panchayats, as is often advocated, is also not likely to be any more efficient or cost effective. In these circumstances, levy of an Agriculture Income Tax, with a sufficiently high exemption limit, as recommended by Kelkar Committee, i.e. no tax on income up to Rs. 1,00,000, is the only way to bring this sector in the tax net.[6]

Another factor, which stresses the need to levy Agricultural Income Tax, is flat rate of land revenue on land holding. As it is a flat rate on fixed land holding which would not tend to increase or decrease with increase or decrease in income, it would be against the principle of progressive taxation.

Improved Economic Conditions of Farmers

Out of India's population of more than 100 crore, less than 3 crore are Income Tax payers, indicating that just 3% pay Income Tax.[5] This is due to the fact that more than 65% of people are dependent on Agriculture, the income of which is exempted from taxation since generations.

Agriculture sector has not been taxed to the extent of justified level for such taxation. Farm sector has not contributed to the exchequer and thus always avoided bearing its due burden of taxation.

Ever since the launching of planned economic development, the Government has made very huge investment in agriculture sector by implementing several rural and priority sector development lending schemes and Rojgar Yojana. The total outstanding rural credit by Financial Institutions has increased from Rs. 2050 crores in 1980 to Rs. 44675 crores in 1999-2000. With substantial investment in Agriculture and improvement in Bio-chemical technology, the Indian Agriculture has shifted from subsistence level to commercial farming.

Farmers in India have enjoyed various types of concessions and subsidies in respect of inputs like irrigation facilities, fertilizers, seeds, Agricultural implements, electricity, credit facilities, support prices, etc.

As a result of the above benefits, Agricultural Sector contributed 26% of GDP of India in 1999-2000. Net agricultural rural income increased from Rs. 134 crores in 1951 to Rs. 21700 crores in 1998. Agriculture Sector contributed 14.6% of total

TABLE 6.3
Indicators of Agriculture Progress

Production (in lakh tones) of Food Grains	*1949-50*	*1999-2000*
Cereals	468	1955
Food Grains	549	2090
Rice	225	595
Wheat	64	756

Source : Ministry of Finance, Government of India, Economic Survey, 1999-2000.

exports of India in 1996-97. The growth rate of agriculture is 2.8% from 1971 to 1997. With recorded highest growth of 7.4% in 1998-99, the production of all Agricultural products has increased manifold :

> As result of the above, the increase in income level provided for a booming market for many consumer durables in the country. According to NCAER, in 1998-99, rural people purchased 47% of the heavy automobiles.

Even after such a high investment, improvement of technologies, subsidies and concessions on Agriculture and increased productivity, there is no logic why Agricultural income should not be taxed.

CRITICAL REVIEW OF CURRENT STATUS AND RAJA J. CHELLAIAH COMMITTEE ON TAX REFORM—RECOMMENDATIONS

At present, Agricultural income of an assessee in India is included in the total income for the purpose of determining the rate applicable to the taxable income. Hence farming has turned into a big business in recent times as it provides a safe heaven free of tax burden and also for converting black money into white.

One of the major recommendations of the Raja J. Chellaiah Committee[9] is taxation of Agricultural incomes, in the hands of those having Non-Agricultural incomes only. In determining the rate of tax on known Non-Agricultural income, the Agricultural income and Non-Agricultural income should be combined in the following manner and order: (i) The initial exemption allowed out of Non-Agricultural income, (ii) Agricultural income, and (iii) Balance of Non-Agricultural income. That means taxpayer having Non-Agricultural incomes and also income from Agriculture above Rs. 25000 shall be brought to tax after obtaining co-operation and consent of the State Government.[6]

The two incomes would be aggregated for working out the tax liability after allowing a basic deduction of Rs. 53000, i.e.

Rs. 28000 on Non-Agricultural and Rs. 25000 on Agricultural incomes.

It is difficult to accept half-hearted attempt of the Committee to Tax Agricultural income partially. There is no justification to grant 100% exemption to those whose income is purely Agriculture and is above minimum exemption level. The Agricultural income must be treated as any other income.

PROBLEMS AND SUGGESTED SOLUTIONS

Right to Recovery is the Matter of State Government

The major argument in favour of not imposing Agriculture Income Tax by Central Government is that Agriculture is the subject of States as per Article 270 of Constitution. According to Mr. N.A. Palkhiwala, "It was a pure historical accident, which resulted in Agriculture income being outside the purview of taxation by Centre. In 1860, when Income Tax was first levied in the country, Mr. James Wilson, member of Finance Committee, recommended, tax on Agriculture income in the shape of cess on Agriculture income. License Tax on Non-Agriculture Income was replaced by Income Tax. Since then, Agriculture income is exempted from Income Tax. After independence, cess on Agriculture has been removed but there is no taxation of Agriculture income again."

According to Kelkar Committee[9] recommendations, Agriculture income should be brought under Central Income Tax purview through a major Constitution amendment. Ideally all income should be included and be subjected to appropriate rate of tax, as cannon of horizontal equity requires that.

However, under Article 252, the State legislatures can pass a resolution authorizing the Central Government to regulate taxation of Agricultural income and related matters. All the State Governments may not cooperate, treating this as an infringement of their autonomy and also due to lack of political will on their part.

Mercy of Nature and Higher Risk

This is another major argument that in India Agriculture is

dependent factor of mercy of nature and hence higher risks are involved. But if we look into it carefully, trade and industry face equal risks like capital risk, which sometimes is unlimited to the extent of claim on private property. With the increase in irrigation facilities, improvement in farm technology, Agricultural production is not as susceptible to seasonal monsoons as it was earlier.

Less Profitability

Another argument for non-taxation of Agricultural income is that prices of Agricultural commodities are very low. But if we look at the present prices of various commercial crops like pulses, flowers, vegetables, fruits and cotton, there is sufficient profit margin and good reason to impose tax on agriculture income.

Less Land Holding as Limited Ability to Pay

It is argued that as a result of land ceiling provisions, consistent fragmentation of holdings and "Bhoodan scheme"[8] Agricultural land holdings are continuously being reduced; this fact is depicted in the Table 6.4.

TABLE 6.4
Number and Area of Operational Holdings in India

	Number in millions		*Area in million hectares*	
	1970-71	*1990-91*	*1970-71*	*1990-91*
Marginal holding (Below 1 hectare)	36(51)	62(58)	15(9)	25(15)
Small holding (1 to 4 hectare)	24(34)	34(33)	49(30)	67(41)
Medium holding (4 to 10 hectares)	8(11)	8(7)	48(30)	45(27)
Large holding (10 hectares and above)	3(4)	2(2)	50(31)	29(17)
Total	71(100)	106(100)	162(100)	166(100)

Note : Figures in bracket are percentages of total in respective column.
Source : Department of Agriculture and Co-operation, Government of India, Annual Report, 1994-95.

From the above table, it means 91% agriculturists have less than 4 hectares holding. Even according to this argument, small and medium farmers will not be liable to taxation; only rich and big farmers are attracted because as per Kelkar committee recommendations, all agriculturists having income above Rs. 1.00 lakh each per year (i.e. Rs. 8333 per month) would be covered under tax net.[5]

Computation of Income from Agriculture

The computation of income from Agriculture with precesion is difficult. Numerous varieties of crops, methods of production, differences in nature of soil, climatic conditions, irrigation methods and facilities, wide fluctuations in prices of farm products and their outputs will lead to wide variations in farm incomes, resulting in an indefinite basis for taxation. Besides, majority of the farmers do not maintain any account due to illiteracy. Such problems exists in trade, industry and in other farms also. Profits in such a situation can be decided on the basis of single entry system where opening capital, closing capital, drawings, additional capital, etc. can be examined and profit figure arrived at.[7]

Sale of Products to PDS

Another argument against the imposition of Agricultural Income Tax is that the farmers bear the burden of supplying their produce to the public distribution system at lower prices (MSP) but the fact is that PDS provides the means of throwing all kinds of inferior quality goods at the poor buyers (BPL families).

Collection and Administration of Agricultural Income Tax

The cost of collection of Agricultural income may be very heavy since the farmer-assesses are widely scattered. Besides, the number of small assessees will be exceptionally large. The inspectors and officers of Income Tax department may exploit the illiterate farmers to till their own pockets. This is probably the most important factor in the imposition of Agricultural

Income Tax. But this difficulty can be removed by giving the power of collection of tax to Panchayats with spreading of education and awareness among the masses and special efforts to keep cost of collection within reasonable limit.[8]

CONCLUSION

Farmers must share the burden of development of economy. Any system of taxation should be based on principles of equality and social justice. As Income Tax is levied on income earned by a person and not on the total revenue received the farmer, he can deduct all expenses incurred by him and only the balance would be liable to taxation. If there is loss, it can be carried forward. Only big and medium farmers would come under the tax purview. The levying of tax on Agriculture is reasonable, timely and justified. Imposing tax on Agriculture will broaden the tax base. This can also make it possible to lower the maximum rate of taxation.

However, looking to the vote bank politics, there is no guarantee that even if empowered by the States (which itself is a day dreaming process), Parliament will ever pass a law to bring Agricultural income in the tax net. BJP-led NDA Government which had given the slogan of "Ram Rajya" was not able to impose tax on Agriculture although in period of the empire of Lord Rama, Tax in shape of "lagaan" as imposed on Agricultural income. The political parties need to come out from cheap politics and try to think about building the nation. It needs a complete set of awareness among the masses. Lets hope for the best from our reformist Prime Minister, Dr. Manmohan Singh who would possibly do something with regard to this!

NOTES AND REFERENCES

1. E.T. Mathew (1999), "Agricultural Taxation and Economic Development", Deep & Deep Publications, New Delhi, pp. 26-29
2. Gandhi, Ved P. (2002), "Tax Burden on Indian Agriculture", Kedar Nath Ram Nath & Co., Publisher, Meerut, p. 2 and Chapters 3-5.
3. Government of India, "Annual Budgets 2001, 2002, 2003, 2004 and 2005".
4. Indira Rajaraman (2002), "Adding Punch to Panchayats", *The Economic Times*, October 10, 2002, p. 5.

5. Madhav Godbole (2002), "Commentary on Task Force Reports on Direct and Indirect Taxes", *Economic & Political Weekly*, December 7, 2002, pp. 4884-90.
6. Madhav Godbole (2002), "Commentary on Task Force Reports on Direct and Indirect Taxes", *Economic & Political Weekly*, December 14, 2002, pp. 4975-82.
7. R.P. Malhotra (2003), "Budget—2003, Making it Less Taxing", *The Tribune*, February 10, 2003, p. 13.
8. Rao, Madhusudan (1994), "Taxation of Agricultural Income", *Agricultural Banker*, April-June 1994, pp. 1-3.
9. Report of Kelkar Task Force on Direct and Indirect Taxes, 2002.
10. Ruddar Datt and Sundhram, K.P.M. (2004), Indian Economy, S. Chand and Company Ltd., Publication, New Delhi, Chapters 31, 33-36.

New Dimensions of Budgeting Process in India

PRANEET RANGI AND SWARNJIT KAUR

INTRODUCTION

Economic reforms in our country were first introduced about 25 years back. The Congress government led by the then Prime Minister, Mr. Rajiv Gandhi, may not have had a clear agenda for the reforms, yet the "R" word had crept in the minds of our governing authorities. The economic crisis of 1991 was perhaps one of the redefining moments in the economic history of our country. The financial help extended by IMF was conditional, the condition being the creation of a market-based open economy in India. Fifteen years henceforth, we are standing at a point where the reforms in our economy are as much needed as they were earlier, the difference being that earlier they were crisis driven, whereas now they need to be strategy driven. The primary objective today is to keep the pace of economic growth stable. However, the outlook to economic growth has undergone a change. The true picture of economic well-being of a country is measured not just in statistical terms alone but also in terms of certain human development indices. One of the important tools in the hands of the government for shaping the economic growth pattern of our country is the budget. The current paper titled "New Dimensions of Budgeting Process in India", is exploring the new and redefined scope of Indian budget.

India's public finance system follows the British pattern. The Indian constitution establishes the supremacy of the bicameral Parliament—specifically the Lok Sabha (House of the People) in financial matters. The Minister of Finance is required to submit to Parliament, usually on the last day of February, a financial statement detailing the estimated receipts and expenditures of the central government for the forthcoming fiscal year and a financial review of the current fiscal year.

Under the Constitution, Budget has to distinguish expenditure on revenue account from other expenditure. Government Budget, therefore, comprises (i) Revenue Budget; and (ii) Capital Budget. The national railroad (Indian Railways), the largest public-sector enterprise, and the Department of Posts and Telegraph have their own budgets, funds, and accounts.

The traditional budget has undergone significant changes in the last few years. There is a realization that the budget reflects and shapes, and is, in turn, shaped by the country's socio-economic life. Keeping this fact in mind, the budgets of recent times are characterized by greater transparency and more achievable targets. The budget follows an inclusive approach so that the benefits do not exclude any section of the society. The current paper examines some significant changes in the Indian budgeting exercise, namely—

- The introduction of outcome budgeting.
- The introduction of gender budgeting.
- Incorporation of fiscal responsibility.

Out of the three emergent dimensions mentioned above, the first and the third easily fit into the budgetary exercise because of their economic nature. The second dimension, however, introduces the concept of social responsibility in the budget. Like a living organism it tends to act like a breather in an otherwise a technical document. The objective behind addressing the three together is to reflect on the possible convergence among them.

I. OUTCOME BUDGETING

The budget that has been presented since 1859, retains a great deal of the same characteristics that were present in it years ago. The budget continues to perform the triple function of planning, control and management. However, the changing economic scenario, changing role of the government and the growing priority of the social sector has forced the budget instrument to move from the traditional administrative budget to an outcome budget. What is this Outcome Budgeting? Outcome Budgeting is basically a pre-expenditure instrument to realize the government's vision through clearly defined outcomes, which will lend greater transparency to the budgetary process [Chowdhary, 2006].

Traditional Budgeting Compares

INPUTS	to	OUTPUTS

Outcome Budgeting Compares

INPUTS	to	OUTCOMES (Result)

The purpose of the outcome budget is that it would list out project-wise outlays for all central ministries and departments for a given fiscal year against corresponding outcomes to be achieved during the year.

If successful, the move may bring about significant changes in the annual budgeting exercise as project targets would come under fiscally monitorable parameters. It would also avoid unproductive use of funds and seek to put a lid on time and cost overruns of projects. The maiden outcome budget was presented in August 2005-06. Although, the first budget is more of a review exercise than a critical analysis, yet if the practice is adopted seriously and continuously, then it would encourage performance, accountability and transparency in the operations of the government.

Prerequisites to a Successful Outcome Budget

Outcome budgeting is a new concept which has found application in some of the developed countries of the world like the US. The journey till date has been rough and it has been a continuous process of trials and errors. The success of outcome budgeting in India requires some major changes in our thought and work process. Some of the important things to remember are :

- The onus of a successful beginning lies with our political leaders. They will have to not only impart sincerity to the exercise but will also have to take upon the task of rejuvenating the Indian bureaucracy. It is a well known fact that change always attracts resistance and outcome budgeting is not a very appealing prospect for the politico-bureaucratic set-up which have the habit of goes into a state of inertia once the elections are over.
- The next essential to outcome budget is that there should be a 'clear definition of the visions of the government'. The ministers need to be more educated on their department's role and responsibilities and fix the targets rationally. Nothing would kill the outcome budget more grievously than poorly planned unachievable targets. This requires that appropriate training should be imparted to the people at the operational level as well as at the policy-making level.
- Further, the parameters against which the performance or the outcomes are to be measured need to be identified. Simply saying that the objective of the education department will be to remove illiteracy does not qualify as an objective. A more close ended statement, containing measurable yardsticks, e.g. number of children to be covered under a primary

education scheme gives us a more definitive target to achieve. The allocations should be combined with a statement of the physical achievements. Till date, we do not have any definite indicators of performance stated.

- Success is all about 'managing effectively', is something that we are all aware of. However, for effectiveness to be achieved, we have to develop a control system that is more effective on the output side than on the input side. The need of the hour is to have integration from top to the lowest level, a system whereby the implementation of the budgetary policies can be monitored and controlled.

The above are some of the very basic prerequisites to start with; they are the foundation on which the effectiveness of the budget can be measured.

II. GENDER BUDGETING

Another pioneering exercise on the budgeting front has been the presentation of gender budget by the finance minister in March 2005. How did 'gender' find its way into budgeting? What is the meaning of gender budgeting?

For long, budget was meant to be a public finance document. The shift in the focus of the budget towards gender can be traced to the success of feminist movement in altering the development paradigm to establish links between gender and development. The transition made possible the cognizance of gender differentials in developments that are not based on any subjective analysis but are based on facts. As a fallout of these developments, feminist activism and advocacy network succeeded in convincing the public policy-makers on the following: It is actually the people who pay for the budgetary expenditure and they get returns in the form of benefits of schemes launched by such budgets and also seek participation in the planning and development process, as of right.

The gender fabric of our county is such that schemes and policies made in the budget affect men and women differently. For instance, in our social set-up, the poor tend to be reluctant in providing medical care to their daughters and even if they provide them then the expenditure incurred will show favour towards boys over girls. Therefore, free public medical care facilities are needed more by girls/women and the budget needs to cater to that [Banerjee, Krishnaraj, 2004]. Similarly, expenditure on social security schemes need to keep in view the enormous number of women workers engaged in the informal and unorganized sectors of the economy. These are just a few examples to illustrate that gender is an integral part of public finance and expenditure and justifies the necessity for gender budgeting.

Gender budget does not mean separate budgets for men and women. It also does not imply separate budgets for women only. On the other hand, the term Gender budgeting means budgeting with a gender perspective [Women Power Connect, 2004]. It is an attempt to dissect the government budget to establish its gender differential impact and to translate the same into budgetary commitments. The aim is to improve the analysis of incidence of budgets, achieve effective targeting of public expenditure and offset any gender specific undesirable consequences of previous budgetary measures. It is looked upon as a tool to engender macro-economic policy-making [http://ed.nic.in/chap11.htm]. One of the important aims of gender budgeting is to evaluate whether allocation contributes to gender equality. Optimization of gender resource allocation to enhance and improve gender situation and position is equally the concern [NCW: 2003].

Genesis of Gender Budgeting in India

The incorporation of gender budgeting may have been the achievement of 21st century but has been preceded by: publication of the report of committee on the status of women in 1974, India's ratification of 1979 international bill of rights of women known as CEDAW (Convention for Elimination of all Forms of Discrimination against Women) in 1981 and more recently due to India's participation in the UN's Fourth World Conference of 1995 and the Beijing Platform for Action that followed it. On the domestic front, focus on women in the eighth, ninth and tenth five year plans seems to have facilitated the move.

The gender budget initiative began in India in 2000 when a workshop on 'Engendering National Budgets in South Asia' was held in New Delhi in collaboration with UNIFEM. This was followed by National Institute of Public Finance Policy (NIPF&P) study on gender-related economic policy issues. The first report submitted by it on 'Status of Women in India and their role in Economy' serves as an input for Economic Survey 2000-01. It was followed by a second report in 2001 which undertook Post-budget assessment of the Union budget 2001-02. The public report was categorized into three main types: (i) Women specific allocations targeting specifically women and girls, (ii) Pro-Women allocations as composite expenditure of schemes with women component, (iii) Mainstream public expenditure having gender differential impacts. The methodology developed by NIPF&P was taken up by the National Institute of Cooperation and Child Development (NIPCCD) to analyze budgets in 15 states. The analysis was carried out for four consecutive years from 2000 to 2004 and this served as a ground work for the gender budget of 2005.

NIPF & P have developed a formula for calculating pro-women allocations both for mainstream social sector ministries where women are significant beneficiaries of almost all the schemes and other ministries where only a few programmes have women interest component. The mainstream ministries included: Health, Family Welfare, Education and Rural Development while other ministries covered were Agriculture and Cooperation, Small Scale Industries, Agro and Rural Industries, etc. The formula is as follows:

For mainstream Ministries

Pro-Women Allocations = (TE WSP)*WC

For other Ministries

Pro-Women Allocations = (SCS)*WC

where TE: Total Expenditure, WSP: Women Specific Programmes, WC: Women Component, a percentage of total outlay, and SCS: Specific Component Scheme.

Challenges and Prospects of Gender Budgeting in India

Gender budgeting promises to focus on the role of rights, freedoms and the choices of women by giving information of content and focus of government policies. Thus, it goes beyond the human development approach that looks at people merely as a resource; the welfare approach that treats people as mere recipients and the basic needs approach that seeks to provide minimal goods and services to people [Banerjee & Krishnaraj, 2004]. Today, gender sensitive budgetary allocations might only constitute 5% of the total budget, yet they stand as a significant attempt at addressing gender inequality. However, gender budgeting exercise needs to be on guard against certain challenges facing it.

Firstly, International Financial institutions that stipulated to initiate economic reform policies in India like IMF, WTO can offset gender budgeting benefits. Imposition of user fees on education, health, water, electricity and other services have the impact of reducing the poor people's access to such services and let us not forget that majority of the poor are women. Lowering of import duties under WTO has resulted in a reduction of government's revenue which in turn translated into lower expenditure on social sector, especially on women.

Secondly, the introduction of VAT has the impact of affecting the people's spending rather than their income and thus tends to hit the poor more. Since feminization of poverty is an established fact, VAT can be more harmful to the interests of the women.

Thirdly, the focus on reducing the fiscal deficit should not imply a cut on the gender equality and women empowerment schemes. Financial constraints have become a reality [Elson: 2005]. But the norms of financial expediency should not push gender budgeting backstage. Reducing fiscal deficit may be a priority but it should not be at the cost of gender budget. Public-private partnership in enhancing expenditure in social sector needs to be encouraged.

Lastly, the scope of gender budgeting needs to be enlarged so as to cover what hitherto have been gender neutral departments or ministries. For instance, it appears illogical to treat the Ministry of Law to be gender neutral. Enhanced allocation for women specific programmes needs to be supplemented by an overall evaluation of budgetary policies from gender perspective.

III. FISCAL RESPONSIBILITY

A word that has proved to be a bane for the governments of our country has been the term 'fiscal deficit'. It is the dream of every government to come up with a low fiscal deficit. So what is this fiscal deficit? The difference between the total expenditure of Government by way of revenue, capital and loans net of repayments on the one hand and revenue receipts of Government and capital receipts which are not in the nature of borrowing but which finally accrue to Government on the other, constitutes gross fiscal deficit [key budget Document, 2006]. High fiscal deficit has been believed to be a major factor responsible for the economic ills of our country. In case of India we can say that India is lucky enough to have sound economic variables like low interest rates, low inflation rates, high forex reserves. The crisis which can erupt due to high fiscal deficit has been avoided till date. But it is no excuse for complacency. As is said, it is politically easier to resolve a crisis, once it happens, than to prevent one. So are we going to wait for it to happen? No. Controlling the deficit has been a major concern with the government and this gets reflected in the Fiscal Responsibility and Budget Management Bill (FRBM).

The Fiscal Responsibility and Budget Management Bill was enacted in 2004 by our parliament. What is the purpose of this bill? The rationale behind this particular bill is that fiscal deficit in our country is responsible for most of the macro-economic variables going off course, hence we need to reduce it. This bill lays down that the government should undertake appropriate measures to eliminate revenue deficit by March 31, 2008. The Bill also seeks to bar the Reserve Bank of India from operating in the primary market for government securities from April 1, 2006. However, extreme situations like natural calamities, exceptional circumstances warrant deviations from the above rigours. The government can borrow directly from RBI and the timetable for zero revenue deficit can be extended in such situations. To critically analyze the FRBM, let us look at some trends in fiscal deficit.

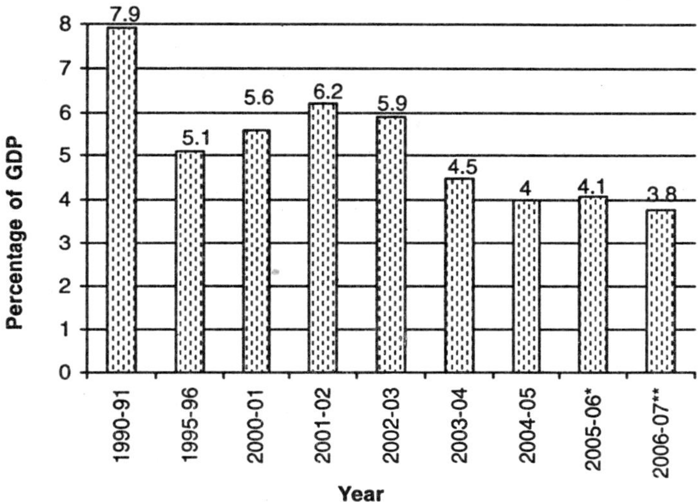

* Revised Figures ** Budgeted Figures.

Source : *India Today*, March 13, 2006, p. 38.

The graph displays the fiscal deficit trends of our country. These trends show that the fiscal deficit has shown a declining trend since 1990-91. The fiscal deficit has been hovering around 4% since 2003-04. Is it a mere coincidence or does it reflect on the efficacy of FRBM ?

Is Fiscal Responsibility and Management Bill Effective?

Too soon to tell. But would it be really bad if our deficit does not fall? Not necessarily, especially if the deficit has arisen because of increased investment activities through public loans. This especially stands true for the Indian economy which has high investment potential. India has yet to achieve its optimal level of utilization for its resources, hence investment is a necessity. Then why was the need to incorporate the Fiscal responsibility management in our budgets. This can be explained by the fact that our deficit has been created not because of investment generating activities but due to non-revenue generating unplanned expenditures of the government.

TABLE 7.1
Trends in Selective Non-plan Expenditure Items

(Figures as %age of aggregate expenditure)

Year	*Interest Payments*	*Defence*	*Subsidies*
1990-91	23.9	14.7	11.0
1995-96	28.1	15.1	7.1
1999-2000	30.3	15.8	8.2
2004-05	25.5	15.2	8.8
2005-06*	25.6	16.1	9.2
2006-07**	24.8	15.8	8.2

*Revised Figures. ** Budgeted Figures.
Source : *Economic and Political Weekly,* April 8-14, 2006, p. 1385.

It is clearly visible that in the past decade and a half, almost fifty percent of the government's expenditure is on interest payments, defence and subsidies. These are items charged against the Consolidated Fund. Interest payments cannot be brought down so soon in the near future. Expenditure on Defence! It can only increase not decrease in the near future when the national security is viewed as of paramount significance, and subsidies, well their share might have fallen but is still a significant amount. In the light of these facts, one can say that the bill has not really addressed the problem of fiscal prudence as yet. Our fiscal deficit may have gone down from 7.9% in 1990-91 to 4.1% in 2005-06. There is a fear that this reduction may be at the cost of economic and social services expenditure.

On the receipt side, the government has gone for popular direct tax reforms which have led to the reduction in the receipts of the government. Introduction of the VAT entails that the VAT rate be kept high if the government wants to get the same revenue that it was getting in the earlier set-up. Care has to be taken that a high rate does not end up in decreasing the purchasing power of the people thereby creating low demand conditions in the economy. Also, the government in the 2006-07 budget may not have stressed on disinvestments, yet the dividends and profits it earns from public sector units are hardly high enough to make a significant contribution to revenue receipts.

Further, the FRBM target of having a zero revenue deficit also seems difficult, as the coming year 2007 is a pre-poll year and expenditures are likely to rise than fall. The fiscal responsibility bill, however, is not a complete failure. As opined by Subir Gokaran, Chief Economist with CRISIL, 'minor slippages in deficit are acceptable if they are for the cause of growth. Budget promotes economic growth with a combination of tax, spending and reform measures. Some deviation from the path of revenue deficit elimination is a small price to pay'. The key word, however, is that these deviations are for the 'growth' of the economy.

CONCLUSION

The government today is seen as an agent of change reshaping the future of our country. It is more of a facilitator than a provider of services. In its new avtar, the government is expected to perform its role in a responsible manner and the budget is an important tool in the hands of the government. As a result, the budgets of today are not just statements of accounts, these are also a reflection of the intentions of the government and a measure of its performance. There have been areas like tax, banking sector, public sector, foreign investment, etc. where reforms have been initiated through the budget, but more than anything else, the budgeting process itself has undergone change through a reform process. This paper has discussed two such major developments, the move from traditional budgeting to outcome budgeting and the incorporation of fiscal responsibility in the budgeting exercise.

It is too soon to clearly measure the impact of these reforms. Critical analysis reveals that the success of outcome budgeting depends on the clear definitions of government's aims and that of the FRBM rests in reducing non-revenue generating expenditures—instead of capital expenditure.

Gender budgeting, on the other hand, requires that mere women specific allocations are not enough, they need to be supplemented by a comprehensive evaluation of the overall budget in terms of their impact on gender differentials. The three emergent dimensions in the 21st century budgeting process in India must converge to make the entire exercise more participatory and inclusive. The important thing is that these measures should not be mere stopovers, but be looked upon as vital tools of development.

References

Banerjee, Nirmala, Krishnaraj Maithrey (2004), "Sieving budgets for Gender", *Economic and Political Weekly*, October 30, 2004.

Bernia, Lourdes and Amy Lind (1995), "Engendering International Trade: Concepts, Policy and Action", GSD Working Paper Series No. 5, Cornell University Gender, Science and Development Programme and UNIFEM.

Chakraborty, S. Lekha (2006), Financial Express Special, www.financial express.com

Chowdhary, Harnita (2006), "Outcome Budgeting—Moving Beyond Rhetoric", *Economic and Political Weekly*, Vol. XLI, No. 25. pp. 2515-18.

Elson, Diane (2005), "Monitoring Government Budgets for Compliance with CEDAW", Report Highlights and Key Conclusions, UNIFEM.

Gender Budget Initiative: http://ed.nic.in/chap11.htm

Kumara, Sarath (2006), "India's 'pro-poor' Budget Boosts Military Spending and Market Reforms", http://www.wsw.org.

Lalvani, Mala (2006), "NDA and UPA Budgets—Continuity or Change", *Economic and Political Weekly*, Vol. XLI, No. 14, pp. 1318-21.

National Commission for Women, (NCW Publication, (2003), "Year of Endeavor, 2003", New Delhi.

Shah, Sonal and Radha Chaurushiya (2004), "The Promise of India: The Challenges Ahead", http://www.americanprogress.org.

Women Power Connect Workshop, (Dec. 13-14, 2004), Workshop Paper Prepared by WPC.

———, (2006), "Key to Budget Documents—Budget 2006-07", http://indiabudget.nic.in.

———, (2001), "Report on Observance of Standards and Codes—Fiscal Affairs", http://www.imf.org.

Critical Evaluation of Union Budgets

MANOJ K. SHARMA

INTRODUCTION

An estimate of all anticipated receipts and expenditures of Union for the ensuing financial year is laid before the Parliament. This is known as 'Annual Financial Statement' or 'Budget' and covers Central Government's transactions of all kinds, in and outside India, occurring during the preceding year, the year in which the statement is prepared, as well as the ensuing year or budget year as it is known.

The presentation of budget is followed by a general discussion on it in both the Houses of Parliament. Estimates of expenditure from the Consolidated Fund of India are placed before the Lok Sabha in the form of 'Demands for Grants'. All withdrawals of money from the Consolidated Fund are, thereafter, authorized by an Appropriation Act passed by the Parliament every year. Tax proposals of Budget are embodied in a Bill (Finance Bill) which is passed as the 'Finance Act' of the year. Estimates of receipts and expenditures are similarly presented by the State Governments in their Legislatures before the beginning of the financial year and Legislature's Sanction for expenditure is secured through similar procedure.

Objectives

To study the budgetary developments in the last 10 years and to analyse patterns in :

1. Revenue Receipts (a+b)

   (a) Tax Revenue
   (b) Non-Tax Revenue

2. Revenue Expenditure

   (a) Interest Payments
   (b) Major Subsidies
   (c) Defence Expenditure

3. Revenue Deficit (2-1)
4. Capital Receipts

   (a) Recovery of loans
   (b) Other Receipts
   (c) Borrowing and other liabilities

5. Capital Expenditure
6. Total Expenditure

   (a) Plan Expenditure
   (b) Non-Plan Expenditure

7. Fiscal Deficit
8. Primary Deficit

   (a) Primary Deficit-Consumption
   (b) Primary Deficit-Investment

Methodology

Comparison of Budgets of last ten years, also comparing budget estimates with the actual from various sources such as web-site of Ministry of Finance, Economic Surveys of various years and literature books on Indian Economy including other books.

The Budgetary position of the Union from 1998-99 onwards is shown in tables.

TABLE 8.1

(in Crore of Rupees)

Particulars/Sources, etc.	*1998-99 Actuals*	*1999-2000 Budget Estimates*	*1999-2000 Revised Estimates*	*2001-02 Budget Estimates*
(1)	*(2)*	*(3)*	*(4)*	*(5)*
1. Revenue Receipts	149510	182840	179504	231745
2. Tax Revenue (net to centre)	104652	132365	126469	163031
3. Non-Tax Revenue	44858	50475	53035	68714
4. Capital Receipts (5+6-6.1+7)	129856	101042	124234	143478
5. Recoveries of Loans	10633	11087	12736	15164
6. Other Receipts	5874	10000	2600	12000@
6.1. of which disinvestment proceeds committed for redemption of Public Debt.	—	—	—	116314
7. Borrowings and other liabilities	113349	79955	108898	375223
8. Total Receipts (1+4)	279366	283882	303738	275123
9. Non-Plan Expenditure	212548	206882	224343	250341
10. On Revenue Account of which	176900	190331	204904	112300
11. Interest Payments	77882	88000	91425	24782
12. On Capital Account	35648	16551	19439	95100

(Contd.)

TABLE 8.1 (*Contd.*)

(1)	(2)	(3)	(4)	(5)
13. Plan Expenditure	66818	77000	79395	60225
14. On Revenue Account	40519	46656	48132	34875
15. On Capital Account	26299	30344	31263	5000
16. Total Expenditure (9+13)	279366	283882	303738	375223
17. Revenue Expenditure (10+14)	217419	236987	253036	310566
18. Capital Expenditure (11+15)	61947	46895	50702	64657
19. Revenue Deficit (1-17)	67909	54147	73532	78821 (3.2)
20. Fiscal Deficit (9+5+6)-16 = (7-6.1)	113349	79955	108898	116314 (4.7)
21. Primary Deficit (20-11)	35467	-8045	17473	4014 (0.2)

Annual Plan

- Central Sector Plan Outlay increased from Rs. 1,03,521 crore to Rs. 1,17,334 crore.
- Gross Budget support for Plan increased from Rs. 77,000 crore to Rs. 88,100 crore.

Agriculture and Rural Development

- Rural Infrastructure Development Fund-VI enhanced from Rs. 3,500 crore to Rs. 4,500 crore and interest rate reduced by 1/2% to 11.5%.
- Credit flow to agriculture through institutional channels to increase to Rs. 51,500 crore in the coming year as compared to the estimated Rs. 41,800 crore this year.
- New initiatives for universalization of elementary education include a new scheme "Sarva Shiksha Abhiyan" to enable enrolment of all children by 2003.

Rural Housing and Social Security to the Poor

- 25 lakh dwelling units to be provided in rural areas.
- Assistance to construct 1 lakh houses for families below annual income of Rs. 32,000.

Small Scale Industries

- Limit of collateral free loans for tiny sector increased from Rs. 1 lakh to Rs. 5 lakh.
- Composite loan limit of SIDBI and banks for small borrowers raised from Rs. 5 lakh to Rs. 10 lakh.
- SIDBI's Technology Development Modernization Fund Scheme extended for another 3 years.

Science and Technology

- Rs. 50 crore provided in the budget of the Technology Information Forecasting and Assessment Council for taking up technology vision projects and boost cooperation between Universities and R&D Institutions.

Capital Market

- Tax regime liberalized and Securities and Exchange Board of India (SEBI) to be made single-point nodal agency for guidelines.
- Access of Indian companies to foreign portfolio investment made more flexible.
- Automatic route for overseas investment by Indian corporates liberalized.

Banking and Finance

- Government not to close any Public Sector Bank. Weak bank to be restructured.
- Banks to be allowed to raise capital from the market to expand operations and for meeting capital adequacy norms.

Reforms in Public Sector Units

- Potentially viable PSUs to be restructured and revived.
- PSUs, which cannot be revived, are to be closed down.
- Government equity in all non-strategic PSUs to be brought down to 26% and below.

Infrastructure Development

- Speedy implementation of PM's National Highways Development Project at a cost of Rs. 54,000 crore.
- Progressive corporatisation/privatization of Public Sector Service Providers in areas like telecommunications, ports and airports.

Subsidies

- Allocation of food grains to below poverty line families under PDS doubled.
- No allocation of sugar under PDS for Income Tax assessees.
- Fertilizer subsidies to be rationalized.

BUDGET ANALYSIS : 2000-01

Presenting the Union Budget 2000, Finance Minister, Shri Yashwant Sinha, proposed to put India on a sustained growth path of 7% to 8% per year. To achieve this, the Finance Minister detailed a strategy which would encompass strengthening the foundations of growth of the rural economy, nurturing growth potential of knowledge-based industries; modernizing traditional industries like textile, leather and agro processing, sustained efforts to remove infrastructure bottlenecks; a high priority to human resource development; strengthening the external sector through high export growth, high foreign investment, prudent debt management and establishing fiscal discipline.

The *budget seems set to promote growth in agriculture, biotechnology, food, IT, power, and telecom.* These areas will bring in a lot of expansion in the coming years. The thrust on basic areas like roads, infrastructure, water, and developing the rural base of the country are growth-oriented. The Finance Minister's focus on strengthening the forex position by relaxing GDR-ADR norms and bringing in $ 10 billion by 2001 into the country will contribute to growth.

Overall, the budget seems to be balanced. *Funds* for rural development, national highways, infrastructure, ports, all show signs of a progressive budget, as does reducing government holding in PSUs to 33 per cent.

But it is disappointing that the *fiscal deficit* has not been adequately addressed; the interest payment as a percentage of deficit is alarming. And reduction in the subsidy by raising the fertilizer prices is a tough decision for the government, but is necessary. With fiscal deficit at over Rs. 1,11,000 crore (it could go up to 1.5 lakh crore at the end of the year), subsidy at Rs. 20,000 crore, the number of government employees continuing to rise and expected to go up to 38 lakh, there is no serious effort to reduce government expenditure.

The raising of *tax on dividend* from 10 per cent to 20 per cent is not a good thing. Companies will be tempted to reduce dividend payout, which will discourage people from making investment in stocks.

On the positive side, Indian firms would get more flexibility for undertaking *capital account* transactions especially for acquisitions for business abroad in the knowledge-based sectors. To facilitate development of the government *debt market,* the legislative framework would be strengthened and modernized through a Government Securities Act which will replace the old Public Debt Act, 1944.

Agriculture and Rural Development

- Corpus of NABARD's RIDF VII increased from Rs. 4,500 crore to Rs. 5,000 crore next year and interest charged reduced from 11.5% to 10.5%.
- Kisan Credit Cards to all eligible agricultural farmers within the next 3 years.
- NABARD to reduce rate of interest for funding the storage of crops, from 10 per cent to 8.5 per cent.

TABLE 8.2
Budget 2001-02 at a Glance

(In crore of Rupees)

Particulars/Sources, etc.	*1999-2000 Actuals*	*2000-01 Budget Estimates*	*2000-01 Revised Estimates*	*2001-02 Budget Estimates*
(1)	*(2)*	*(3)*	*(4)*	*(5)*
1. Revenue Receipts	181513	203673	206166	231745
2. Tax Revenue (net to centre)	128271	146209	144403	163031
3. Non-Tax Revenue	53242	57464	61763	68714
4. Capital Receipts (5+6+7)	116571	134814	129357	143478
5. Recoveries of Loans	10131	13539	14885	15164
6. Other Receipts	1723	10000	2500	12000@
7. Borrowings and other liabilities	104717	112275	111972	116314
8. Total Receipts (1+4)	298084	338487	335523	375223
9. On Plan Expenditure	221902	250387	249284	275123
10. On Revenue Account	202309	228768	23041	250341
11. Interest Payments	90249	101266	100667	112300
12. On Capital Account	19593	21619	18853	24782
13. Plan Expenditure	76182	88100	86238	95100
14. On Revenue Account	46800	52330	53104	60225
15. On Capital Account	29382	35770	33134	34875
16. Lump sum provision for Additional Plan expenditure linked to investment receipts				5000
17. Total Expenditure (9+13)	298084	338487	335523	375223
18. Revenue Expenditure (9+14)	249109	281098	283535	310566
19. Capital Expenditure	48975	57389	51987	64657
20. Revenue Deficit (18-1)	67596 (3.5)	77425 (3.6)	77369 (3.6)	78821 (3.2)
21. Fiscal Deficit 7-(1+5+6)	104717 (5.4)	111275 (5.1)	111972 (5.1)	116314 (4.7)
22. Primary Deficit (21-11)	14468 (0.7)	10009 (0.5)	11305 (0.5)	4014 (0.2)

Management of the Food Economy

- Greater involvement of State Governments in procurement and distribution of foodgrains for PDS. Financial assistance would be available to the State Governments to enable them to procure and distribute foodgrains to BPL families at subsidized rates.

INFRASTRUCTURE

Power

- A specific programme for deduction and eventual elimination of power theft.
- Tariff determination by SERCs and compliance thereof.
- Commercialisation of distribution.
- SEBs restructuring.

Telecom

- Competition being introduced in all service segments.
- Convergence Bill to cover telecommunications, information technology, and information and broadcasting sectors in an integrated manner to be introduced.

FINANCIAL SECTOR AND CAPITAL MARKETS

- Financial sector and capital market reforms to continue.

Debt Market

- A Clearing Corporation for further orderly development of money market (including repo), Government Securities market and settlement of forex transactions will be set-up.
- Removal of taxation anomalies to promote the issuance of STRIPS, zero coupon bonds, deep discount bounds, and the like.

- Public Debt Act to be replaced by Government Securities Act.

Capital Account Liberalization

Indian companies may now invest abroad up to US $50 million annually through the automatic route without being subject to the three year profitability condition.

- Indian companies that have ADRs/GDRs, may acquire shares of foreign companies up to an amount of US $100 million or an amount equivalent to ten times their exports in a year, whichever be higher.

Foreign Investment

The 40 per cent limit of investment in a company under the portfolio investment route by FIIs being increased to 49 per cent.

Industrial Restructuring

- SICA to be repealed.
- 14 items related to leather goods, shoes and toys being de-reserved.
- The exemption limit has been doubled to Rs. 1 crore from September 1, 2000.

FISCAL CONSOLIDATION

Expenditure Management

- All requirements of recruitment will be scrutinized to ensure that fresh recruitment is limited to 1 per cent of total civilian staff strength in PSUs and Government.
- Postal rates will be revised moderately to contain the rising postal deficit.
- Facility of LTC to Central Government employees suspended for 2 years.

Interest Rates

- Administered interest rates being reduced by 1 to 1.5 per cent points as of March 1, 2001. Government guarantees and tax incentives for these schemes to continue.
- The benefit of reduction in interest rates on Small Savings Deposits will be fully passed on to the States.

PUBLIC SECTOR RESTRUCTURING AND PRIVATIZATION

- Privatization to be accelerated.
- An amount of Rs. 7,000 crore out of the expected receipts of Rs. 12,000 crore from disinvestment will be used for providing restructuring assistance to PSUs, safety net to workers and reduction of debt burden.

Principles of Tax Proposals

- Need for growth in revenues, simplification and rationalization of the tax regime, and effective tax compliance through measures, which are friendly for the honest taxpayers, and deterrent to the evaders.

Budget Estimates

- The target of 5.1% of fiscal deficit in 2000-01 has been achieved first time in many years.
- Total expenditure in the budget estimates for 2001-02 has been estimated at Rs. 3,75,223 crore, of which Rs. 1,00,100 crore is for plan and Rs. 2,75,123 crore for non-plan.

BUDGET ANALYSIS : 2001-02

One central feature of the Central Government finances during the 1990s has been the decline in both the share of taxes and expenditure in the GDP. The latter has been brought about through compression in capital expenditure rather than revenue component of expenditure. The erosion in tax-to-GDP ratio has to some extent prevented fiscal adjustment on a sustained basis. Therefore, erosion in tax-GDP ratio needs to be reversed. The potential for increase in tax-GDP ratio does exist. This is reflected in a rising share of non-agriculture GDP, which augurs well for a higher overall tax-GDP ratio. Besides, resumption in overall growth and particularly industrial growth in future is likely to bring in higher corporate tax collections and excise revenues. Also, a concerted effort would be required to tax untapped potential of direct taxes through improvement in direct tax administration by focusing on measures to foster increased compliance and wide spread computerization.

The trends in the Central Government finances during the current year show considerable slippage on the revenue side due to the slowdown in the economy and industry in particular. Government has responded to slowdown by cutting down the tax rates in both the direct and indirect taxes. The slower economic growth not only leads to revenue shortfalls but also puts pressure for fiscal stimulus. As a deliberate policy, the Government has avoided cutting or compressing capital expenditure. In the backdrop of economic slowdown, the issue of quality rather than quantum in fiscal adjustment assumes importance. Higher Government spending with low capital expenditure content may not translate into much needed higher aggregate demand to stimulate the economy. A major feature of the inter-temporal profile of Government expenditure has been the erosion of capital expenditure. Capital expenditure, which has been cut out in both Central and State Government budgets needs to be restored by budgetary allocation and higher Internal and Extra Budgetary funding. As a result, we are not investing enough for future. Further, such expenditure would have to be in growth augmenting infrastructure sectors. Government investment and reforms should focus on leveraging private sector participation in these sectors rather for furthering the objective of ownership. Besides, the composition of revenue expenditure has to shift to social sector like education and health.

TABLE 8.3
Budget 2002-03

(*Rupees in Crores*)

Particulars/Sources, etc.	*2000-01 Actuals*	*2001-02 Budget Estimates*	*2001-02 Revised Estimates*	*2002-03 Budget Estimates*
(1)	*(2)*	*(3)*	*(4)*	*(5)*
1. Revenue Receipts	192624	231745	212572	245105
2. Tax Revenue (net to centre)	136916	163031	142348	172965
3. Non-Tax Revenue	55708	68714	70224	72140
4. Capital Receipts (5+6+7)	132987	143478	151864	165204
5. Recoveries of Loans	12046	15164	15143	17680
6. Other Receipts	2125	12000	5000	12000
7. Borrowings and other liabilities	118816	116314	131721	13524
8. Total Receipts (1+4)	325611	375223	364436	410309
9. Non-Plan Expenditure	242942	275123	265282	296809
10. On Revenue Account, of which	226782	250341	242471	270169
11. Interest Payments	99314	112300	107257	117390
12. On Capital Account	16160	24782	22811	26640
13. Plan Expenditure	85669	95100	99154	113500
14. On Revenue Account	51076	60225	61834	70313
15. On Capital Account	31593	34875	373200	43187
16. Lump Sum provision for Additional Plan expenditure linked to disinvestment receipts	—	5000	—	—
17. Total Expenditure (9+13+16)	325611	375223	364436	410309
18. Revenue Expenditure (10+14)	277858	310566	304305	340482
19. Capital Expenditure (12+15+16)	47753	64656	60131	69827
20. Revenue Deficit (18-1)*	85234 (4.1)	78821 (3.2)	91733 (4.0)	95377 (3.8)
21. Fiscal Deficit* {17-(1+5+6)}	95377 (5.7)	116314 (4.7)	131721 (5.7)	135524 (5.3)
22. Primary Deficit (21-11)*	19502 (0.9)	4014 (0.2)	24464 (1.1)	18134 (0.7)

Budget Strategy

- Continue the emphasis on agriculture and food economy reforms.
- Enhance public and private investment in infrastructure.
- Strengthen the financial sector and capital market.
- Deepen Structural reforms and regenerate industrial growth.
- Provide social security to the poor.
- Consolidate tax reforms and continue fiscal adjustment at both the Central and State levels.

Agriculture and Rural Development

- Removal of small scale industry reservations related to various agricultural equipment items.
- Decimalization of the export of agricultural commodities and phasing out of remaining export controls.

Rural Roads

- Allocation of Rs. 2,500 crore for the Pradhan Mantri Gram Sadak Yojana (PMGSY).

Rural Electrification

- New interest subsidy scheme called the Accelerated Rural Electrification Programme to be introduced. An outlay of Rs. 164 crore provided.

Management of Food Economy

- Number of steps taken by the Government to reduce high food stocks.

Power

- APDP being redesigned as the Accelerated Power

Development and Reform Programme (APDRP), with an enhanced plan allocation of Rs. 3,500 crore for 2002-03. The focus of reform has shifted from generation to transmission and distribution.

Roads, Ports and Civil Aviation

- The Golden Quadrilateral will be completed substantially by December 2003, a year ahead of schedule.
- Major ports to be corporatised in phased manner. Regulatory structure will be strengthened.
- International airports at Delhi, Mumbai, Chennai and Kolkata to be upgraded.
- Private sector participation in Greenfield airport projects will be encouraged through a package of concessions.

Debt and Capital Market

- Legislative changes will be proposed in the SEBI Act 1992 for investor protection, and to enhance the effectiveness of SEBI as the capital market regulator.
- FII portfolio investments not to be subject to the sectoral limits for foreign direct investment except in specified sectors.

Banking Sector

- Additional fiscal relief is being offered to help banks and financial institutions to make provisions for NPAs.
- IDBI to be corporatised.
- Foreign banks to either operate as branches of their parent banks or to set-up subsidiaries.

Capital Account Liberalization

- Full convertibility of deposit schemes would be put in place for Non-Resident Indians. The schemes, which do not offer full convertibility to NRIs are to be discontinued from April 1, 2002.

- NRIs will be free to repatriate in foreign currency their current earnings in India.
- Indian companies may now invest abroad up to US $ 100 Million on an annual basis through the automatic route, up from the existing limit of US $ 50 million.
- Indian companies may make overseas investment in joint ventures abroad by market purchases without prior approval up to 50 per cent of their net worth.

Administered Pricing Mechanism (APM)

Petroleum

- Administered Price Mechanism (APM) in the petroleum sector to be dismantled as of April 1, 2002.

Fiscal Consolidation

Expenditure Management

- Of the identified surplus manpower of 42,200 in 36 Ministries/Departments where ERC completed its work, nearly 12,200 posts are expected to be abolished by the end of March 2002.
- Decision to limit fresh recruitment to 1 per cent of total civilian staff strength to continue over the next 4 years.

Small Savings and Interest Rates

- Most of the administered interest rates to be reduced by 50 basis points from March 1, 2002. Future adjustments to be made annually on a non-discretionary automatic basis. The benefit of reduction in interest rates on small saving deposits will be fully passed on to the States.

Principles of Tax Proposals

- Tax proposals are against the backdrop of the current economic slow-down. Intended to revive demand, promote investment, accelerate economic growth, enhance productivity, widening the tax base, rationalization and simplification of tax structure and encouraging voluntary compliance.

BUDGET ANALYSIS : 2002-03

The Union Budget for 2002-03 was formulated in the background of *falling industrial growth, falling revenue receipts, tense security environment* and a *slowdown in world economic growth.* Keeping these constraints in view, the Budget is aimed at consolidating the gains of economic reforms and hastening this process further to the State level through a strategy of reforms linked to public funding. The Budget adopted a strategy of continuing the emphasis on agriculture and food economy reforms, enhancing public and private investment in infrastructure, strengthening the financial sector and capital markets, deepening structural reforms and rejuvenating industrial growth, providing social security to the poor, consolidation, tax reforms and continuing fiscal adjustments at both the Central and State levels.

Disconcerting Features

The revenue deficit which was estimated at Rs. 78,821 crore in 2001-02 had increased alarmingly and stands at Rs. 91,733 crore, much more than in 2000-01. The fiscal deficit of the centre for the year 2001-02 had later been placed at 5.7 per cent of GDP, as compared to the budget estimate of 4.7 per cent. If the deficit of public sector undertakings and local bodies is added to this, the total public sector deficit is clearly unsustainable.

Fiscal Discipline

Adoption of zero base budgeting has remained a mere paper slogan. The 10 reports submitted by the Expenditure

Reforms Commission (ERC) are gathering dust. A Voluntary Retirement Scheme (VRS) was announced for the staff declared surplus but there was no move to abolish the surplus posts at the end of the year if the staff did not opt for VRS.

Interest Rates and Savings

An important point which needs to be emphasized is that till such time as the large public sector borrowings came down, the pressure of interest rates would continue, despite efforts to reduce the administered rates. Yet another matter of concern is that most of the borrowings by the centre and the states are for consumption expenditure.

Economic Reforms

The mounting food stocks and the need for revision of food procurement policy is an area requiring urgent attention.

Issues regarding restructuring of railways, privatization of nationalized banks, the All-Indian public financial institutions and the coal sector and similar other major issues seem to have been put on the backburner. The unfinished agenda of economic reforms is truly large.

TABLE 8.4
Budget : 2003-04

(*Rs. in Crores*)

Particulars/Sources, etc.	*2001-02 Actuals*	*2002-03 Budget Estimates*	*2002-03 Revised Estimates*	*2003-04 Budget Estimates*
(1)	*(2)*	*(3)*	*(4)*	*(5)*
1. Revenue Receipts	201449	245105	236936	253935
2. Tax Revenue (net to Centre)	133662	172965	164177	184169
3. Non-tax revenue	67787	72140	72759	69766
4. Capital Receipts (5+6+7)	161004	165204	167077	184860

(*Contd.*)

TABLE 8.4 (Contd.)

(1)	(2)	(3)	(4)	(5)
5. Recoveries of Loans	16403	17680	18251	18023
6. Other Receipts	3646	12000	3360	13200
7. Borrowings and other Liabilities	140955	135524	145466	153637
8. Total Receipts (1+4)	362453	410309	404013	438795
9. Non-plan Expenditure	261259	296807	289924	317821
10. On Revenue Account of which	239954	270169	268979	289384
11. Interest Payments	107460	117390	115663	123223
12. On Capital Account	21305	26640	20945	28437
13. Plan Expenditure	101194	113500	114089	120974
14. On Revenue Account	61657	70313	72669	76843
15. On Capital Account	39537	43187	41420	44131
16. Total Expenditure (9+13)	362453	410309	404013	438795
17. Revenue Expenditure (10+14)	301611	340482	341648	366227
18. Capital Expenditure (12+15)	60842	69827	62365	72568
19. Revenue Deficit (17-11)	100162 (4.3)	95377 (3.8)	104712 (4.3)	112292 (4.1)
20. Fiscal Deficit {16-(1+5+6)}	140955* (6.1)	135524 (5.3)	145466 (5.9)	153637 (5.6)
21. Primary Deficit (20-11)	33495 (1.5)	18134 (0.7)	29803 (1.2)	30414 (1.1)

Note : Percentages are given within brackets.

ANALYSIS OF BUDGET : 2003-04

Finance Minister, Jaswant Singh, while presenting the budget for 2003-04, had to keep in mind the *Report of Kelkar Committee* on Direct and Indirect Taxes on the one hand and the imperatives of an impending election the following year. Thus, he had to balance the economic and political compulsions. The Finance Minister decided not to accept immediately the Kelkar Committee Recommendations on direct taxes.

Kelkar Committee while making all these recommendations, did not provide an answer to the basic question whether the recommendations would improve tax-GDP ratio of the Central Government or be revenue-neutral or whether it would result in a decline in tax-GDP ratio. In order to promote fiscal consolidation, it is imperative to use the words of the Finance Minister that the Central Government goes in for "expenditure reprioritization or revenue augmentation". There is no doubt that the Government has undertaken expenditure reprioritization and as a consequence, "the revised estimates of expenditure for the year 2002-03 show a decrease in expenditure of Rs. 6,296 crore as compared to the budget estimate. There is addition of Rs. 339 crores, if the entire arithmetic is translated into reality. There were certain sops for the middle classes and high income groups in the budget.

Certain *Schemes* to benefit the poor and senior citizens have also been announced by the Finance Minister. Among them are : Extension of Antodya Anna Yojana to another 50 lakh families, LIC Varishta Pension Bima Yojana; making credit available to the SSI sector at a rate of interest 2 per cent above the PLR. But the basic problem is that there is a wide gap between profession and practice.

The government has *failed to reduce subsidies*. Though the average rate of interest on market borrowing has declined due to debt swap at lower rate of interest, yet increase in the quantum of borrowing year after year to meet the revenue deficit, does not allow the total interest payments to register a decline.

To sum up, it may be stated that the budget (2003-04) has offered some *carrots for the middle and upper income groups* and thus provided relief to the vocal section of our society. *But it has failed to address the need for fiscal consolidation.*

The budgetary proposals are tax revenue neutral and thus will not improve the tax-GDP ratio. The projections of receipts from major *taxes* for 2003-04 are very optimistic and can be considered as over estimates. Budget raised the issue of agricultural development with a bang but its measures of implementation ended with a whimper. It has not seriously addressed to the social concerns of education, health, women and child developments. In nutshell, budget betrays a serious gap between rhetoric and reality.

TABLE 8.5
Budget : 2004-05

(In Crore of Rupees)

Particulars/Sources, etc.	*2002-03 Actuals*	*2003-04 Budget Estimates*	*2003-04 Revised Estimates*	*2004-05 Budget Estimates*
(1)	*(2)*	*(3)*	*(4)*	*(5)*
1. Revenue Receipts	231748	253935	263027	290882
2. Tax Revenue (net to Centre)	159425	184169	187539	220132
3. Non-tax revenue	72323	69766	75488	70750
4. Capital Receipts (5+6+7)	168648	184860	211228	16652
5. Recoveries of Loans	34191	18023	64625[1]	14100
6. Other Receipts	3151	13200	14500	16000
7. Borrowings and other Liabilities	131306	153637	132103	136452
8. Total Receipts (1+4)	400396	438795	474255	457434
9. Non-plan Expenditure	288942	317821	352748	322363
10. On Revenue Account of which	268074	289384	284801	295359
11. Interest Payments and Debt Servicing	117804	123223	124555	129500
12. On Capital Account	20868	28437	67947[2]	27004
13. Plan Expenditure	111455	120974	121507	135071
14. On Revenue Account	71554	76843	78086	85383
15. On Capital Account	39901	44131	43421	49688
16. Total Expenditure (9+13)	400396	438795	474255	457434
17. Revenue Expenditure (10+14)	339627	366227	362887	380742
18. Capital Expenditure (12+15)	60769	72568	111368	76692
19. Revenue Deficit (17-11)	107879 (4.4)	112292 (4.1)	99860 (3.6)	89860 (2.9)
20. Fiscal Deficit {16-(1+5+6)}	131306* (5.4)	153637 (5.6)	132102 (4.8)	136452 (4.4)
21. Primary Deficit (20-11)	13502 (0.6)	13502 (1.1)	7548 (0.3)	6952 (0.2)

* Based on provisional estimates Actuals for 2002-03.

1. Excludes repayments to National Small Savings Fund.
2. Includes receipts from States on account of Debt Swap Scheme.

RURAL DEVELOPMENT

Sampoorna Gramin Rozgar Yojana

- 5100 crore rupees provided for the scheme. The objective of the scheme is to provide additional wage employment in rural areas as also food security.

Pradhan Mantri Gram Sadak Yojana

- 2468 crore rupees provided for Pradhan Mantri Gram Sadak Yojana with the objective of providing connectivity to unconnected rural habitations through good all weather roads.

Rural Housing

- 2500 crore rupees provided for rural housing for rural poor to be built by themselves.

Agriculture and Cooperation

- 350 crore rupees provided for Crop Insurance Scheme.
- 719.94 crore rupees provided for Macro-management in agriculture.
- 200 crore rupees provided for Technology Mission in Horticulture in North Eastern Region, Jammu & Kashmir and Uttaranchal.

Fertilizers

- 117.09 lakh tonnes of Nitrogenous fertilizer production targeted.

Elementary Education and Literacy

- 3057 crore rupees provided for Sarva Shiksha Abhiyan. It is meant for implementation of universal elementary education in a mission mode with a clear distinct focus to provide quality elementary education to children of the age group of 6-14 years.

Information Technology

- 750 crore rupees provided for the development and promotion of Information Technology.

Telecommunications

To install—

- 105 lakh direct exchange lines by BSNL & MTNL.

Agro-based and Rural Industries

- 164 crore rupees provided for Prime Minister's Rozgar Yojana to assist educated unemployed youth.
- 248 crore rupees provided for Rural Employment Generation Programme to generate additional employment in the rural industries/sector through development of Khadi and village industries.

Small Scale Industries

- 176 crore rupees provided for Credit Guarantee Funds for SSI to provide collateral free loans to SSI sector.

Non-conventional Energy Sources

- 420 villages and hamlets proposed to be electrified.
- 525 MW power generation capacity to be added from renewable energy sources.

Science and Technology

- 216 crore rupees provided for Multi-Disciplinary Research in Science and Technology Programme under the Science and Engineering Research Council (SERC).

Space

- 490 crore rupees provided for Geo-synchronous Satellite Launch Vehicle (GSLV) Mark-III Development.
- 430 crore rupees provided for INSAT operation.

ANALYSIS OF ALL PREVIOUS BUDGETS

Politics of Economic Policy and Reforms

After a decade and more of economic reforms, the internal contradictions amongst the *major political parties*, namely the BJP. The RSS as well as the Swadeshi Jagran Munch (SJM), which shares the same parentage as the BJP, are opposed to foreign investment, to globalization, to the World Trade Organization, to privatization, all of which are part of the agenda of the ruling alliance led by the BJP. Indeed, on many of these and other issues like labour law reform, RSS/SJM are closer to the left parties like the CPI (M) than the BJP.

Nor does the Congress seem to have any kind of coherent and consistent economic policy stance. It was the party which initiated economic reforms under the stewardship of P.V. Narasimha Rao as the Prime Minister and Manmohan Singh as the Finance Minister. To be sure, the trigger for the reform process was the compulsions following the *balance of payments* crisis. On the other hand, by then, it was surely evident that the 40 year old model of economic policy had made as a laggard in the Asian growth league, and that major changes were needed. These were implemented by the Congress government but almost by stealth, with nobody 'marketing' the changes and explaining to the voters their need. Out of power, and under the second leadership of Mrs. Gandhi's, the party seems to have gone back even further on the policy agenda as witnessed, for example, by the famous Pachmarhi Resolution. One blatant contradiction increasingly emerging in Congress policy is that the party opposes at the centre what it practices in the states it rules.

Besides the internal contradictions in the two major policies, the politics of economic policy also has to contend with opposing coalitions controlling the two houses of parliament. Since our *democracy* has not matured much beyond the scoring of points, this also hampers needed legislative changes.

In terms of the resources constraint, perhaps the most important is the issue of *subsidies* to those who are not really needy. Chidambaram's finance ministry has brought out a White Paper on subsidies a few year back—it evidenced that the explicit and implicit subsidies at the centre and states taken together add up to about 15 per cent of GDP, clearly an unsustainable burden when the aggregate revenues of the centre and states barely reach this level. More importantly, the white paper argued that 75 percent of the subsidies are aimed at not the really poor, but the relatively better off. It is of course a moot factor what part of the balance is eaten up by middle-men before reaching the 'poor' over whose plight ritual tears continue to be shed in each policy announcement.

But BJP and Congress apart, the lasting legacy of the third front government led by Gujral is the utterly irresponsible decision on the report of the Pay Commission. Compensations were increased beyond what was recommended, and the proposals about economizing completely glossed over. This has crippled the finances of the centre, and even more so of the states, whose plight is unenviable. *Like Enron, they have gone in for massive amounts of 'Off balance sheet' financing* and the chicken are coming to roost. An estimated Rs. 44,000 crore worth of state government-guaranteed bonds are maturing upto 2007 and massive defaults are inevitable.

While changes in subsidies even to the less-than needy are not feasible under the current dispensation, the resultant pressure on resources means that the availability of fund for primary schools, village roads, water supply and other rural infrastructure, etc., is crippled. This, in turn, means that agro-processing industry cannot come up where it will do most good in terms of jobs and cost efficiencies. Other financial time bombs are also ticking—even after the change in the last budget, the government's pension liability will keep growing for many years to come, and there is also the large gap between the return on employees provident funds to them and what the investment of Fund's investments can earn.

Take the question of *labour law reform* which has become a hurdle to job creation. It is worth noting that despite 6 per cent per annum GDP growth for a decade, there has been hardly any increase in employment in the organized sector. Job protection seems to be coming at the cost of job creation. In theory, economic liberalization should lead to investments in areas where we have a comparative advantage. In our case, it has led to huge investments in say refineries—not in world class toy manufacture ! Interestingly, the dangers of total *job protection* were foreseen very clearly by Mahalanobis, the father of the planning process in India. To quote him, "Welfare measures tend to be implemented in India ahead of economic growth. Indian labour laws are probably the most highly protective of labour interest in its narrowest sense in the whole world". He had argued, according to T.N. Srinivasan, that Indian labour laws would be an obstacle to growth and would increase inequalities. He was right then, his analysis is true even today.

In the process, we have vacated labour intensive manufacture of toys, low-tech electronic goods, etc. to China, and that too without even a token fight. It is worth remembering that much of the rapid growth in China has come in the 'special economic Zones' in which job protection laws do not apply. Will there ever be a political consensus on withdrawing protection at least for those earning x times the per capita income ?

Institutional Weaknesses

If financial constraints are one part of the political economy, major institutional weaknesses are another. Amongst these, perhaps the legal is at the top. The delays, the focus on procedures rather than substance, the unwillingness to reform have crippled the system to such an extent that even the guardian of law and order namely the police, prefer, "encounters" to prosecution of criminals, and the otherwise vociferous human rights activists watch in silence.

But the legal system is by no means the only one suffering from inefficiencies and poor governance. While any number of instances could be cited, let me list only three:

The UTI's *US 64 fiasco.* It is truly amazing that, even after the Deepak Parekh Committee report, nothing was done to overhaul the fund's investment policies, until matters reached such a stage that thousands of crores are now being spent for a bailout.

Take, again, the case of *Enron's power project* in Maharashtra. After Enron's bankruptcy, for reasons unconnected with the Dabhol Power Project, the matter is now drifting for the last two years, between MSEB, the state government, the lenders, the centre and umpteen other agencies. It is obvious now that Maharashtra needs the power and the Rs. 12,000 crore plant was/is ready to produce it. The way we are going about would mean that no solutions would come till the plant rusts if it has not already done so. Surely, given that all the agencies involved are arms of the state, some acceptable solution, at least an interim one, to get the plant running, can be found. But our political and administrative system seems incapable of sorting out the problem in any purposeful way.

On March 17, *The Economic Times* reported that the CBDT had started examining the issue of tax treatment of derivatives. How many years has it taken after trading in derivatives started in India? As if the system does not have a surfeit of tax disputes already.

GDP Growth

In our focus on the domestic sector of the economy, we often tend to overlook how critically important the external sector has become to industrial and GDP growth. Consider the data in the following table:

Growth Rates

(Per cent)

	IIP	*Exports*
1994-95	9.1	18.4
1995-96	13.0	20.8
1996-97	6.1	5.3
1997-98	6.7	-4.6
1998-99	4.1	-5.1
1999-01	6.7	10.8
2000-01	4.9	21.0
2001-02	2.6	-1.6

The co-efficient of correlation between export growth and the growth in the index of industrial production is as high as 0.7

per cent. Perhaps a wonder since ¾ths of our exports consist of manufactured goods. Too long have we looked upon exports from a balance of payments, rather than GDP growth, perspective.

Paradigm Shifts

Thanks to competition, price rises in manufactured goods have been subdued. In fact, there have been periods when manufacturing inflation had been negative. Certain sectors, for example, auto-ancillaries, are finding that the buyers are insisting on price reduction each year. Inflation would, therefore, be increasingly a phenomenon of energy prices and agricultural output, both broadly outside the direction of monetary policy.

Manufacturing industry has become far more efficient in the use of capital. According to CMIE study, the average working capital cycle has gone down from 60 days in 1990-91 to 14 days in 2001-02.

There seems to be an increasing awareness that high *interest rates* can as much be a cause of fiscal deficit as the other way round, given our total debt. This is a point one has been arguing for a few years. The low interest rates, at least in nominal terms, have benefited not only in lowering the government's interest burden, but also given a fillip to the housing sector—housing loans would have otherwise been unaffordable to a large segment of today's borrowers, at higher interest rates.

Easy money and low interest rates have also persuaded the banking system to aggressively pursue the consumer market not only for housing finance, but also for consumer durables. This is a major and welcome shift if financing Maruti is virtuous so should the financing of the buyer of its output be, without which Maruti itself may suffer. The liberalisation of trade and exchange control and a wise exchange rate policy have led to a surplus on current account for the first time in decades. That foreign exchange is no longer a constraint is a major paradigm shift in the macro-economy—we suffered for decades through export pessimism, and self-inflicted BoP constraints.

On the service side, apart from IT and ITES, one can hope for major increases under say pharma and biotech research, hospitalization services, etc. Even in merchandise exports, once the quotas are removed in the next year or two, one should see sharp growth in textile exports. Besides, auto-ancillaries and indeed vehicles should became star performers, if only for their own viability. It is difficult to see the capacity created being used fully by the domestic sector alone. The sector will demonstrate, if any such demonstration is needed, that exports result not by imposing obligations but through the economics of the business.

The public/private partnership: The Finance Minister referred to this which by itself is also a major change—less than a couple of decades back, Delhi used to be so suspicious of the private sector.

If one change signifies the paradigm shift, it is our policy-makers' stance on *gold.* For decades, we banned gold imports which did nothing to reduce imports, except that they came illegally, and strengthened only the smugglers and 'hawala' market operators. What a refreshing change to see the Finance Minister even talking about making India an international gold trading centre.

Miscellaneous Issues

A few more refreshing, qualitative changes are as under :

The efficient implementation of the *golden quadrilateral road* and Delhi metro projects.—Investments by Indian companies abroad have become almost routine, particularly in IT and pharma sectors.

Increasing consolidation in domestic industry through *mergers/takeovers/sales,* no longer unwilling to sell assets.

EVALUATING QUALITY OF BUDGETS WITH A COMPOSITE INDEX

Proposed Quality Index of Budget

The various measures that are often considered in assessing a government budget, more specifically in the case of the budget of the central government, are: (a) gross fiscal deficit,

(b) revenue deficit, (c) primary deficit, (d) composition of expenditures in terms of spending on 'productive purposes', and (e) composition of revenues that have implications to sustainability of revenue strategy.

(1) Quality of revenue expenditures: measured by the share of revenue expenditures other than interest payments, subsidies and defene;
(2) Quality of capital expenditure: share of capital expenditure other than defence;
(3) Qualify of revenue: ratio of net tax revenue of centre to GDP, on the ground that dependence on taxes as a source of revenue is a more sustainable revenue generation strategy;
(4) Degree of fiscal prudence 1: fiscal deficit to GDP ratio; and
(5) Degree of fiscal prudence 2: revenue deficit to GDP ratio.

Are the Budgets Getting Better?

The *quality of revenue expenditure* deteriorated over the years due to larger volumes of interest payments, salaries and subsidies.

Some improvements for 2000-01 and 2001-02 (BE).

The quality index of capital expenditure has gone down more or less steadily during the 1980s and 1990s. The value of the index during recent years fluctuated between one-third and one-fourth of level in early 1980s.

From the point of view of *fiscal consolidation,* the year 1996-97 happens to be the best year and 1986-87 the worst year for the central government. The fiscal prudence index remained low for most of 1980s, shows significant upturn in first half of 1990s and downturn in the closing years of 1990s.

Position given in the Table 8.6 is self-explanatory.

Recent years get the lowest scores from the revenue side: 2000-01 for revenue deficit control and 2001-02 (RE) for tax revenue generation. The current trends on these variables are worrisome and call for priority attention to reverse the trends.

Considering all factors together, the highest overall score was

TABLE 8.6

Composite Index of Budget Quality and Indices of Components

Year	Quality Indices of Individual Components					Composite Index	Composite Index (with 1980-81=100)
	Revenue Expenditure	Capital Expenditure	Revenue Measures	Fiscal Prudence	Revenue Prudence		
(1)	(2)	(3)	(4)	(5)	(6)	(7)	(8)
1980-81	75.5	63.2	30.2	64.5	64.6	59.6	100.0
1981-82	58.6	67.7	36.9	77.2	94.2	66.9	112.3
1982-83	64.7	68.6	38.3	67.1	82.6	64.3	107.8
1983-84	60.4	63.9	40.7	61.3	71.1	59.5	99.8
1984-85	55.0	62.1	43.8	38.1	57.0	51.2	58.9
1985-86	65.1	59.4	52.1	22.7	47.0	49.3	82.7
1986-87	57.8	57.5	56.3	10.7	37.5	44.0	73.8
1987-88	67.5	44.5	58.1	27.4	35.5	46.6	78.2
1988-89	58.3	42.1	60.1	33.3	37.6	46.3	77.6
1989-90	50.8	40.9	57.8	33.4	38.7	44.3	74.3
1990-91	47.1	39.6	51.2	23.0	18.4	35.9	60.2
1991-92	44.4	29.3	53.3	68.8	37.8	46.7	78.4

(Contd.)

TABLE 8.6 (Contd.)

(1)	(2)	(3)	(4)	(5)	(6)	(7)	(8)
1992-93	52.4	24.8	44.4	72.6	38.0	46.4	77.9
1993-94	52.3	22.3	24.4	39.7	4.8	28.7	48.2
1994-95	49.4	24.5	33.2	66.0	23.4	39.3	65.9
1995-96	55.9	17.6	37.9	78.6	37.4	45.5	76.3
1996-97	45.3	16.7	37.0	82.5	40.3	44.4	74.4
1997-98	41.4	20.9	25.7	63.2	23.7	35.0	58.7
1998-99	45.2	21.5	19.0	51.1	3.4	28.0	47.0
1999-00	45.3	22.5	31.1	47.4	13.6	32.0	53.7
2000-01	57.1	14.1	24.2	49.6	3.4	29.7	49.8
2001-02RE	57.8	18.8	3.5	66.0	16.6	32.5	54.6
2002-03BE	55.2	17.2	16.4	72.0	19.8	36.1	60.6

Note : The basis of indices: Revenue expenditure measure; percentage of expenditure other than interest payments, subsidies and defence: Capital expenditure measure; percentage of non-defense expenditure; Revenue measure: percentage of tax revenue in receipts; Fiscal prudence; ratio of fiscal deficit to GDP; Revenue prudence; ratio of revenue deficit to GDP. Composite index is the simple average of the components and the last column is scaling of the index with base as 1980-81.

achieved in 1981-82 when the index reached the level 112 (with 1980-81 value =100). The overall index then slipped for several years, exhibited moderate fluctuations, reached the lowest point in 1998-99 and took a small upturn after that. The overall score of the quality of the central government's budget in recent years is only about half the 1981-82 peak level.

The *2002-03 budget appears to be better* than the previous budget and actually better than the budgets of the previous five years—four of which were presented by the current Finance Minister himself. Taking into account all the indicators that do not necessarily move in the same direction, this year's budget is a 'better budget' on three counts: proposed reduction in fiscal and revenue deficits and expansion of tax revenue.

There is, of course, always the point that budget estimates are often way off the mark by the end of the year. For example, net tax revenue collection for 2001-02 was budgeted at Rs. 1,63,031 crore, but it is likely to come down to Rs. 1,42,348 crore as per the revised estimate, a fall of 13 per cent. The budgets of the 1990s show more 'volatility' as compared to the more stable budgets of the 1980s.

In the case of government budgets, assessments are made based on a number of different perspectives. It is difficult to perceive that there would be one common set of indicators that can be used to judge the budget by all. Through the 1990s, the central government budgets have become more varied, attempting to achieve fiscal stabilization 'gradually'. This year's budget (2002-03), on the basis of the index presented here, is one of the better budgets in the last five. But, again, going by the budget estimates alone, 2001-02 budget was superior to a few of the previous ones.

Fiscal Consolidation

The Union Budget of 2003-04 has listed five priorities: (a) poverty eradication and social capital (health, housing, education and employment) formation; (b) development of infrastructure; (c) fiscal consolidation through tax reforms; (d) agriculture and related aspects; and (e) enhancing manufacturing sector efficiency. To be fair, the Finance Minister has indeed addressed all the priority areas. In many ways, however, fiscal consolidation would seem to be prerequisite for attaining the other four objectives listed by the Finance Minister.

Contribution of Budget to Fiscal Consolidation

Thus dividends are to be free from tax in the hands of investors, the tax on long-term capital gains has been abolished for investment in equities made during the next financial year. A rationalization of the excise duty structure have been put in place with three rates of 8 per cent, 16 per cent and 24 per cent. The VAT is to be introduced from April 1, 2003, the rate of service tax has been increased to 8 per cent and 10 new items are to pay the service tax, the peak rate on customs duties has been lowered to 25 per cent. There have been some changes in respect of the surcharge on income tax, and the deduction on income from interest, mutual funds, etc. has been raised.

Fiscal consolidation is a desirable goal in itself and would also facilitate the attainment of the other four objectives of the 2003-04 budget. The attainment of such consolidation would require, primarily, a substantial increase in India's tax/GDP ratio. Pruning of subsidies is probably less important than their fine-tuning and targeting. In the absence of a substantial expansion of the tax base, it is difficult to contemplate how significant rise in the *tax/GDP ratio* can take place. The current budget has not made any significant effort in this direction. On the other hand, the effect of changes in the existing tax rates and exemptions and change in the debt policy make the attainment of revenue target even more difficult.

Budgetary Position—Synoptic View

Sr. No.		1992-93 (Actual)	1993-94 (Actual)	1994-95 (Actual)	1995-96 (Actual)	1996-97 (Actual)	1997-98 (Actual)
(1)	(2)	(3)	(4)	(5)	(6)	(7)	(8)
1.	Revenue Receipts	74128	75453	91083	110131	126279	133886
2.	Revenue Expenditure	92702	108161	122112	139861	158933	180335
3.	Revenue Deficit	18574	32716	31029	29730	32654	46449
4.	Capital Receipts	36178	55440	68695	58338	61544	99077
5.	Recoveries of Loans	8317	6143	11952	7902	7995	9230
6.	Borrowing and other liabilities	27861	49297	56743	50436	53549	89847
7.	Capital Expenditure	29916	33684	38627	38414	42074	57718
8.	Total Receipts	110306	130893	159778	168469	187823	232053
9.	Total Expenditure	122618	141853	160739	178275	201007	232053
10.	Budgetary Deficit (9-8)	12312	10760	961	9806	73184	910
11.	Fiscal Deficit [(1+5)-9 = 6+10]	40173	60257	57704	60246	66773	88937

(Contd.)

TABLE (Contd.)

Sr. No.		1998-99 (Actual)	1999-2000 (Actual)	2000-01 (Actual)	2001-02 (RE)	2002-03 (BE)	2003-04 (BE)
(1)	(2)	(9)	(10)	(11)	(12)	(13)	(14)
1.	Revenue Receipts	149485	181482	192624	212572	245105	253935
2.	Revenue Expenditure	216461	249078	277858	304305	340482	366227
3.	Revenue Deficit	66976	67596	85234	91733	95377	112292
4.	Capital Receipts	130064	115707	131790	148060	165204	184960
5.	Recoveries of Loans	16507	11855	14171	20143	29680	18023
6.	Borrowing and other liabilities	113557	103852	117619	127917	135524	153637
7.	Capital Expenditure	62879	48975	47753	60131	69827	72568
8.	Total Receipts	279540	298053	325614	360436	410309	438795
9.	Total Expenditure	279340	298053	325611	364436	410309	438795
10.	Budgetary Deficit (9-8)	209	864	1197	3804	—	—
11.	Fiscal Deficit [(1+5)-9 = 6+10]	113348	104716	118816	131721	135524	153637

Reforms with Human Face

P.K. Saini

Populist politics gained ascendancy in the mid-70s with the "Garibi Hatao" planks of Mrs. Indira Gandhi's populist politics. But populist politics is not and can never be credible platform of sustainable and pro-people socio-economic development. It is a political tactic and an electoral ploy.

Welfare schemes for sectional interests have been announced by the successive P.M.s from time to time which have not been put into practice. Populist politics, therefore, lost its relevance. It is wholly invalid in the context of market economic growth path and has become vulgar and flippant.

Since the advent of economic reforms in 1991, India has been aiming to integrate itself with global economy and is also aiming to reap the benefits of the process of liberalization and globalization. The maximum benefit from the globalization can be drawn if both rural and urban segments of the economy participate in it on equal footing.

The axioms 'India lives in its villages' is true even after decades of independence. The social base of economic growth in

India has since tended to shrink rather than expand. This has provided mass discontent and resistance. The people of India, however, have by now a keen awareness of their democratic right. The ordinary Indian is demanding the bare necessity of life—drinking water, food, power, education, health services and security of life.

The growth rate of the economy in 2004-05 is expected to be 7.5% to 8% with the inflation rate of 4%. Industrial growth would be 6%. The major emphasis of the budget is on the poor sections of society, agriculture, agro-processing, water resources, rural development, education and health, to improve the lives of the people. Students, senior citizens, the salaried class and farmers will gain from this budget. It has been tried to balance demand of agriculture and industries. There will be no tax on income up to Rs. 1.00 lakh. The senior citizen will get 1% more on their bank deposits. The pensioners are exempted from the purview of one by six setting. But there is no change in the small savings interest rate. Students will also be benefited as no guarantor is required for education loan up to Rs. 7.5 lakh.

The common man will also be benefited due to downward revision of indirect taxes on a variety of goods. They will have to pay lower prices for some items such as computers, LPG stoves, footwear, writing instruments, braille writers and typewriters, crutches, walking frames and artificial limbs. Reduction in duties on goods favoured by the middle class as well as sops for the salaried and pensioners is clearly aimed at elevation the "feel good" factor to a "feel better" feeling.

Before one runs away with the impression that the government's budget would bring relief to the common man, one must remember that the Government has already effected a sharp hike in the LPG, diesel and petrol prices. Besides, it has imposed 2% education cess on almost all taxes. The service tax has been increased from 8% to 10% and coverage extended. Everyone will, therefore, end up paying more taxes—for a noble cause.

Five percent tax exemption is given to rural hospital which will go a long way in building health care infrastructure in the rural areas. The decision to exempt the ambulance from custom duty will help in providing the rural people with quality primary health care. The government has reduced custom duty on parts of artificial limbs and specified rehabilitation aide to 5%. While the domestic manufacturers of these products do have to pay excise duty, it has been slashed from 16% to 8% for medical, surgical, dental and veterinary furniture. The universal health insurance for the poor is to be re-worked. All these benefits have a measurable impact on the welfare of the poor.

These measures which are in conformity with the government's intent to make India a health destination by bringing down the cost of hospitalization and creating modern facilities would make specialty hospitals more profitable. Besides, project cost of organization, setting up of hospitals, would come down. The government's proposal is expected to give a fillip to fresh investments in the capital intensive sector. The reduction in duty on medicine and hospital equipment is pro-active measure by the government to reduce the cost of health care and make it more accessable to the common man.

As regards food consumption and employment, one in every 200 households in the rural India goes "chronically hungry" according to National Survey, June 2000 to 2004. It found that over 2/5th of population in the villages was unemployed. The average per capita monthly consumer expenditure in villages was only Rs. 498. Further, the hungry millions have been spending less in villages on food. The total expenditure on food has declined over the years. This is true for both towns and villages. This share of food in total expenditure has declined to 43% in urban centres in 2001-02 from 56% in 1987-88. For villages, the decline was to 55.5% from 64%. This does not signify improvement in the living conditions of the poor but it does bring to light the increase in malnutrition among the large sections of the population.

The position, with respect to food consumption and employment opportunity with job security, in rural as well as urban areas, has worsened more rapidly after 2001-02 when economic growth picked up and touched 7% in response to market-oriented economic reforms policy of the successive governments of different political ideological hues. This has made the contradiction between market driven economic growth and living conditions of the mass of the people more glaring. So, the government has launched the food for work programme in 150 most backward districts, under which 100 days work to every able bodied person from the poor households will be provided. A sum of Rs. 6,000 crore is available for the scheme. The budget provided an additional Rs. 10,000 crore to implement other the poverty alleviation programmes.

The budget expanded the benefits of their produce to the farmers. Earlier, the farmers were forced to sell their products to *mandis* where it is taxed. The model agriculture market law replaces the *Agriculture Marketing Commodity Act* which will free the farmer to sell his produce wherever he can get a better price. Crop diversification will also get a boost. The decision of the government to exempt water supply projects for industrial and agricultural use from excise and custom duties on par with drinking water supply projects, spells boom time for the farming community. Even so, this may give only partial relief to the working people in rural areas. It can not end their exploitation and misery.

To encourage and support the small scale industry, the government proposes to increase the rate of subsidy from 12 to 15% and raise the loan limit from Rs. 40.00 lakh to Rs. 1.00 crore. Integrating the tax system across goods and services will result in great benefits. The respite in import duty will help to absorb any external pricing pressure. Investment Commission will be set-up which will be entrusted the job of attracting foreign investment in India. This will improve the environment for investment and generation of productive jobs.

This is a part of the overall so called economic "reform" to boost the income and consumption of the affluent even as working people suffer cuts in living standards and deprivation of essential goods and services for want of purchasing power and their rising prices. A concentrated campaign is on for providing sources for access to these goods to the poor consumers. Presently, the access is limited to those who can afford to pay the price. The price is determined on the basis of cost of production of the growers with guaranteed returns at least 16% on capital employed in their production and marketing.

The reformists within the Government have criticized that the policies pursued during the 1990s lacked the human face. During the first three decades upto the early 1980s, the proportions of the population living below the poverty line remained unchanged. The total population was rising when the liberalization began, the income rose rapidly due to inflationary trend (measured at macro-level) and thus the proportion of rural and urban poverty statistically declined. All those schemes operated for poverty alleviation were good but touched only the tip of the Ice-berg.

The Budget of 2004-05 will be remembered as the one containing 'Reforms with Human Face.' Attempts have been made to balance the needs of various sections of society. This exercise can result in India growing stronger in economy. The last two decades belonged to the India's urban middle class, the next could well belong to the poor, marginal farmers in the country side. This budget clearly signals the change of economic and political direction—welcome change indeed !

Part II

Management of Public Expenditure

Expenditure Management— A New Paradigm

B.P. MATHUR

All State activities depend first on Treasury. Therefore, a King shall devote his best attention to it.

—*Kautilya: Arthashastra*

Most of our leaders assumed that the only way to cut spending is to eliminate programs, agencies and employees. But waste in government does not come tied in neat packages. It is marbled through our bureaucracies. It is embedded in the very way we do business. It is employees remaining idle, working at half speed—or barely working at all. It is people working hard at tasks that aren't worth doing, following regulations that should never have been written, filling out forms that should have never been printed . . . . Waste in government is staggering, but we cannot get at it by wading through budgets and cutting out items. . . . Our government is like

> fat people who must lose weight to stay healthy. They need to eat less and exercise more; instead when money is tight they cut off a few fingers and toes . . . . To melt the fat, we must change the basic incentives that drive our governments.
>
> —*Osborne and Gaebler: Reinventing Government*

Every year when budgets are presented in Parliament, considerable heat is generated regarding government's taxation policy, funds allocated to various sectors of the economy, subsidy given for certain activities and the level of public debt to be raised. However, very little attention is given to the fact whether money voted by Parliament has been wisely spent and best value for money has been secured. Issues of public concern like provision of quality education, effective health services and lack of infrastructure facilities like road and irrigation net work are side-tracked pointing to shortage of funds as a constraint. Public officials are rarely questioned whether resources already made available are optimally used. It is widely perceived that a good part of public expenditure goes waste and value for money is not realized. Late Rajiv Gandhi when he was Prime Minister made a startling statement that only fifteen paisa of public money reaches the intended beneficiary. The problem seems to be inherent in the budgetary and expenditure management practices followed by the government—a result of highly centralized, input-oriented control system and unless systems are overhauled there is little possibility of achieving optimization in public expenditure.

Budget Implementation

Articles 112 to 115 of the Constitution lay down the procedure for presentation and approval by Parliament of the Budget of the Central Government. The Appropriation Act passed by Parliament contains the authority to appropriate the specified sums from the Consolidated Fund of India for specified services. The Comptroller and Auditor General of India (C&AG) conducts appropriation audit under Article 149 of the Constitution to ascertain that expenditure actually incurred under various Grants is within the authorization given by the Appropriation Act and whether the expenditure has been incurred in conformity with the law, relevant rules, regulations and instructions. Five different Appropriation Accounts pertaining to different sectors of government are prepared under 118 Demands/Appropriations for which sanction has been obtained as under : Civil Ministries 96; Railways 16; Defence Services 5, Postal services 1. Table 10.1 contains estimates and actuals of disbursements of the Union Government for Civil Ministries for seven years from 1997-98 to 2002-03.

TABLE 10.1
Budget Provision and Expenditure of Civil Ministries

	1	*2*	*3*	*4*	*5*	*Saving as % of Grant (5.3)*
	Original Grant	*Supple-mentary Grant*	*Total*	*Actual Expen-diture*	*Unspent Provision*	
2002-03	343279	18884	362163	34196	20216	5.58
2001-02	310416	24112	334528	315049	21367	6.72
2000-01	300005	22444	322449	269539	52909	19.62
1999-2000	258411	26949	285360	273148	12212	4.28
1998-99	269661	26273 (1444+ 11825)	295934	285488	10446	3.52
1997-98	233019	40668	273687	253421	15033	5.49
1996-97	211662	7327	218989	206223	14744	6.73

Notes : (1) The figures exclude provisions under Public Debt, Loans and Advances and 90 days Treasury Bills.
(2) Civil Ministries refer to all departments of Central Government other than Defence, Railways and Post and Telecommunication.
(3) For 1998-99 sanction for supplementary grant of Rs. 11825 crores was taken after March due to dissolution of Parliament.

Source : Extracted from Report of the CA & G, Union Government, Civil No. 1 of 1998 to 2004.

The budget implementation process shows major deficiencies as indicated below:

(1) *Heavy savings and surrenders have been taking place under several Grants, while at the same time, many schemes of*

national importance are starved of funds, distorting the entire budgetary process. As is evident from the table above, around Rs. 15000 to Rs. 20000 crores of budgetary allocation of Civil Ministries get surrendered every year. There were persistent savings every year in the Departmental of Education, Health, Rural Development, Road Transport. For example, in the year 2002-03, the Department of Elementary Education and Literacy surrendered Rs. 429.60 crores, and Department of Secondary Education and Higher Education Rs. 291.27 crores, and in 2001-02 amounts of Rs. 264.16 crores and Rs. 122.34 crores, respectively, of the budgeted Grant. In the year 2000-01, the surrender of money of Department of Elementary Education was Rs. 504.76 crores (14% of the Grant) and Department of Higher Education Rs. 162.49 crores (3% of the Grant). The Non-utilization of large amount of money by Ministry of Education is an annual feature as would be evident from the following amounts surrendered in earlier years; Rs. 596.84 crores in 1999-2000 (8% of the Grant), Rs. 724.69 crores during 1998-99 (10% of the Grant), Rs. 603.58 crores during 1997-98 (11.54% of Grant) and Rs. 792.12 crores during 1996-97 (18% of Grant). Budgeted money could not be utilized for schemes such as free education for girls, adult education, setting up of Navodaya Vidyalayas, primary schools in rural areas, special projects for eradication of illiteracy, vocationalization of secondary education, non-formal education, etc. despite their being national priorities.

(2) Supplementary Grants of heavy amounts are made every year which shows that proper forecast of expenditure by various ministries and departments was not made.

(3) Re-appropriations made under power delegated to Finance Ministry were injudicious as the original provisions under the heads where re-appropriations are made were not utilized. This also showed that spending departments had no clue of trend of expenditure on various schemes and programmes or

made incorrect forecast of expenditure even when they were half-way through the financial year.

(4) Excess expenditures over budget provisions were made under several Grants showing lack of exchequer control.

(5) There was heavy rush of expenditure in the month of March, and in large number of cases, the entire budgeted money was released in the last fortnight of financial year. As it is not feasible to constructively utilize the money within the financial year, most spending departments circumvent rules and commit financial irregularities to escape the lapse provision. March rush also creates serious cash management problem for Finance Ministry.

ISSUES IN EXPENDITURE MANAGEMENT

A large part of the problem in expenditure management arises due to a highly centralized system of allocating resources with all powers concentrated in Finance Ministry, the overlapping jurisdiction of Planning Commission in respect of plan schemes and the system of annual budgetary appropriation. Some of these issues are listed below :

(1) Budgetary outlays for plan schemes and projects are reflected in annual Budget after the Planning Commission has given in principle approval for the same. However, actual investment/expenditure can be incurred only after detailed scheme has been formulated and approved, and approved by the prescribed authority. Under the existing arrangement, all investment/expenditure proposals above a certain limit (Rs. 100 crores in case of PSUs and between Rs. 50 crores to Rs. 100 crores in other cases where financial returns are not quantifiable) need approval of Cabinet Committee on Economic Affairs (CCEA), after it has been approved by Public Investment Board (PIB)/ Expenditure Finance Committee (EFC). Powers have also been delegated to EFC headed by Secretary, Expenditure (between Rs. 15 crores to Rs. 50 crores)

and to Standing Finance Committee headed by Administrative Secretary (between Rs. 1.5 crores to Rs. 15 crores) to approve schemes below the monetary limit required for CCEA approval. A great deal of consultation with various ministries/departments is required to determine justification and socio-economic viability of such schemes before the proposals are placed before the PIB/EFC. The procedure is long and tortuous and may take from few months to several years and is the main reason why substantial funds lapse at the end of the financial year. The Planning Commission also funds a large number of centrally sponsored schemes whose implementation is with the State governments. Very often, the State governments are not able to fulfil the conditions under which schemes have been sanctioned, there are delays in implementation of the schemes or there is unutilized balance of previous year which result in central ministries not releasing the money and hence its surrender.

There is need to have a medium-term expenditure framework. Most developed countries such as UK, Australia, New Zealand, Scandinavian countries have developed highly disciplined and consistent approach to preparing multi-year budgets and ensuring proper linkages with the annual budget.[1] In Nordic countries and Japan, investment budgets are approved for the duration of the projects. *For capital projects and plan schemes, there is a strong case for budgeting for full life of the project/scheme so that funds are allowed to be rolled over for the next year.*

(2) The present planning and budgeting process leads to severe distortion in funds allocation for activities which could be called sovereign functions of government. Due to resource crunch, Financ Ministry is not able to make increased money allocation to traditional departments like Police, Judiciary, Health and Public Works as they are classified as non-plan. Thus, funds are not made available for critical activities such as modernization of police force,

upgradation of Courts and upkeep of hospitals and maintenance of buildings and roads. The allocation of funds by the Planning Commission has shown severe deficiencies and many schemes of dubious value get funded. The planning process has degenerated into intense competitive games of size and numbers among different Ministries and among States. Aspects relating to techno-economic feasibility studies and availability of resources are neglected. *The criterion of financial rate of return was given up not only for social sector projects but also for economic sector projects. This has resulted in building up of vast projects with poor financial returns.* The Planning Commission, as per its existing policy, funds a scheme for five years and, thereafter, it is shifted as a non-plan activity. Once the activity gets shifted as non-plan, there is a problem of finding money—the biggest casualty is the maintenance of capital assets created out of plan funds which languish. *The distinction between plan and non-plan schemes and budget allocation is artificial, it severely distorts the system of scientific budget making and needs to be given up.*

(3) The rush of expenditure in March leads to considerable wastage of money and puts heavy pressure on government's cash resources. Osborne and Gaebler[2] observe that the existing system gives no incentive for saving money and normal government budgets encourage managers to waste money. "If they don't spend their entire budget by the end of the fiscal year, three things happen: they lose the money they have saved; they get less next year; and the budget director scolds them for having requested too much last year. Hence the time honoured government rush to spend all funds by the end of fiscal year. "There is a strong case to allow roll over of certain category of expenditure particularly bills and invoices that have been committed over previous fiscal year but have not been paid because of delays in deliveries. Several developed countries (e.g., Australia) have this system. *Thus departments could keep a portion of money, say upto 25 percent of appropriation for the next year so that rush of*

expenditure at the end of financial year leading to waste could be avoided.

(4) Due to highly centralized system of budget-making and with little powers to the administrative ministries to allocate funds, they develop a tendency to inflate their demands, both for the existing schemes as well as new schemes. On the other hand, due to resource constraint, the Finance Ministry develops a psychology to allocate the minimum necessary funds sought by the administrative ministries irrespective of the merits of the scheme. In the process, the whole exercise of budget formulation becomes a bargain rather than need-based. Finance Ministry by itself has no expertise to judge the requirement of administrative ministries and understand the complexities of the schemes proposed by them. *Thus the annual non-plan budgets have become routine incremental budget exercise*—if last year you were allotted x amount of money, this year you should do with x + 5% increase over last year, giving allowance for inflation and normal growth of expenditure and maintain the same level of activity. Finance Ministry has been making efforts to prune unnecessary schemes and cut down expenditure by introducing measures such as Zero Base Budget (ZBB) but has not been very successful due to unwillingness on the part of administrative ministries.

(5) One of the major problems with the existing budgetary practice is its "input orientation", viz. funds are sanctioned without correlating them to output. Performance budget, which implies that public expenditure be presented in terms of functions, programmes and activities and correlates output with cost was introduced in early 70's following the recommendations of Administrative Reforms Commission. Performance Budget, in considerable detail, is prepared by every ministry and placed in Parliament every year but it has largely remained a ritualistic exercise. Periodical budgetary releases made by the ministries are not linked with physical progress of work or targets as set out in performance budget

document. *There is need to change the focus of budget to output and results in terms of quantifiable physical targets and delivery of services to the public.*

STATE GOVERNMENTS—EXCESS EXPENDITURE OVER VOTED GRANTS

Appropriation audit conducted by CAG shows that State Governments have been spending money much beyond the ceilings imposed for each department while passing the Annual Financial Statement (Budget) and no serious action has been taken to obtain sanction of legislature to regularize it. A staggering sum of over Rs. 1,79,585 crores was spent over voted Grants by 25 States as on March 2002. Excess expenditure of Rs. 41321 crores over voted Grant has been incurred from 1980-81, onwards; Rs. 23248 crores by UP which includes excess incurred from 1984-85 onwards, Rs. 23206 crores by Assam which includes excess incurred from 1983-84 onwards; Rs. 6956 crores by Bihar which includes excess incurred from 1977-78 onwards and Rs. 23412 crores by West Bengal, where excess was incurred during three years from 1999-2000 to 2001-02. Excess expenditure has not been regularized for periods as long as ten to twenty five years. Gujarat is the only State where excess expenditure has been regularized upto 2000-01. Era Sezhiyan,[3] a former Chairman of Public Accounts Committee, observes, "More than the huge amounts involved, it is the enormity of the misuse and the monstrocity of the misappropriation that makes the entire parliamentary system and the cherished objectived of accountability and control over public purse a huge mockery."

Non-regularization of excess expenditure is fraught with serious consequences and may result in fraud as was the case with Animal Husbandry scam in Bihar. In Bihar, there was *excess expenditure* in Grant of Animal Husbandry department in each of the years from 1987-88 to 1995-96 (thus, for example, for 1993-94 while the budgetary Grant was Rs. 77.14 crores, an expenditure of Rs. 199.17 crores was incurred, in 1994-95 against Grant of Rs. 74.40 crores, a sum of Rs. 245.01 crores was spent; and in 1995-96, against Grant of Rs. 82.12 crores, Rs. 228.61 crores was spent). The Bihar PAC never met to examine the issue and put a stop to such serious violation of financial rules, as a result the irregularity continued for years.

According to Article 113(2) and 203(2) of the Constitution, the estimates of expenditure in the form of Demands for Grants is required to be submitted to Parliament/State Legislature (to lay down ceiling of expenditure for each department such as Health, Police, Public Works, etc.) at the time of presentation of Annual Financial Statement. The Comptroller and Auditor General (C&AG) conducts appropriation audit under Articles 149 and 151 of the Constitution to ascertain that the expenditure actually incurred under various Grants is within the authorization and the expenditure is in conformity with the law, rules and regulations. The Constitution has a provision that in an exceptional case where expenditure exceeds the Grant, it should be regularized by the Legislature. Articles 115(b) and 205(b) state, "if any money has been spent on any service during a financial year *in excess* of the amount granted for that Service and for that year", a statement showing the amount of that expenditure and the demand of that excess should be laid before the House. The *excess expenditure* is regularized on the basis of the recommendation of the Public Accounts Committee after it examines the explanatory notes furnished by the Ministries and Departments giving reasons leading to the *excesses* under each Grant. As PACs are not functioning effectively in most States, huge amount of *excess expenditure* remains unregularized.

In India, we do not have a system of exchequer control which ensures that no money can be drawn over the budgetary grants. In UK, New Zealand and other countries, law empowers C & AG to exercise this power and no money can be drawn from government treasury unless Audit Office has certified that it can be lawfully paid.

TIMELY SUBMISSION OF ACCOUNTS

Effective control of expenditure can be exercised only if Appropriation Accounts are timely submitted to Parliament/ State Legislature and desired remedial action taken. Most countries have statutory provision regarding date of submission of audited accounts to parliament. In UK, under the Exchequer and Audit Department Act of 1886, the Treasury is required to submit Accounts to C & AG by 30th September and C & AG is required to submit certified accounts to Parliament by January of the following year to which they relate. In New Zealand, under the Public Finance Act of 1989, the Treasury is required to forward the Annual Financial Statement to the Audit Office by 31st August following the end of financial year and the Audit Office is required to give its opinion within 30 days of its receipt for placing it in the House of Representatives.

There is considerable delay in submission of Appropriation Accounts, even of the Union Government to the Parliament. A study for 8 years from 1992-93 to 1999-2000 by this author, shows that it takes over 15 months from the close of the financial year for the audited accounts and the audit report thereon to be placed in the Parliament. It takes another year for the PAC to examine and submit its recommendations and Parliament to approve excess expenditure. There is need for accelerating the time cycle for preparation of Appropriation and Finance Accounts and its audit by C & AG and regularization of excess expenditure by PAC. A statutory provision needs to be made, prescribing time limit within which Appropriation accounts audited by C & AG are submitted to Parliament and examined by Public Accounts Committee and excess expenditure, if any, regularized by Parliament/State Legislature as under :

(i) The Appropriation and Finance Accounts should be prepared and finalized by the Controller General of Accounts for Union Government and Accountant General (Accounts) for the State Government by 30th of September of the following financial year to which they relate.

(ii) C & AG should certify the accounts within two months of its receipt and submit his report to Parliament/State Legislature by November of the following year, to which they relate.

(iii) The PAC should consider the accounts and make its recommendations regarding regularization of excess expenditure by January so that Parliament could approve the same by February of the following year to which the accounts relate (before presentation of next year's budget).

CENTRALIZED CONTROL OF FINANCE MINISTRY—LINE ITEM BUDGETING

The allocation of funds by Ministry of Finance to each ministry is done under Demands of Grants, which are estimates for gross amount of expenditure by Major Heads of Account. Ministry of Finance decides the number of demands for Grants and their coverage. The break-up under each major Head shows the estimates under Charged and Voted, Revenue and Capital and Plan and non-Plan. These Demands for Grants and broken into Detailed Demands known as detailed head and sub-head running into six tiers as follows: (a) Major Head—4 digits (function), (b) Sub-major Head—2 digits (Sub-function), (c) Minor Head—3 digits (programme), (d) Sub-minor Head—2 digits (Schemes), (e) Detailed Head—2 digits (Object head). Standardized code numbers allotted to the Major, sub-major and Minor Heads in the List of Major and Minor Head of Account meant for accounting classification is used for individual ministries' demands for Grants. At the object head level, standard heads and codes prescribed by Ministry of Finance are used.

At the time of presentation of Budget in Parliament, only Demands for Grants are presented. However, before Lok Sabha starts discussion on the budget, Detailed Demands for Grants which constitute huge bulk of printed pages in which details are available in six digit classification upto object head is presented. The adoption of accounting heads meant for classification of expenditure, for presentation of Budget leads to several problems. Once funds get sanctioned, these take the form of parliamentary/finance ministry approval and there remains practically no scope for the administrative ministry to shift funds from low priority activity/unit to high priority activity during the course of the year. Thus if funds are allotted for Gobar gas project, there is very limited authority with Ministry of Non-Conventional Energy to shift funds to Solar energy programme, if it finds that it has greater priority. *This problem is fundamental in line budgeting system where expenditure limits for every item are fixed giving no scope to a particular department to spend money as per priority.* Osborne & Gaebler[4] observe, "Most public budgets fence agency money into dozens of separate accounts, called line items. This was originally done to control the bureaucrats—to them from all sides, so that they could not spend a penny more than the council or the legislature originally mandated on each item of government. But once again *our attempt to prevent bad management made good management impossible*". A committee appointed by government to review the Integrated Financial Adviser scheme known as Eswaran[5] the Committee points out, "Itemised control is unwieldy and is usually ineffective as compared to bulk control of expenditure. This points to the need of making Budget an instrument of expenditure management and providing flexibility to administrative ministries in expenditure on individual items". The Fifth Pay Commission[6] has recommended that, "It would be more appropriate if Finance Ministry approves the overall budget for different ministries and thereafter allows them sufficient flexibility to manage the financial resources in the most productive manner irrespective of various heads under which it is spent."

Administrative ministries have been given very limited powers to re-appropriate expenditure from one head to another. Presently, there is a limit of Rs. one crore which is inadequate. Money also cannot be shifted from plan to non-plan and *vice versa*. Towards the end of March, hundreds of files get referred to ministry of Finance for re-appropriation of funds. *There is need to do away with itemized budgeting. More discretion needs to be given to field units to utilize the money with an overall budgetary cap so that money can be more optimally used.*

The economy instructions issued by Finance Ministry from time to time have taken away even the limited delegation, which the administrative ministries enjoyed. Finance Ministry routinely issues instructions to regulate expenditure on staff car, telephone and other sundry items relating to office maintenance and upkeep. Instructions have been issued that government officers cannot undertake domestic travel on any airlines other than Indian Airlines. Travel expenditure has been broken into local travel and foreign travel with a cap fixed at a level of expenditure incurred some years back. This seriously affects the operations of ministries whose officers have to make journey abroad in exigencies of public purpose. Such rules get circumvented by officers charging their foreign travel bills to PSU's, under their ministry's control and which prove counter-productive.

REFORM MEASURES—ZERO BASE BUDGETING (ZBB)

One of the major initiatives for expenditure optimization taken by government has been introduction of ZBB. ZBB is intended to help in the judicious allocation of scarce resources at the national level and deriving the maximum benefits from the resources thus allocated. The objective is to make public expenditure programs more effective by purposive allocation of scarce resources. ZBB thus requires identification and sharpening of objectives, examination of various alternative ways of achieving those objectives, selecting the best alternative through cost effectiveness analysis, prioritization of objectives and programs, switching resources from programmes of lower priority to higher priority and elimination of programmes which have outlived their utility. ZBB was introduced with considerable fanfare by government of India in 1987-88 but it hardly made any dent on improving the quality of government expenditure. The Finance Minister, Yaswant Sinha, again resurrected it and in his budget speech for 1999-2000, re-emphasized the need to adopt ZBB by various spending departments. ZBB has, however, not been successful due to inadequate response on the part of budget executing agencies. ZBB by definition is a management process that provides for systematic consideration of all programmes and activities and without the active support and cooperation of executive agencies, it cannot be implemented. If budget formulation and resource allocation process ignores the genuine concerns of administrative ministries, an exercise of expenditure optimization cannot have much success.

REFORM MEASURES IN ADVANCED COUNTRIES—NEW PUBLIC MANAGEMENT

Some of the developed countries which faced the problem of inept functioning of public bureaucracies and fiscal profligacy have met the challenge by taking some bold reform measures, which have come to be known as New Public Management. The NPM emphasizes deregulating internal management of public bureaucracies, decentralizing and streamlining various management processes such as budgeting, personnel and procurement. The approach includes market driven management practices, creation of an internal market or competition to reform the public sector from inside and introduction of private sector management practices.

UK launched Financial Management Initiative (FMI) in 1982, when Margaret Thatcher was Prime Minister. Its thrust was budgeting for results and providing value for money. The objective was to mould budget into a contract for performance. FMI implies delegated budgeting in which responsibility for resources is pushed down the line to budget holders who are to be given sufficient flexibility and incentive to produce value for money. These reforms were followed by Next Steps Initiative under which most departments concerned "with delivery of services to the public were converted into autonomous agencies. As part of reform, the methods of appointment and promotion to top grades of civil service was changed. A contract regime and a system of lateral entry model effectively replaced the old closed entry system for top posts. These reforms have continued with introduction of Citizen's Charter for all public services. In 1997, UK introduced Fiscal Responsibility Code whose main feature is *comprehensive spending review with expenditure planned firmly for three years and public service agreements which are quasi-contracts between Treasury and each departments about what they would deliver in return for budget funding*. As part of Comprehensive Spending Review, the government brought out a White Paper in July 1998, which gives measurable targets in the form of Public Service Agreements (PSAs). They are expressed in terms of end results that taxpayers' money is intended to deliver. They cover areas such as improvement in health, educational achievements and reduction in crime. They include service standards such as smaller class sizes, reduction of waiting lists for patients, swifter justice, etc. *The idea is to set Specific, Measurable, Achievable, Relevant and Timed targets related to outcomes, in what is called SMART.*

USA

A series of legislative measures has been taken in USA to improve financial management. The most significant of those is the Government Performance and Results Act of 1993. The act seeks to improve efficiency and effectiveness of federal programmes by establishing a system that sets goals for programme performance and to measure results. Legislative action has been taken to reduce deficit and reduction of public debt. Gramm-Rudman-Hollings Act (1987) sets deficit reduction targets and sequestration procedures. The budgetary strategy is governed by Budget Enforcement Act of 1990 and 1993 and Balanced Budget Act of 1997 which has helped in successfully controlling discretionary spending by setting caps on government investment and consumption. If the annual appropriation exceeds the cap, the law invokes an automatic sequestration, which means any excess spending over the specified limits is subject to sequestration by a uniform percentage across activities. As the result of these measures adopted, the general government deficit had declined since 1992 and USA achieved budget surplus, which was 2.4 percent of GDP in FY 2000. However, due to tax cuts by Bush administration and heavy spending commitment, the USA has again moved into heavy deficit and the fiscal discipline brought about by Clinton administration has vanished.

New Zealand

Financial reforms in New Zealand had their genesis in governmental attempt to control deficits and increase the efficiency of public spending. In exchange for increased accountability, management of government departments was decentralized so that personnel, contracting and many purchasing decisions were made in the department. New Zealand's public financial system is governed by three key pieces of legislation. State Sector Act, 1988: The main objectives of the Act is to improve productivity, to ensure that managers have greater freedom and flexibility to manage effectively, and at the same time to ensure that managers are fully accountable to government for their performance. This has lead to formulation of performance contracts between ministers and chief executives. Public Finance Act, 1989 : The driving principle behind the act is a shift of focus of what the departments consume to what they produce. Hence, budgeting and reporting is on output basis rather than relying solely on information how outputs are produced. The Act requires the Crown and all its sub-entities to report on a basis consistent with Generally Accepted Accounting Practices (GAAP).

The Fiscal Responsibility Act, 1994

The objective of the Act is to promote consistent good quality fiscal management. The Act requires Governments to follow : (a) A legislated set of principles of responsible fiscal management, and publicly assess their fiscal policies against these principles, (b) Publish a Budget Policy statement well before the annual Budget containing their strategic priorities for the upcoming budget, their short-term fiscal intentions, and long-term objectives, (c) Fully disclose the impact of their fiscal decisions over a three-year forecasting period in regular economic and fiscal update, (d) Present all financial information under GAAP. These requirements are that the Government of the day has to be transparent about both its intentions and the short-term and long-terms impact of its taxation decisions, which would lead to sustainable fiscal policy. The Act establishes a set of principles for use as a benchmark against which the Finance Expenditure Committee evaluates spending. One of these principles is: to run operating surpluses until prudent debt levels are achieved. The act states, "Once prudent levels of total Crown debt have been achieved, maintaining these level by ensuring that, on average, over a reasonable period of time, the total operating expenses of the Crown do not exceed its total operating revenues". The other principles are: to achieve levels of net worth to provide buffer against adverse position; to manage the risks facing the Crown and to pursue policies that are consistent with a reasonable degree of predictability about the level and stability of tax rate. The prudent debt level is interpreted to mean net public debt in the region of 20 percent to 30 percent of GDP.

As a result of these bold reform measures, fiscal deficit in New Zealand was eliminated in the year 1994, after 10 years of difficult political decision-making and management reform. New Zealand's public debt had fallen to 26.8 percent of GDP by fiscal June 1997.

A New Maastricht Treaty (1991)

Governing European Union seeks to place a limit of 3 percent for the ratio between Public Deficit and the Gross Domestic Product (GDP) at market prices and a limit of 60 percent for the ratio between Public Debt and GDP. Most EU countries now adhere to the Measures. Several developed countries are enjoying a period of budget surpluses. Norway and New Zealand are having budget surpluses since 1994. Australia, Canada, Sweden, and UK have achieved budget surpluses from 1997 and 1998.

A New Paradigm—Budgeting for Results

Fiscal discipline can be brought only by changing the management culture in government. A key component of New Management philosophy is budgeting for results or what is known as mission driven budgets. Besides countries cited above, Australia, Canada, Denmark and Sweden have moved towards a management culture which is attentive to performance when funds are parceled out. *Mission driven budgeting, instead of present system of input budgeting, should be moulded into a contract for performance. In exchange for obtaining the agreed resources, managers would be expected to achieve specified targets. Decentralisation of authority and delegation are important components of budgeting for results. Mission driven budgets have the following advantages : they give incentive to employees to save money, give managers autonomy they need to respond to changing circumstances, create predictable environment to operate, simplify budget process and give managers opportunity to experiment to fulfil their assigned tasks.*

Mission driven budgets imply that public servants be made accountable for their performance. If Administrative Ministries, Department Heads and Chief Executives are to be made accountable for results, they should be give the necessary authority, flexibility and tools. This was recognized by the Eswaran Committee which put it in following words, "In financial matters, the gap between the decision-making authority and the implementing agencies be minimized. *The Committee is clear that the administrative ministries, as the authorities concerned with detailed policies and programmes for implementing them, should be empowered to take decisions and take responsibility for them fully. This implies all round delegation of authority within the Government and continuing review of the scheme of delegation of powers to enable administrative ministries and their agencies to respond quickly to changing conditions at field level.* Delegation and accountability should not be viewed separately. Promotion of one should lead to another". The Committee emphasized that, *while delegating,* the approach should be to delegate the *maximum possible rather than the minimum necessary and the delegation should be formal and unambiguous, by amending the Rules rather than informal through executing instructions. The Committee observed that financial prudence should not be the sole responsibility of Ministry of Finance and should permeate the system of government.*

Fiscal Responsibility Act, 2003

The fiscal situation in the country has been a matter of great concern. Central Government finances during the last two decades are characterized by heavy revenue deficit and fiscal deficit and ballooning public debt, the three key indicators of the health of an economy. The average revenue deficit during five years from 1999-2000 to 2003-04 was 4 percent and fiscal deficit 5.58 percent of GDP. Presently (2003-04), the interest burden (Rs. 125000 crores) constitutes almost half (47 percent) of Central government revenue receipts (Rs. 263000 crores), 26 percent of total expenditure (Rs. 475000 crores). The total liabilities of the Central Government constitute 67 percent of GDP, up from 51 percent in 1998-99. If this trend continues, government will have very little money left for critical development programmes. A high fiscal deficit affects growth, leads to inflation and puts pressure on balance of payments. It also raises issues of equity as heavy debt puts unnecessary burden on future generation.

A committee appointed by government, which was chaired by Finance Secretary (July 2000) to study the problem of fiscal stress suggested legislation with a view to have a mechanism to promote fiscal prudence. Based on the committee's recommendations, Government introduced Fiscal Responsibility and Budget Management Bill, in Parliament in December 2000. *The original Bill envisaged that within a period of five years ending March 2006, Government shall reduce revenue deficit to nil and fiscal deficit to not more than two percent to GDP for that year. The original Bill also stipulated that within a period of ten years ending March 2011, the total liabilities at the end of financial year will not exceed fifty percent of GDP of that year.* The bill was referred to Parliament's Standing Committee on Finance (November 2001) which watered down the proposals of the original bill and has suggested doing away with numerical ceilings and time frame for achieving the targets of revenue and fiscal deficit. Based on Parliamentary Committee's recommendations, a Fiscal Responsibility and Budget Management Act was passed in August 2003. The Act stipulates that, 'Government shall take appropriate measures to reduce fiscal deficit and revenue deficit so as to eliminate revenue deficit by 31st March 2008' and, 'Government shall by rules specify annual targets for deduction of fiscal and revenue deficit (Section 4 of the Act). By not specifying firm date by which fiscal deficit shall be eliminated or ceiling limit beyond which fiscal deficit should not be incurred and leaving it to Government to frame rules for reduction of fiscal and revenue deficit, the Act simply becomes a statement of pious intentions. It was desirable that Parliament gave firm directive to Government to observe basic rules of fiscal prudence.

At the time of presentation of Budget for 2004-05 to Parliament, the Finance Minister has presented Medium Term Fiscal Policy Statement, Fiscal Policy Strategy Statement and Macro-Economic Framework Statement as required under rules framed under FRBM Act. The targets for 2004-05, 2005-06 and 2006-07 have been set as follows: Revenue deficit as percentage of GDP: 2.5% ; 1.8% and 1.1%; Fiscal Deficit : 4.4%, 4% and 3.6%; outstanding liabilities as percentage of GDP: 68.5%; 68.2% and 67.8%. Even the soft targets set in rules framed under the FRMB

Act are not going to be met. *The rules stipulated elimination of revenue deficit by 2007-08, but the Government now proposes to amend the rules to achieve this by 2008-09.* The position of outstanding liability is more alarming—government seems to have no intention to reduce the size of public debt which is 68 percent of GDP. Prudent management requires that it should be no more than 50 percent of GDP.

Accounting Reforms

Financial reforms should include reforms in disclosure and reporting of government accounts. Countries such as Australia, New Zealand, UK and USA have moved to commercial system of accounting with a view to provide a more balanced judgment on the financial status of the country. They prepare annual balanced statement on uses and sources of funds and income and expenditure statement together with income due and liabilities. A Government Accounting Standard Board has been set-up to specify accounting standards. New Zealand has gone a step further and presents budget on accrual basis.

In India, accounts are prepared on cash basis. The Central government accounts have been departmentalized and the Controller General of Accounts attached to Ministry of Finance compiles and prepares the accounts. In the States, however, all payments are made through the old Treasury system and accounts are prepared by Accountant General (who functions under C & AG). Given the complexities, it does not seem feasible to move towards accrual accounting system at present. However, it is necessary that Annual Accounts disclose committed liabilities on account of major works, supply contracts, revenue demands raised but not realized, contingent liability, etc. This should help in making more realistic preparation of budget estimates every year. An Accounting Standard Board has recently been set-up under the chairmanship of Dy. Comptroller & Auditor General. It is hoped that the Board will work towards transparency in presentation of Government Accounts and adopt modern management techniques.

The System of Financial Adviser

Under the Integrated Financial Adviser Scheme (IFAS), Financial Advisers (FAs) of the rank of Joint Secretary or Additional Secretary are posted in each ministry and assists the ministry in planning, budgeting and expenditure management responsibilities. Certain financial powers have also been delegated to administrative ministries which are to be exercised in consultation with FA. The scheme has evolved over time from 1950's onwards when we had launched our developmental plans, as it was felt that there should be demarcation and division of financial responsibility between the ministry of finance and administrative ministry and budgetary control should be strengthened by developing an internal financial machinery in each ministry. The FA is selected jointly by the administrative and finance ministries and is accountable for his work both to the administrative as well as finance ministry. There is a conceptual dualism about his role which makes his position anomalous. If the FA makes a sincere attempt to follow the guidelines of the Ministry of Finance, he is dubbed as "unhelpful" and "obstructionist" and if he whole heartily supports the proposal of administrative ministry, he is dubbed as "ineffective" and "pliable". Eswaran Committee, appointed by Ministry of Finance (November 1996) expressed itself against the existing system of dual control and felt that FA should become an integral part of the administrative ministry and be accountable to the Secretary of the ministry. This will help in giving greater freedom to administrative ministries in their day-to-day functioning and make them more accountable for their performance. However, no action was taken on committee's recommendations.

One of the problems in the existing scheme of FA is lack of professionalism. FA's job is a highly specialized and technical job where one deals with appraisal procedures of projects, viability of schemes, financial job where one deals with appraisal procedures, viability of schemes, financial instruments available in the capital market, understanding of balance sheets, etc. Lately, there has been an increasing tendency to post-generalist administrators drawn from IAS to the FA's post instead of drawing officers from Central Finance & Accounts

Services whose officers possess the necessary background and training. Even for junior posts of Section Officers and Under Secretary, officers are drawn from Central Secretariat Service without exposing them to requisite experience and training. Eswaran Committee has observed that officers well equipped with experience and background appropriate to the ministries should only be selected for the job.

In USA, with a view to improve financial management, a provision has been made for appointment of a Chief Financial Officer (CFO) in all federal government departments and agencies. The Chief Financial Officers Act of 1990 prescribes the functions required to be performed by CFO: He is expected to oversee all financial management activities relating to the agency's programme and operations; develop and maintain an integrated accounting and financial management system; ensure that agency's system provides complete, reliable, consistent and timely information; and monitor the financial execution of the budget. In order to provide leadership, the act envisaged a cadre of trained financial management professionals. *In order to make the integrated Financial Advice system effective, it is necessary that only persons of proven professional competence are appointed as Financial Advisers and they are integrated as part of administrative ministries.* There is also need to build a cadre of professional managers to man the IFA wing of the ministries.

CONCLUSION

There are two key elements for a successful strategy of managing national finances. *First, improving the quality and productivity of public expenditure. This can be achieved by giving emphasis on performance, decentralization and enhanced accountability. Second, the overall size of public expenditure needs to be reduced by restricting, borrowing and taking strong deficit reduction measures.* This cannot be done through traditional instruments of managing government finances and controlling expenditure. There is need for a new management culture in government. The new approach as discussed in this essay is summarized below:

1. Annual budgets consume enormous amount of time

and energy of administrative ministries and executing units in securing budget grants and spare very little time to management to deliver performance and evaluate the effectiveness of various programmes and schemes. *There is need to have a medium-term expenditure framework covering at least two to three years, integrated into annual budgetary cycle. For capital projects, budgeting should be done for full life cycle of the project/scheme and funds saved at the end of financial year be allowed to be carried forward to the next year.*

2. The doctrine of lapse at the end of financial year results in rush of expenditure in the month of March leading to considerable wastage of public funds. *Administrative departments be permitted to keep a portion of money, say upto 25 percent of appropriation, for the next year for meeting committed liabilities so that rush of expenditure at the end of financial year and consequent wastes could be avoided.*
3. The distinction between plan and non-plan budget is artificial and should be abolished. Expenditure needs to be classified as "Revenue" and "Capital" only. Traditional departments such as Police, Judiciary, Health, Roads and Buildings, which presently fall under non-plan should be given treatment at par with Roads and Buildings, which can be said to be performing sovereign functions of the government, which presently fall under non-plan should be given as much priority for money allocation as plan schemes. *Allotment of funds should be need-based and the practice of incremental budgeting should be discarded.*
4. Centralized control of Ministry of Finance, with very little delegation to administrative ministries, is the main reason for most budgetary mal-practices. *Once budgetary allocations are made, the ministries be given sufficient flexibility and incentive to produce value for money. Line item budgeting should be done away with.*
5. There is need for budgeting for results and to formulate mission-driven budgets. *The focus of the budget should be output and results in terms of quantifiable physical targets and delivery of services to the public.*

Budget should become a contract for performance. In exchange for obtaining agreed resources, managers should be expected to achieve specified targets.

6. A *statutory provision needs to be made for prescribing of Appropriation Accounts by Controller General of Accounts/ AG (Accounts),* its audit by CAG and presentation to Parliament and State Legislature, and excess expenditure over voted Grants should be regularized by Public Accounts Committee, before the end of next financial year to which the accounts relate. Urgent steps need to be taken to regularize excess expenditure of Rs. 180000 crores incurred by State governments. An effective control mechanism should be put in place so that budgetary grants are not exceeded.
7. A *conscious policy of securing budgetary surplus on the lines of some developed countries needs to be pursued.* While Fiscal Responsibility Act reflects intention of the government to eliminate or at least to cut deficits, it does not bind the government to eliminate deficit or restrict fiscal deficit within the prudent limit of 2 percent of GDP in foreseeable future. *There is need for a legislation stipulating that the government cannot borrow for current consumption (revenue expenditure) and borrowings would be used for capital projects and productive investment only.*
8. While preparing Annual Accounts, there is need to introduce *accrual accounts, disclose committed liabilities on account of major works, supply contracts, revenue demands raised but not realized, etc. so that the objective of greater transparency in presentation of accounts is achieved.*
9. A professional cadre for financial managers be created in each ministry and department. *Professionals with proven competence, background and training should only be appointed as Financial Advisers (FAs). FA should be accountable to the Secretary of the administrative ministry and should form an integral part of the ministry.*

We need a paradigm shift in our thinking regarding expenditure management practices. If we do not change and innovate, most control systems will result in meaningless ritual without public spending serving the avowed purpose of securing economic development and social change.

Notes and References

1. For a detailed discussion, see Salvatore Schiavo-Camp and Daniel Tommasi: Managing Government Expenditure; (ADE, 1999) and A Premchand: Control of Public Money, (Oxford University Press, New Delhi, 2000).
2 David Osborne and Ted Gaebler: Reinventing Government, (Addison Wesley, London 1992).
3 Era Sezhiyan: Appropriation and Misappropriation of Excess Expenditure; *Mainstream*, July 19, 2003.
4. *Op. cit.*, p. 117.
5. V.B. Eswaran, *et. al.*: Report of the Committee to Review Integrated Financial Adviser Scheme : Ministry of Finance, Government of India, November 1996.
6. Ministry of Finance: Report of the Fifth Pay Commission, Vol. I, January 1997, p. 155.

Management of Public Expenditure : A Performance Orientation

ANJALI A. SRIVASTAVA

INTRODUCTION

The box 1 is only a small excerpt from a large number of appraisals carried out each year by the Comptroller and Auditor General of India. Every year, his report reveals a dismal scenario of good intentions going awry in implementation. An annexure to this paper reveals uncanny similarities in the deficiencies

Box I

Rural Housing Schemes, which aimed to remove shelterlessness by the end of the Ninth Five Year Plan failed to achieve the desired success. As against the target of 109.53 lakh housing units, only 50.34 lakh houses were constructed/upgraded as of March 2002. The multiplicity of schemes without proper linkages led to overlapping of objectives and failed to ensure convergence of various interrelated activities for providing cost effective and hygienic rural houses. Misdirected targeting resulted in expenditure of Rs. 58.56 crore on ineligible beneficiaries. There were instances of excess payment of Rs. 7.38 crore to the beneficiaries depriving the eligible beneficiaries to that extent. Payment to the beneficiaries less than the prescribed norms led to underpayment of Rs. 42.11 crore in 10 States and one Union Territory. Contrary to the guidelines of the scheme, Rs. 198.55 crore were spent through contractors depriving the beneficiaries of their involvement in construction of houses. Basic amenities, like smokeless chulah and sanitary latrine, intended to promote healthy environment and hygienic habitations in rural areas, were not provided in almost fifty percent of the houses. Rs. 1162 crore released for rural housing were not spent on the programme. Poor fund management led to large amounts being diverted or retained in deposits, misappropriation of funds and expenditure in excess of the approved norms. Inadequate and inefficient monitoring of the programme, both at the Ministry and state levels failed to enhance the quality of the delivery mechanism thus raising questions on the willingness and efforts of the agencies involved in accomplishing the objective of ending shelterlessness by the end of Ninth Plan period.

In April 1999, Govt. of India launched *Swarnjayanti Gram Swarojgar Yojana (SGSY)* as a single holistic programme to cover all aspects of self-employment for the rural poor. The funding pattern of the programme was to be shared by the Centre and the State in the ratio of 75:25. This was not strictly followed and there was a significant shortfall in the release of matching State share particularly by the special category States. There were large scale diversions, misutilization and parking of funds curtailing the actual funding for the programme. Resultantly, coverage of at least 30 percent of the BPL families under the scheme in 5 years also appears difficult as only 4.59 percent of the total BPL families were covered during 1999-2002. Per family investment of Rs. 19,678 against the contemplated level of income was inadequate and had largely failed to generate desired level of income. The focus did not shift from individual beneficiaries to Self-Help Groups as emphasized in the Scheme guidelines. Conceived as a process-oriented programme, the complex design and networking could not establish the identified processes. There were several deficiencies at all stages of implementation. None of the special projects due for completion by March 2002 could be completed as of June 2002, depriving the beneficiaries of the intended benefits. Monitoring was also deficient. The programme has not emerged as an improvement over the earlier IRDP and other complementary schemes, which it had replaced.

National scheme for Liberation and Rehabilitation of Scavengers and their dependents aimed at putting an end to the de-humanizing practice of manual scavenging by providing alternative, dignified and viable occupations to scavengers and their dependents by the Eight Plan period (1992-97). However, even after a decade of its implementation (1992-2002), the Scheme failed to deliver its social vision and more than 40 percent of the estimated beneficiaries remained unrehabilitated.

[Excerpts from the Report of the Comptroller and Auditor General of India for the Union Government- "Performance Appraisal" for the year 2001-02.]

in implementation of wide ranging schemes controlled and implemented by different Ministries of Govt. of India in different States in far flung districts. At the same time, the overall economic scenario as revealed in the Mid Year Review published by the Govt. of India, Ministry of Finance in December 2004 indicates that the Indian economy recorded an impressive broad-based growth of 8.2 percent in 2003-04 supported by a turnaround in agriculture. In addition to agriculture bouncing back from a decline of 5.2 percent in the previous year to a growth of 9.1 percent in 2003-04, industry and service sectors also grew by 6.7 percent and 8.7 percent, respectively.

It is difficult then, to attribute the abysmal human development indices for Indians to a lack of resources. Mark Tully's recent collection "India in Slow Motion" reflects a complete failure of governance. What was brought out with startling contour by the then Prime Minister, Sh. Rajiv Gandhi, in a public speech is now commonly accepted as a fact that the citizens of India get only value of about 15 paise out of a rupee spent on government programmes. A common explanation for this is corruption, both political and bureaucratic. While this argument cannot be rejected outright, it will be simplistic to attribute all ills to this factor. A recent study carried out by National Institute of Financial Management in the implementation of four schemes in the rural development sector viz., Employment Assurance Scheme, Indira Awaas Yojana, Swarnjayanti Gram Samridhi Yojana and Jawahar Gram Samridhi Yojana corroborated many of the CAG's observations. Some common observations were lack of planning and delays in decision-making, deficiencies in identification of beneficiaries, defective systems for delivery of funds, mismatch between receipt of funds needed, in terms of adequacy as well as time, etc. It was observed that funds were delivered to implementing organizations without reference to their capacity to absorb funds or their readiness for delivery of services.

In the schemes for housing, such as Indira Awaas Yojana (IAY), the resources were phased in such a manner that houses partially constructed out of funds released lay unattended for want of further funds. In many cases, these partially built houses deteriorated, rendering the earlier investment infructuous.

Swarnjayanti Gram Samridhi Yojana (SGSY) scheme faltered mainly due to misunderstanding of its objectives by those responsible for its implementation. Some deficiencies in the implementation also arose due to the social and cultural realities in the target areas, not having been factored in, while planning. For example, large amounts of cash delivered to beneficiaries for house construction under Indira Awaas Yojana were found often diverted to other social and personal needs of the recipients.

A PERFORMANCE ORIENTATION TO PUBLIC SPENDING

The deficiencies pointed out in the foregoing paras are not isolated instances but manifestation of systemic defects. The deficiencies in implementation of social sector schemes are often related to deficient structures and systems adopted. The present budgetary system allocated funds without correlation to expected results. The governance systems adopted lay emphasis on the observance of archaic rules and procedures and not on delivery of services. There appears to be no concern with actual 'output' or 'performance'.

The traditional bureaucratic systems also tend to forget the real purpose of spending monies from the public funds. An exaggerated fear of error and unrealistic expectations of "Zero error" systems leads the bureaucracy to create tighter and tighter controls. These regulations become so restrictive that action or activity become almost impossible.

Widespread dissatisfaction with government employees in delivery of services, their unresponsiveness to the ultimate beneficiaries, the burgeoning size of government and the consequent pressure on public finances has once again brought the concept of performance-based administrative structures to the forefront. Greater access to literacy and benefits of the information boom since the spread of television and other communication systems has changed the mental horizon and level of awareness of the citizen of India. He is no longer the stoic, long suffering "common man" and has understood his rights and demands his due. The Civil Society has helped bring about this change and it is now for the government organizations to adapt to these changes in the environment.

The New Public Management starting with the United Kingdom's reforms of 1980's and systems attempted in New Zealand in 1990s emphasized on performance as the primary instrument for efficient utilization of public resources and ensuring public good. No doubt, these international experiences provide models, which can address the issue of non-delivery of results. However, before adopting these systems, it will be useful to revisit the fate of the first attempt at focusing on performance through a Performance Budgeting initiative and draw lessons from it.

Performance Budgeting was a fascinating management mechanism, which many countries embraced with enthusiasm in the 60s and 70s. In India, too, adopting a functional classification system for the budget and accounts created the necessary structures. Preparation of performance budgets was made mandatory for development-oriented departments, especially those given plan funds in the early 70's. Government departments have carried out the annual exercise of preparation of performance budgets with instructions for correct preparation of this document reiterated year after year by the Ministry of Finance. However, even a cursory look at most of the Performance Budgets prepared by Ministries will indicate that the real purpose of establishing a performance-based management mechanism has not been achieved. The complete exercise of setting of output targets has been brought to naught by the concerned organizations by offering "activities" in the guise of "outputs". For example, an education-based scheme may offer "number of trainings conducted" as an output target for a given size of input, instead of offering "number of students passing out" as the output target. The advantage in the latter case will be the quality of education imparted. Similar instances abound in most of the performance budgets.

Performance Budgets of the Central Ministries, which offer "milestones" instead of "units of output" for justifying budget demands. The recent Zero Based Budgeting initiative is showing similar signs of bureaucratic obfuscation and it is likely that unless lessons are learnt from the failure of Performance Budgeting, fresh initiatives on "accountability for results" will suffer a similar fate.

The second important factor to be kept in view while adopting a performance-based public expenditure management system is that input controls and quality controls be continued alongside the output indicators being introduced so that while measuring output, the quality and consequently the outcome, is not neglected. For example, for a "vaccination" scheme, not only the administering of a requisite number of vaccines is important but also the quality of the vaccine cannot be ignored otherwise the actual outcome expected from the expenditure on vaccination will not be achieved.

A careful understanding of the formal or informal systems and rules of the organization where the performance measurement systems are to be applied and an assessment of the capabilities of the organization should precede introduction of performance budgeting system.

Properly applied, performance measurement can substantially improve the service delivery systems in government. Good data collection and good monitoring are prerquisites for the success of the performance measurement-based system adopted. The system will also need to be backed up with an appropriate system of incentives. Performance measures will be used not only for benchmarking the performance for comparison purposes but will also identify opportunities for achieving economy, efficiency and effectiveness in the system. This benchmarking can be against data from other organization working in the same area of activity or against performance of the same organization during earlier periods.

The road ahead for public management certainly appears to be leading towards a performance orientation to the public sector activities. Measuring performances in terms of result and providing for consequences for non-achievement while not neglecting the 'effort' which goes into activity, will definitely improve delivery of service to the citizen.

Recent Initiatives

Performance orientation to public sector activities cannot be possible unless government systems are restructured to permit those responsible for delivering results to have a reasonable amount of operational flexibility. Deficiencies in delivery of results have been addressed to some extent recently in a variety of ways by the central government. Restrictive and inflexible rules for government are the hurdles or barriers. Certain recent initiatives in this regard have taken the shape of review of the financial management rules for government, a review of procurement systems followed in government, etc. One such effort has been to update the General Financial Rules of the Central Government. These rules provided instruction for guidance of government officers in dealing with matters of a financial nature and basically served as mother regulations for systems established in various State Government and semi-government formations.

These rules have been reviewed recently to give a framework, ensuring efficiency, effectiveness and transparency while transacting government's financial business. A system of financial rules characterized by a genuine delegation of powers, flexibility in operation and direct accountability of officers entrusted with powers and authority, has been established. The government system for procurement has been liberalized and made more transparent and fair, ensuring fair competition as well as quality in government purchases. A greater decentralization and delegation of powers and responsibility has been envisaged.

There is also an attempt at rationalization of central scheme for social welfare by careful planning of schemes in consultation with the filed formations and tailoring new schemes to needs of a specific area rather than centrally determined and top driven ones as at present. The programmes in future will focus on attainment of objectives and not on expenditure only. Towards this end, the new systems envisage a project management orientation to implementation of social welfare schemes with close monitoring of implementation and proper evaluation and impact studies for gauging the effectiveness of public expenditure on these schemes. The new systems suggested by the Task Force for Review of General Financial Rules, 1963 (which the author had the privilege of assisting in the capacity of Member Secretary) have been adopted recently by the Central Government with effect from 1st July, 2005. The new General Financial Rules of the Government of India are available on Ministry of Finance, Govt. of India, website http//www.finmin.nic.in

In the past fifty years, India has moved from being a newly independent colony with a teeming and hungry population and archaic systems inherited from rulers to being a fairly self-confident and economically stronger nation. From being a leader of the deprived, it has moved to being acknowledged as a potential superpower of the 21st century. However, better governance systems that ensure that development intentions do not merely remain on paper but get translated into concrete results on ground are needed. The resources are now available, effective utilization of resources is the need of the hour, to place India where it should belong, right alongside developed nations.

Annexure I

RURAL HOUSING SCHEMES

The objective of the national Housing Policy to provide 'Housing for all' and that of the Special Action Plan to end all shelterlessness by the Ninth Five Year Plan were largely defeated. Against the target of 109.53 lakh housing units, only 50.34 lakh houses were constructed or upgraded as of March 2002 under various Rural Housing Schemes.

Overlapping objectives of multiple Rural Housing Schemes blurred the focus on providing cost effective, hygienic rural houses. No genuine effort appeared to have been made for convergence of the activities of various schemes to achieve the desired objectives.

Targeting of beneficiaries was misdirected, resulting in selection of 34,542 ineligible beneficiaries utilizing funds to the extent of Rs. 58.56 crore in 19 States and one Union Territory. In seven States, beneficiaries were allotted houses on the recommendations of MPs/MLAs, District authorities, Sarpanches, etc.

The system of funds transfer to beneficiaries was not uniform. In 10 States and one Union Territory, Rs. 7.38 crore were paid in excess of the prescribed norms whereas short payment of Rs. 42.11 crore was made in 10 States and one Union Territory.

In 16 States, Rs. 198.55 crore were spent on construction of houses through contractors, defeating the objective of involvement of beneficiaries in the construction with objective of ensuring cost-effectiveness and quality.

Rs. 171.56 crore were diverted to activities and schemes beyond the scope of the programme in 21 States and one Union Territory. In 20 States, Rs. 682.97 crore were drawn and retained in civil deposits, fixed deposits, and in treasuries outside Government account. Advances of Rs. 222.81 crore were paid to implementing agencies in five States and Rs. 4.04 crore were spent on unapproved works. Such leakages, besides reducing the actual expenditure on the programme by 31.55 per cent, adversely affected its implementation.

In 20 States and 2 Union Territories, smokeless *Chulhas* and sanitary latrines were provided in only 50 per cent and 57 per cent of the houses constructed respectively, thus depriving a large section of the beneficiaries of a clean, pollution-free environment and hygienic habitations.

In 17 States and 2 Union Territories, 37.75 per cent of the allotments were made in favour of male members, defeating the objective of empowerment of rural women.

In 26 States and 2 Union Territories, inventories of constructed/upgraded houses were not maintained in the absence of which verification of actual construction of the houses and the extent to which benefits reached the target group was rendered difficult. Monitoring of the implementation and execution of the programme was inadequate and ineffective both at Central and State levels.

Evaluation of impact of the programme was not conduced in almost all the states.

Swarnjayanti Gram Swarozgar Yojana

A central allocation of Rs. 2,668.24 crore was provided for SGSY during 1999-2002, of which only Rs. 1,723.62 crore (64.60 per cent) was released. Of the total funds of Rs. 3,326.16 crore available, Rs. 3,061.33 crore (92.04 per cent) were reported as having been spent, leaving an unspent balance of Rs. 264.83 crore.

Out of the expenditure totaling Rs. 988.41 crore, subjected to test check, Rs. 529.18 crore (53.54 per cent) were diverted, misutilised, misreported, etc.

Key performance parameters indicated that even though it was projected as a holistic programme, integrating all components of the erstwhile rural employment and proverty alleviation programmes, it failed to make the desired impact.

As against the targeted coverage of 30 per cent (167 lakh) of the BPL families, to be covered in a period of five years, only 25.60 lakh (4.59 per cent) could be covered in the initial three years of implementation. There was no acceleration in the pace of implementation as the number of BPL families assisted under the erstwhile IRDP was 17 per cent higher in the last two years of its implementation in relation to the first three years of implementation of SGSY.

In most of the States, there was no evidence of proper planning which was crucial for setting in motion the processes identified for implementation.

Selection of key activities was carried out without involving the agencies concerned, including banks, as conceived in the scheme. Project reports for the selected key activities were either not prepared or were deficient. This led to delay in disbursement or non-disbursement of funds to the Swarozgaris by the banks.

Identification of Swarozgaris and formation of Self Help Groups (SHGs) was not in accordance with the guidelines as there was little evidence of involvement of line departments and banks.

There was no evidence of overall shift of focus from individuals to SHGs. Proper evolution of SHGs could not ensured by the implementing agencies.

Regarding releases from the Revolving Funds to sustain evolution, SHGs were irregular and deficient.

There were delays in disbursement of loans and subsidy by the banks and under-financing of the projects to the Swarozgaris to the extent of Rs. 25.94 crore.

Systematic identification of infrastructure needs, for completing forward and backward linkages, was lacking in most of the States.

Implementation of special Projects was deficient as the guidelines lacked clarity. 15 Special Projects targeted for completion by 2002 remained incomplete. Utilization of funds on most of the Special Projects was negligible and unproductive.

Monitoring of the programme was deficient and ineffective.

National Scheme of Liberation and Rehabilitation of Scavengers and their Dependents

The Scheme was not calibrated to relate its parameters to the legal framework provided by the Employment of Manual Scavengers and Construction of Dry Latrines (Prohibition Act), 1993.

The base-line surveys conducted in the states, which intended to locate, specify and particularize the beneficiaries and their needs for training and rehabilitation, suffered from various infirmities. Even after the lapse of ten years since initiating action in this regard (June 1992), the Ministry/ implementing agencies did not have a reliable database of targeted beneficiaries.

Contrary to the Scheme stipulations, no special curriculum was developed for training of scavengers. As against 3.50 lakh eligible scavengers and their dependents targeted for training during 1992-97, only 2.02 lakh scavengers could be imparted training by March 2002. Shortfall in training during the Ninth Plan Period (1997-2002) was as high as 77 per cent.

Of the 4.00 lakh scavengers and their dependents targeted by the Eighth Plan period (1992-97), only 2.68 lakh beneficiaries could be rehabilitated by 1997. The Ninth Plan period showed quantitatively even a lesser achievement (2.02 lakh) than the Eighth Plan period. Audit review of occupational rehabilitation revealed misapplication of resources, preponderance of unavailable low cost projects and, rehabilitation of untrained scavengers, while trained scavengers remained un-rehabilitated, mismatches between skills acquired and occupations provided, etc.

The implementing agencies were casual in project formulation and estimation of its viability, as was evident from the rejection of a large number of loan applications by banks.

Expenditure of Rs. 22.78 crore remained unfruitful due to the houses remaining incomplete for periods ranging between one and 12 years or having been abandoned.

Provision of basic amenities like smokeless *Chulha* and construction of sanitary latrines could not be ensured in 24 States/Union Territories.

In 17 States and 2 Union Territories, 37.75 per cent of the allotments were made in favour of males, defeating the objective of empowerment of rural women.

Non-maintenance of inventories of houses in almost all the States rendered difficult the verification of the status and occupation of the beneficiaries and their actual existence.

Funds amounting to Rs. 1162 crore, though released, were not spent on the programme. Financial shortcomings relating to diversion of funds to unauthorized activities, execution of unapproved works, unauthorized retention of funds in various deposits, misappropriation of funds, inflated reporting of expenditure and advances treated as final expenditure were noticed during audit.

Monitoring of the programme at the Ministry and State levels was ineffective and inadequate. No proper evaluation had been carried out in the States.

Sustainability of Public Debt

Subhash Chandra Pandey

Taking a synoptic view, the first 3 decades were characterized by moderate growth rate of average 3% (the "Hindu rate of growth") but without the burden of debt and deficit. The moderate level of borrowing was then confined to financing capital expenditure as it was generally a period of revenue surplus. It was also the period when the foundation of modern industry, agriculture, science and education were laid. In the decade of eighties, we saw sharp increase in fiscal deficit and emergence of revenue deficit in the accounts of the Central Government with a gradual opening up of the economy and fiscal expansion, the doubling of the average growth rate with accentuation in indebtedness leading to the BoP crisis of 1990-91.

The Government had to resort to high levels of borrowings from the Reserve Bank of India which had an expansionary effect on money supply and inflation. High fiscal deficits also contributed to a large current account deficit and aggravated the problem of external indebtedness. We have risen, phoenix-like, from a Balance of Payments crisis in 1991 when our foreign exchange reserves had falled to below US $ 1 billion barely sufficient to finance a month's imports. True to our tradition, we had even pledged gold to avoid default and maintain our good name ih international community. We have steered clear of subsequent crises relatively unscathed and maintained our position of being one of the fastest growing economies in the world.

Economic reforms undertaken since then have yielded credible gains in external and monetary sector policies and paved the way for tax improvement. Foreign exchange reserves have swelled in recent years bringing a new set of problems in its wake. Inflation has climbed down from a peak of 17% in August, 1991 to about 4% till recently when a combination of factors like delayed Monsoons, excess liquidity, sharp rise in crude oil prices and surging demand put pressure on inflationary trends. The economy has grown at an average of over 6% p.a. Tax reforms during this period have laid the foundation of a robust, expanding tax base. Out of our total external debt of nearly US $ 112 billion, only about 5% is short-term debt. Gradual and cautious liberalization of capital account has sought to control short-term capital inflows and keep the maturity profile, end use, etc. within prudential norms. These are very impressive achievements. However, we cannot afford to rest on our laurels. Achieving stability in external sector and unshackling the central bank in conduct of an autonomous monetary policy has been not without a cost. The burden has mainly been borne in a significant measure by the fiscal sector, which was already in dire straits. The continuing high level of fiscal deficit for the last 20 years or so is the proverbial Achilles' heels that is a cause of serious concern. The fiscal stress, which peaked in the aftermath of the 5th Central Pay Commission and the economic slowdown, has since eased, mainly due to improvement in tax collections and softening of interest burden consequent upon increased liquidity from foreign exchange inflows. The fiscal crisis currently enveloping both the Centre and the States is serious and calls for timely and decisive action.

Fiscal deficits used to pre-empt a significant portion of savings in the economy, crowing out productive private investment and raising the cost of borrowing for the commercial sector. With excess liquidity in the system, the private investment is no longer being crowed out. But the relatively high levels of inflation, high capital inflows and relatively abundant liquidity should not lead us into complacency. Fiscal drag on the economic growth is still very significant and we have a huge backlog of infrastructure and social development. It is necessary to carry the fiscal consolidation efforts forward so that both public and private investments increase. Studies of the experience of a cross-section of countries suggest that large public sector deficits reduce growth by crowing out productive private investment. A study by World Bank (2000) suggested that in India, during the period 1986-87 and 1997-98, an increase in the central government's fiscal deficit (inclusive of oil pool deficit) by one percent of GDP was associated with a reduction in private corporate investment by one percent of GDP. However, the situation is different today. Government borrowings for meeting fiscal deficit is now at market determined rates of interest and with excess liquidity in the system, even the argument that private investment is being crowed out, may not be fully valid. Moreover, according to conventional economic theory, high levels of debts and deficits are associated with symptoms of fiscal or economic crisis. In India today, no such symptoms are evident. The relatively high levels of growth, low interest rates, relatively low levels of inflation, higher capital flows and relatively abundant liquidity in India seem to go against the conventional theory.

However, it would be a fallacy to be complacent about persistence of fiscal deficit and a high level of Public Debt and contingent liabilities of both the Central and State Governments that are not all comprehensively documented. A potential debt-trap can arise if the nominal interest rate of debt exceeds the rate of growth of nominal GDP, as debt service payments would outstrip output growth. The situation today is favourable but as the economy becomes increasingly globalised, there is no certainty that business-as-usual approach may not lead to a crisis again. Government dis-saving means potential growth foregone. India has to go into a higher trajectory of growth and realize its full potential. Fiscal consolidation is, therefore, essential for rapid and sustained growth.

The seriousness of Government's commitment to pursue a path of fiscal prudence is reflected in the enactment of Fiscal Responsibility and Budget Management (FRBM) Act. Lest the relative easing of fiscal stress in recent years should lead to complacency about the potentially damaging impact of fiscal indiscipline on macro-economic parameters, the Parliament had passed this Act in August 2003, which has recently been brought into force on 5th July 2004. This is a comprehensive legislation covering rules relating to borrowing, deficit and debt. The centrepiece of this landmark legislation is the Golden Rule: Governments must refrain from borrowing for consumption: they should borrow only for prudent investment. Hence, we must ensure that we put an end of using borrowed funds for current Government consumption as soon as feasible. Under FRBM Act, we have targeted to do so by 2008-09 in a steady manner by reducing revenue deficit to zero at the minimum rate of 0.5% of GDP every year. Other targets set under the Act include bringing down the fiscal deficit by at least 0.3% of GDP every year, limiting accretion to stock of fiscal liabilities in any year to 9% of GDP and limiting accretion to stock of guarantees in any year to 0.5% of GDP. The reporting and disclosure requirement has also been enlarged under the enhanced fiscal transparency. FRBM represents a discipline and an institutional framework within which the Government has committed to pursue a prudent fiscal policy aimed at achieving sustained growth and inter-generational equity. Annual targets for the reduction of revenue deficit, fiscal deficit, tax-GDP ratio and outstanding liabilities will define the Government's path to achieving end-period targets. These targets mean a lot of discipline.

FRBM Bill was introduced in the Parliament, in December 2000 based on the Report of the Committee on Fiscal Responsibility Legislation, which submitted its report to the Finance Minister on 4th July, 2000. To build consensus on the issues contained in the Bill and honouring the accepted best parliamentary practice in this regard, the Bill was referred to the Standing Committee on Finance for detailed examination and report thereon. The committee deliberated upon the various provisions of the Bill and after recording evidence of the officers of Ministry of Finance, Reserve Bank of India, Non-Official

Experts, etc., placed its recommendations on the Table of the Lok Sabha in November 2001. The Finance Ministry accepted most of the recommendations of the Standing Committee and amended the Bill accordingly. The amended Bill was deliberated upon and approved by Parliament in May 2003. The Bill, which had the support of the majority of the members cutting across party lines, got the Presidential assent on August 26, 2003 and became an Act. It has been brought into force along with the FRBM Rules on 5th July 2004.

The Report of the Committee on Fiscal Responsibility Legislation came in July 2000. To appreciate the context of the Committee's recommendations, we have to see the trend of revenue and fiscal deficits in the decade of 90s and even before. While fiscal deficit has always been there, the revenue deficit emerged after 1979-80 and continued to build up from an average of 1.02% of GDP in 1980-85 and peaked to 3.82% of GDP in 1998-99 after the Pay Commission's recommendations were implemented. Fiscal deficit, on a comparable basis excluding Small Saving loans to states, used to be less than 3% of GDP in 1970-75 but then began to rise to about 3.81% in 1975-80, 5.13% in 1980-85 and peaked to 6.57% in 1985-90 leading ultimately to the BoP crisis. It was subdued in early nineties till the 5th Pay Commission's report implementation upset the declining trend.

Despite recent modernization in fiscal deficit, there is still a large overhang of accumulated liabilities of the past. Total liabilities of Central Government by the end of current financial year are estimated to be about 2,000,000 crores including over Rs. 500,000 crores liability to depositors of small saving schemes. This level of outstanding liabilities is nearly 6.5 times. Central Government's annual revenue and nearly two-thirds of our Gross Domestic Product, compared to Rs. 12,00,000 crore, about 60% of GDP in 2000, when the Sarma Committee recommended the FRBM legislation. The sharp increase in the liabilities is noteworthy: from Rs. 2,865 crore at the end of 1950-51 to Rs. 59,749 crore at the end of 1980-81, Rs. 538,611 crore at the end of 1994-95, Rs. 778,294 crore at the end of 1997-98. With an average of 10% direct and indirect cost of servicing the liabilities, the interest burden is enormous. It is evident that if these trends were to continue unabated, the debt burden of the

Government would grow to such an extent that the Central Government would very soon find it difficult to find resources for investment in critical development programmes. It may also be noted that external debt as reported in the budget is at historical cost, which implies an understatement of these liabilities because most of these were contracted at officially controlled exchange rate that has since been given a go by.

Against the outstanding liabilities of the order of Rs. 2,000,000 crore, the assets of the Central Government are only about Rs. 1,200,000 crore, ignoring any adjustment of depreciation in value or appreciation in value over time. This means that cumulatively as much as Rs. 800,000 crore has been borrowed by successive governments for consumption. Government borrowing is nothing but deferred taxation. Therefore, if the present generation lives beyond its means, it will leave an unbearable burden of debt to the future generations and also damage the prospects of sustainable economic growth. The accumulated burden of the past considerably constrains the Government's ability to sustain current levels of spending. We are continuously and dangerously living beyond our means. Worse is that we are financing even day-to-day consumption expenditure through borrowing whereas the prudence demands that the borrowings be limited only to adequately productive investments. We are borrowing not only to repay past debts but also to pay interest thereon. In order to cap, decelerate and reduce the fiscal deficit without affecting the developmental programmes and investments, it is more than ever necessary to prune low priority public expenditures, to effect maximum economy, efficiency and effectiveness in the use of public resources, cut down cost of public services, review the role of government in various activities and so on. Persistently high level of deficit and consequent build-up of debt stock meant substantial pre-emption of Government revenues by debt servicing costs. It was as high as about 50% at the time FRBM legislation was planned. Such high pre-emption of revenues by interest, coupled with commitments on subsidies and defence and internal security, salaries, pension, etc. ensured that the Government hardly has any headroom available to finance developmental expenditure at any meaningful level. One of the key objectives of FRBM is to reclaim this fiscal space for development financing. By elimination of revenue deficit and generating revenue surplus, the entire borrowing plus revenue surplus will then be available for capital expenditure. That would be the most positive outcome of the FRBM discipline.

According to the Tenth Status Report on India's external debt, India's external debt stock stood at US $ 112.1 billion as on December 31, 2003 as against US $ 105.3 billion as on December 31, 2002. Notwithstanding an absolute increase in external debt stock, India's external debt indicators have continued to improve. The incidence of external debt burden as measured by Debt-to-GDP ratio came down from 38.7 per cent in 1991-92 to 20.2 per cent during 2002-03. The share of short-term debt in total debt declined from the peak of 10.2 per cent at the end of March 1991 to 5.1 per cent at end-December 2003. Short-term debt as a proportion of foreign exchange assets too declined from a high of 38.21 per cent to 5.9 per cent during the corresponding period. Similarly, debt servicing as a proportion of gross current receipts dropped from 30.2 per cent in 1991-92 to 15.8 per cent in 2002-03. However, debt service ratio rose to 18.1 percent during 2003-04 (April-December) mainly because of redemption of Resurgent India Bonds (RIBs). According to the latest Report of the World Bank entitled "Global Development Finance, 2004", India improved her rank from the position of third in 1991 to eighth in 2002 in the list of the top fifteen debtor countries. (World Bank classifies countries into three broad categories, i.e., severely, moderately and less indebted countries by relating ratios of Present Value of total debt service to exports of goods and services and Present Value of total debt service to GNP. With 76.1 billion US $ Present Value of external debt in 1997, India was classified as Moderately Indebted, ranking 10th in the world in indebtedness). Besides, India's external debt indicators compare well with that of other developing countries. For example, the ratios of short-term debt to total debt and short-term debt to foreign exchange reserves are the lowest. While the ratio of concessional to total debt is the highest, the debt to GNP ratio is the second lowest after China in the year 2002. The improvement in India's external indebtedness as measured by inter-country comparison is encouraging and the position of India's external debt appears to be sustainable. Significantly, external financing of fiscal deficit is negligible.

So in the public debt management, the focus is on domestic debt management, how to reduce the cost of debt, how to prevent bunching of repayments, how to increase the share of long-term debt in the total portfolio of public debt. There is a discernible shift in the composition of Government liabilities towards increasing share of market loans as regulatory pre-emption of investible funds and deficit monetization gives way to market loans. Year after year, the liabilities are increasing as repayments due to be made during any year are financed by new borrowings during the year. Thus, liabilities are being merely rolled over or refinanced. When will this borrowing from Peter to repay Paul (or to Peter himself) as well as to meet other expenses end ? This has raised serious problem of sustainability of increasingly higher gross market borrowing programme.

It is noted that sustainability of debt and deficit may be examined from two angles: Continued capacity to borrow or capacity to repay from own resources. One or the other or both may be unsustainable in a given time frame and a given macro-economic context. "Continued capacity to borrow" as a measure of debt/deficit sustainability is also linked to the issue of being sustainable, at what cost and how long ? The debt sustainability tests or solvency tests based on discount value of primary balances indicate the level of debt and deficit that is unsustainable because it cannot be financed from government's own resources. However, governments can, after exhausting their own resources, resort to further borrowing from within and outside the country, to repay or service their debt and this can continue so long as it can find lenders. So long as there are lenders willing to lend or there are "captive lenders" within the control of the Government, it can continue to borrow whether or not it has the capacity to repay from own resources. However, as the compulsions for marginal borrowings increasing the cost of borrowing and as continued rolling over or refinancing borrowings becomes increasingly difficult, the situation will lead to a crisis. As the governments become more and more desperate to borrow, lenders' attitude will harden and the successive borrowings would become more and more costlier.

Interest rates on government debt will rise and Government's pre-emption of resources from market will leave all non-government borrowers in lurch and that will hurt economic growth. When a stage is reached that no one is willing to lend to government, it can theoretically start printing currency notes leading to runaway inflation and Balance of Payments crisis. Nothing of this sort has happened because for various reasons, the supply of money is exceeding its demand.

The sustainability of debt and deficit is often examined from the perspective of liquidity risk and insolvency risk, i.e., whether the inability to repay debt is temporary or permanent. Particularly in the case of a Government's fixed nominal interest rate on domestic currency debt, solvency of the Government is not the issue, it is the cost and consequences of remaining solvent. Governments can retain their "creditworthiness" on the ruins of their central bank, banking system, economic growth and public welfare. Governments can remain solvent [especially in respect of fixed nominal interest rate on domestic currency debt], if necessary by printing currency notes, returning worthless paper to lenders. A rupee is borrowed and a rupee is returned. It is a different thing that the rupee taken may be equivalent to lot of goods and services in terms of purchasing power and the rupee returned may not be worth the paper on which it is printed! Hence, debt/deficit sustainability cannot be considered in isolation, it is not a static and context—free measure. How far drinking is sustainable? For a person of means, drinking may be sustainability at the cost of his health and his family's welfare. Sustainable drinking level has to be measured in terms of acceptable health levels. Government's situation is similar in many respects. Likewise, sustainability of Government debt has to be similarly considered in the context of acceptable costs and consequences. A certain level of debt is sustainable with reference to a certain acceptable level of inflation, growth rate and Balance of Payments situation within a certain time frame. Any increase beyond this level will mean either higher inflation, lower growth and worse Balance of Payments situation.

Since 1991, a number of reform measures have been taken and are still being taken to develop a broad-based, deep and well regulated capital market so that, on the one hand, the investors have a wider choice in terms of avenues of investment and on the other hand, the borrowers can also minimize their cost of borrowing by cutting through cartels of financial intermediaries. The small saving schemes were started at a time when the banking and capital market were relatively undeveloped and confined to a few urban areas. People looked upon the government as a reliable trustee/banker with whom they could lodge their hard earned savings. That fiduciary bonding is still intact but now the banking and capital markets are fairly well-developed and their coverage is also pretty widespread. In the interest of economic growth, we would like to see the banking and capital markets grow stronger. Therefore, what we need is an effective regulatory mechanism in banking and capital markets so that people can repose greater trust in them and on the other hand, to wean them away from looking up to the government for providing assured high yield, risk free avenues of investment. Ironically, the small saving scheme which could have been an instrument of offering Minimum Support Price for investible funds, have actually become Maximum Support Price for investible funds. While the people may be justified in such expectations, the experience so far has shown that the governments have not been able to put borrowed funds to good, revenue earning uses and, therefore, these liabilities have become an albatross round their neck, something they rather cheerfully carry around because it helps them to postpone unpopular but economically prudent decisions on taxation and cost recovery of services.

Borrowing *per se* within prudential limits is not bad. In fact, it is inevitable for a developing economy. But what is important is the end use of borrowed funds. If these are deployed for creation of income generating quality assets and the income is at least sufficient to cover the cost of borrowing, then such a borrowing is prudent though there may be other limiting factors such as those arising out of monetary policy. But borrowing to finance current consumption for a long period is a prescription of disaster. It is axiomatic not to borrow for consumption purposes. The expected rate of return from public spending should at least be equal and preferably higher than the cost of borrowing. Therefore, the revenue deficit should be the central concern of fiscal policy. For long the Governments have been shying away from legitimate taxation and, instead, resorting to the softer option of more and more borrowing. Borrowing is nothing but deferred taxation and sooner or later, we will have to address the inter-generational equity issue in fiscal policy. We have no right to borrow for consumption and burden the future generations with debt without leaving durable assets for them. If we want to maintain and increase economic growth rate, enjoy the pleasures of modest inflation, stay away from balance of payment crisis, nurture the health of our banking system, we need to reverse current fiscal stance towards greater fiscal rectitude.

Management of Forex Reserves : Innovations and Opportunities

G.I. DEWAN

Foreign Exchange reserves of India which today stand at about USD 165 bn., represent the accumulated excess of inflows over outflows. There are different degrees of comforts attached at various levels of reserves for the country. The higher the level of foreign exchange reserves, the higher are the opportunities and options available for effective utilization and deployment of reserves. Large reserves are needed by emerging markets to withstand any crisis and, to some extent, these reflects confidence in the superprising and complex international financial situations. It may be worthwhile to recognise that reserve accumulation, in some sense, reflects the savings-investment balances.

As reported by the Bank for International Settlements (BIS), the Emerging Market Economies (EMEs), during 2000 and 2005, accumulated reserves at an annual rate of US $ 250 bn. which was almost five times higher than the level seen in the early 1990s. The bulk of the reserve accumulation was concentrated in Asia, with countries like China, Korea, India, Malaysia and Taiwan witnessing large increases, while countries in Latin America and Central Europe had a fairly modest increase in reserves during this period.

Reserves Driven by Capital Account Surplus

It is important to identify the sources of reserve accumulation. There are some countries like Russia where the reserves are built out of current account surplus while the countries like China, Korea and Taiwan built up their reserves both from current and capital account surpluses. In India, the reserves accretion was driven more by capital account surplus and not due to current account, broadly implying that net capital inflows have remained much larger than what could be absorbed in the domestic economy. When the reserve accumulation is due to large capital in flows, it is relevant to distinguish between debt and non-debt flows as also between foreign direct investment and generally less stable portfolio flows. In fact, the stock as well as flow in each category would be relevant for reserve management with varying degrees of volatility.

Difficulties in Computing Quasi-Fiscal Cost of Reserves

A simple method of calculating net cost of carrying reserves, to the central bank, is the difference between the interest rate on domestic securities and the rate of return earned on the foreign exchange reserves adjusted for any exchange rate change. The magnitude of the cost, which is often difficult to estimate, varies with the extent of sterilisation and the yield differentials. These are termed "quasi-fiscal" costs in the literature since the costs to the central bank are passed on to the sovereign through a lower transfer of profits. In countries where local interest rates are well above international levels, such carrying costs could be positive, while if the reverse is true, such carrying costs could be negative. A recent study by the BIS has shown that carrying costs are negative in a number of countries at current interest rates. The study states that in China, for instance, one year interest rate in June 2006 was less than half the comparable US Treasury bond rate. Hence the central bank is earning a positive carry. However, it can be argued that given the inherent cyclical nature of interest rates, such negative carrying cost could reverse over a period of time. Moreover, one has to keep in mind that these hypothetical cost calculations do not capture capital gains or losses.

While assessing the fiscal cost of holding reserves, it would be worthwhile to set-off the benefits that the country may have in holding reserves. In any country risk analysis by the rating agencies and other institutions, the level of reserves generally has high weights. Moreover, it is essential to keep in view some hidden benefits which could accrue to a country holding reserves and which may, *inter alia,* include: maintaining confidence in monetary and exchange rate policies; enhancing the capacity to intervene in foreign exchange markets; limiting external vulnerability so as to absorb shocks during times of crises; providing confidence to the markets that external obligations can always be met; and reducing volatility in foreign exchange markets. It is true that beyond a point, when the credit rating reaches appropriate investment grade, addition to reserves may not lead to further improvement in the credit rating. It is necessary to recognise that, as in the case of costs, there are difficulties in computing the benefits too.

Changing Investment Opportunities of Reserves

An important objective of holding the reserves is to be prepared for contingencies, but the range of instruments available to satisfy this need is limited. Nevertheless, the management of reserves has been changing and there has been a quest for higher returns within these traditional objectives. To quote Mr. Philip D. Wooldridge of the BIS, in his latest article on "The Changing Composition of Official Reserves" in the September 2006 issue of the *BIS Quarterly Review:*

> "Continuing a trend that began in the 1970s, when reserves were first reallocated from US Treasury bills to bank deposits, reserve managers have been gradually shifting into higher-yielding, higher-risk instruments. They seem

most comfortable managing market risk but are beginning to take on more credit and liquidity risk too. The currency composition of their portfolios, while volatile, has not changed as much as the instrument composition."

It is essential to recognise that reserve managers are already shifting into higher-yielding instruments with a higher risk-return equation, presumably as a result of progressively rising level of reserves. Consequently, the financial returns on the free reserves at the margin could be far higher than the average return.

Quasi Reserves

With the positive shock emanating from large capital flows resulting in significant reserves accumulation in many EMEs, a new development in reserve management is to hold a part of the reserves which could be used by the public sector in a country in a manner different from the strictly defined pattern of holding of the external assets by the monetary authorities. Such foreign exchange reserves could be termed as quasi reserves. In terms of its holding, such quasi reserves could be easily retrievable when the situation demands. In Singapore, the Monetary Authority of Singapore (MAS) and the Government of Singapore Investment Corporation (GIC) basically manage foreign exchange reserves. GIC is the Government's principal investment agent, handling the bulk of the nation's investments while the MAS holds reserves to maintain the stability of the Singapore dollar.

On the pattern of the Singapore's GIC, South Korea has recently established the Korean Investment Corporation (KIC). Another interesting example is China, where foreign exchange reserves have been utilised to strengthen the banking system without foreign securities being sold. China has transferred funds from its international reserves, held with the Peoples' Bank of China (PBC) to a new company, Central Huijin Investment Company (CHIC), set-up in 2003 and jointly managed by the government, PBC and the State Administration of Foreign Exchange. In the PBC's balance sheet, the said amount of reserves was replaced by claims on the CHIC. The CHIC used the assets to purchase shares in banks which were to be recapitalised.

INNOVATIVE IDEAS

It is useful to explore some of the innovative ideas that have been put forward in the recent period for using reserves:

1. *In March 2006, Prof. Lawrence Summers* while delivering the L.K. Jha Memorial Lecture in Mumbai, argued that the level of reserves in many countries far exceeded the traditional measures of reserve levels required to guard against a foreign exchange crisis. Prof. Summers suggested creation of an international facility by the International Monetary Fund (IMF) and the World Bank, under which the countries could invest their excess reserves. The proposal provides an option to a country holding reserves to place a part of them with the IMF/World Bank entities to operate, *de facto,* as external asset managers, if the envisaged entity could assure that it had the expertise to function as such an external asset manager and to provide a higher risk-weighted return than the domestic reserve managers.
2. *In 2005, Eswar Prasad and Raghuram Rajan* of the IMF proposed for a controlled approach to capital account liberalisation for economies experiencing large capital inflows. The proposal essentially involves securitising a portion of capital inflows through close-ended mutual funds that issue shares in the domestic currency, use the proceeds to purchase foreign exchange from the central bank and then invest the foreign exchange so acquired, abroad. It is argued that such an arrangement would eliminate the fiscal costs of sterilising these inflows, provide the domestic investors opportunities for international portfolio diversification and stimulate the development of domestic financial markets; more importantly, it would allow central banks to control both, the timing and the quantity of capital outflows. It is advocated that this

proposal could be a part of a broader tool kit of measures to liberalise the capital account cautiously when external circumstances are favourable.

In fact, in India, domestic mutual funds are permitted to invest in foreign securities, apart from ADR/GDR of Indian companies, up to an aggregate limit of USD two billion. In addition, a limited number of qualified mutual funds are also permitted to invest cumulatively up to USD one billion in overseas exchange traded funds (ETF).

3. *An idea which received some attention in March 2002* during the gathering on 'Finance for Development' in Monterrey, Mexico, is that instead of holding the reserves in the US dollars, a new form of global money, akin to IMF's Special Drawing Rights, namely, 'global greenbacks' could be issued, which countries could hold in their reserves. The corpus would be created by countries setting aside a part of reserves every year as an insurance against contingencies. The amount of money held by these countries in 'global greenbacks' could be given to developing countries for financing their development programmes as well as global public goods like environmental projects, health initiatives, humanitarian assistance, and so on. For countries that receive less than the amount that they need to put into reserves, the new 'global money' would go into reserves freeing dollars that these countries would otherwise set aside. Countries that receive more than they must put into reserves, could exchange the new money for conventional currencies. Eventually, all the new money will find its way into reserves, which in effect represents a commitment by the countries to help each other in times of trouble.
4. In the aftermath of the Asian financial crisis, two related developments took place.

   (a) *In the year 2000,* ASEAN countries mutually agreed to form a network of bilateral swap agreements to provide mutual protection from financial emergencies, popularly known as the Chiang Mai

Initiative (CMI). The success of such an initiative is reflected in the recent proposal of the Asian Finance Ministers to double the size of the Asian Central Bank Swaps under the CMI.

(b) *In the year 2003,* Asian Bond Fund Initiative was launched reflecting the efforts to develop a regional bond market for catering to the medium and long-term financing needs of the Asian economies. The Asian Bond Fund provided an arrangement for pooling of a portion of foreign exchange reserves of a few East Asia and Pacific countries and the Fund's portfolio is invested in the liquid US dollar denominated bonds issued by the major Asian economies. The second ABF, launched in June 2005, aims to promote local currency bond markets, by establishing a Pan-Asian Bond Index Fund (PAIF) and eight single-market funds (SMFs).

COMFORT LEVELS

The concept of adequacy of reserves is popular but it is also possible to view reserves in terms of degree of comfort they provide at various levels. Certainly, at a very low level of reserves, which we in India had in the early 1990s, the degree of comfort was very low, and with rising level of reserves, the comfort also increases. The level of comfort and discomfort could be linked to the problem of plenty and the problem of scarcity. For a country, it could happen that initially the degree of comfort with the level of reserves may be too low for sometime but with rising level of reserves, the country might reach a 'comfort zone', and as the reserves level keeps on rising to reach a still higher level, then at some point, a portion of the reserves would cease to be strictly 'foreign exchange reserves' and could be characterised as a corpus of funds available for deployment in a higher risk-return portfolio.

Opportunities alongside Comfort Levels

We can now look at the availability of various

opportunities linked with the degree of comfort.

1. It may be useful to view the adequacy of reserves in terms of degree of comfort they offer at a given time.
2. While considering the level of reserves and comfort derived therefrom, it will be necessary to take into account the investment and the stabilisation funds, transferability from official reserves to such funds and *vice versa*. The extent of liquidity required also needs to be considered in assessing the comfort level.
3. Relative emphasis on safety, liquidity and return keeps changing with the degree of comfort at a given level of reserves.
4. It must be noted that from a national balance sheet point of view, official reserves have to reflect the potential market infirmities in the private sector. So, if there are high returns derived from high risks assumed due to larger risk appetite of the external asset managers, then deploying official reserves too in the high-risk assets would exacerbate the risks. Official reserves may be needed as a cushion when markets get suddenly risk averse and hence, safety and liquidity should normally have higher orders of priority in the management of reserves.
5. It is possible for a central bank to have tranches—each tranche reflecting a different combination of safety, liquidity and return. Each tranche can be managed by the central bank or an external asset manager, or both, in parallel, to benchmark their relative performance.
6. Above all, the criticality of the accountability in the use of reserves must be recognised. It is useful to note that the reserve management policies normally involve joint responsibility of the Government and the central bank—irrespective of the situation in whose balance sheet they appear.

Now, with the global rise in the interest rates, there is always a lurking fear in the EMEs, that the level of capital flows may not be maintained. Thus, the comfort level of reserves should not be viewed with respect to the current situation alone but should also reckon the assessment of the emerging risks.

Moreover, at this moment, the global economy has not been tested on the eventuality of a not-so-orderly correction of the current global imbalances. In that eventuality, disruption in financial markets in the form of large cross-currency volatility and sharp rise in interest rates are not unlikely in the global economy. Several factors impinge on the comfort level of reserves and the relative weights assigned to safety, liquidity and return. When, how and through whom should the search for higher returns be pursued, depending upon the level of comfort, is a matter of convenience and opportunities, which should always be kept open.

PART III

Economic and Social Infrastructure Development : Public-Private Partnership

Private Sector Participation in Economic and Social Infrastructure

RAJAN KASHYAP

Infrastructure is taken as "the basic systems and services, such as transport and power supplies, that a country or organization uses in order to work effectively" (Cambridge Advanced Learner's Dictionary). In so far as a state or a country is concerned, its economic infrastructure would include all physical items that form the base of development. Social services, on the other hand, such as education and health, constitute the social infrastructure. Both these forms of infrastructure are the basic foundations over which any system of economic development can be built.

THE PROBLEM OF ECONOMIC INFRASTRUCTURE

It is recognized that the availability of infrastructure facilities is imperative for the acceleration of economic development of a country. Traditionally, governments have accepted direct responsibility for building up most forms of infrastructure including railways, roads, power, telecommunications, seaports and airports, water supply, sanitation and sewerage. The India Infrastructure Report, 1996 observes a new wave of privatization and deregulation of infrastructure sectors the world over in the preceding 10 years or so. The Report identifies five major reasons for the growing trend of commercialization in infrastructure development:

(1) Massive requirements of investment to fuel high economic growth coupled with fiscal stringency in most countries.
(2) An increasing emphasis on specified/service agencies in laying down user charges for providing infrastructure services.
(3) Technological changes that justify agencies in laying down user charges for providing infrastructure services.
(4) Pressures of globalization that persuade countries to provide cost effective and efficient infrastructure services and serve to attract external investments in other sectors of the economy.
(5) A new dynamism and integration of world capital markets, which encourage flow of capital funds on commercial basis for investment in infrastructure.

The India Infrastructure Report had pointed out that for the Indian economy to grow as projected from 6% in 1996 to 7.5% by 2001 and 8.5 by 2006, implying a rise in the investment from 25% of the GDP in 1996 to 29% in 2000 and 31.5% in 2005, then the requirements of investment in infrastructure would be of the order of Rs. 4000 billion in the five year period 1996 to 2001 and Rs. 7500 billion from 2001 to 2006. Quite clearly such gigantic investments were beyond the capacity of the budgets of the Central Government and of the State Governments to provide. The rate of growth in the 5-year period 1996-2001 turned out to be less than 4.5% per annum, even as infrastructure struggled to grow.

While the national policy determines the approach to infrastructure, the creation and management of most infrastructure is the responsibility of state governments. The status of infrastructure in a progressive state like Punjab puts in perspective the magnitude of the problem facing the country.

Conservative estimates suggest that the State of Punjab requires a minimum investment of Rs. 5000 crore per annum in infrastructure in the next five years if the growth rate projected above is to be sustained. An analysis of investments made in the past shows that the public sector (the state government and its agencies) would find it difficult to provide directly more than Rs. 1000 crore per annum toward infrastructure development. This leaves a resource gap of Rs. 4000 crore per annum in the infrastructure sector. The National Centre for Agricultural Economics and Policy Research, New Delhi assesses that investment on infrastructure in the rural sector in Punjab declined from 13.46% of the Net State Domestic Product at current prices 1974-79 to only 4.76 in the period 1991-96. This shows that the resources available for infrastructure in the rural sector have been declining as a percentage of the state domestic product. Apart from conventional loaning from institutions such as HUDCO (Housing and Urban Development Corporation) in rural areas, the national policy now allows state governments to seek investment from private sector institutions, many of which has foreign partners. Each state is free to determine the manner in which its infrastructure is financed.

In this scenario, most state governments, including Punjab, are looking for external investments in all fields in the infrastructure sector. Several models such as Build-Operate-Transfer (BOT), Build-Operate-Own-Transfer (BOOT), joint ventures and direct borrowing for specific projects have been adopted in various parts of the world, especially in countries in South East Asia and the Far East. A number of state governments such as Maharashtra, Gujarat and Andhra Pradesh have also taken certain initiatives. Basically, there are two approaches. First, seeking loans from external sources (including foreign sources), the repayments of which is guaranteed by the Government over a stipulated period of time. Secondly, direct external investment from whatever source, which can be a part of BOT or BOOT or under any other arrangement.

The first route, that is, obtaining a loan from an external source, holds certain attractions for every government. When there is an assurance of a State guarantee, bonds can easily be floated in the open market by specialized financial institutions on behalf of the State Government. Various departments of the government, urban local bodies, public sector undertakings such as the State Urban Development Authority, the State Tourism Corporation, etc. have in position machinery that can immediately take up the work if any additional funds are infused. This route is found convenient as per the established pattern of expenditure by the agencies concerned.

The obvious shortcomings of such direct borrowing by the State Government are :

- It increases the indebtedness of the State to levels that might be beyond the capacity of the Government to sustain, eventually leading to debt trap for the government.
- It also entails no increase in efficiency in delivery. The construction agency may often not be equipped to handle the higher quantum of additional funds, which must be utilized in a shorter time frame.
- There is a tendency to utilise the funds not only for creating new infrastructure but also for repairs and maintenance of existing infrastructure. Thus borrowed funds tend to be used on revenue account.

Loans for such infrastructure as roads are available from several sources. There can be variations in the terms of such loaning, including ease in procurement, the rates of Interest, the period for repayment, etc. The chart below gives some indication of this.

As against this, the BOT or BOOT route envisages maximum exploitation of the strengths of the State Government and its institutions while bringing in qualitative upgradation of performance in construction activities. This route is in tune with the needs of a market economy, but the flow of funds is usually tied to the recovery of minimum user charges from the beneficiaries. Whether they be vehicles on a super highway or a railway over bridge, or urban dwellers who are provided a

Comparative Terms of Loans for Roads from Agencies

	HUDCO	*RIDF^*	*World Bank*	*Infrastructure Bonds (Negotiable)*
*Rate of interest % per annum	15.91	12.00	9	10-12
Period for repayment	7-10 years	5 years		6-8 year
Service charge	1.25 one time	—		10 to 25%
Moratorium, if any	—	3 years		
State Government's contribution as seed money	30%	10%		Nil
Period of time for negotiation of loan and flow of funds	1 month	2 months	18 months	1 month

*Rates as prevalent in the year 1999.

^ Rural Infrastructure Development Fund.

sanitation and water supply scheme in a town, or even consumers of electricity supplied from a power project. The determination of user charges clearly conflicts with current populist trends whereby the public has become used to facilities which are heavily subsidized.

An important decision in funding economic infrastructure is to balance a certain level of direct borrowing by the State and its agencies with the maximization of direct external investment in its infrastructure projects.

AN APPROACH FOR STATE GOVERNMENTS

Quite clearly, private investment in physical infrastructure in any state in India will be guided by the perception and visions of development of the state government concerned. Each state would indeed have to design its own model for attracting external investment. In an open, and now globalizing environment, all private players have a free choice in selecting partner states for investing their resources. The states are thus competing for the flow of resources from external institutions, public and private. For success in the long-term, therefore, the model of partnership must incorporate several features that afford comfort to both partners. These include the following :

(1) The framework for infrastructure development should be as simple and practically oriented as possible.
(2) The evaluation of potential investors should be as per objective empirical indicators and there should be total transparency in decision-making.
(3) The system should encourage initiative of the agencies directly involved in infrastructure development. There should be maximum decentralization and delegation. Various departments and institutions involved in infrastructure should be free to arrange funding for their specific projects under the overall guidelines of the government, which are based on fiscal prudence.
(4) Strong systems of project appraisal and monitoring have to be in position before the funds are actually utilized. A professional agency is to be selected from

the open market for assisting in the monitoring systems.

(5) Credit rating of the state government, as well as of its agencies, must be a part of the exercise.

(6) The capacity of the State Government to repay loans must be carefully appraised before offering any state sovereign guarantee. In other words, the status and implications of indebtedness have to be fully evaluated. Several states have a statutory restriction on the level of borrowing that they can undertake, and even on the amount that they can pledge as government guarantee for any institutional borrowing. The legislation in Punjab is called the Fiscal Responsibility Act, 2001.

(7) An appropriate mix of borrowing and direct investing, including establishment of joint ventures in infrastructure development is to be adopted.

(8) The systems need to be dynamic, in order to adjust to market conditions in the infrastructure sector.

PRIVATE SECTOR PARTICIPATION IN SOCIAL INFRASTRUCTURE

The Nobel laureate, Amartya Sen, considers an efficient social welfare network to be the *sine qua non* of a democracy. It is the basic responsibility of the State to provide quality service in such sectors as healthcare and education. What role can the private sector play in strengthening and enlarging these facilities?

Government institutions as well as numerous private hospitals and nursing homes provide medical and healthcare in India. Apart from doctors following the western (allopathic) system of medicine, there are many practitioners of traditional systems of medicine serving all parts of the country, especially the remote areas. The private allopathic doctors operate mainly in the urban and sub-urban areas, which are considered lucrative for professionals. Mainly, the government institutions dispense what is categorized as primary healthcare in the rural areas. In respect of secondary healthcare the Government has a strong presence in small and large towns. The Government also dominates tertiary care thought reperal hospitals and medical colleges and post-graduate institutions. The common perception is that the government healthcare is inefficient and inadequate, whereas the private sector is expensive and exploitative.

Both forms of institutions are firmly entrenched, delivering, even if perceptively imperfectly, some level of healthcare. Without passing a value judgment on performance of the existing system, one can consider if a partnership can deliver better value for money. Any linkage must couple the strengths of each sector. Many states are grapping with the issue. Basically, good healthcare has three components, good physical infrastructure (hospitals, dispensaries, etc.), good personnel (doctors, para-medical staff, etc.) and good systems of management. With the support of the national government and external institutions, many states have upgraded their secondary healthcare institutions. A similar scheme for primary institutions is currently being drawn up. In Punjab, for example, all 155 secondary hospitals in the state have been modernized with a Rs. 460 crore World Bank Loan. In regard to the quality government doctors, in terms of technical qualifications and skills, they are second to none. Where the state system is deficient is in effect management control and motivation. It is accepted that within the government oriented system, accountability is inadequate. The reform process will impact both primary and secondary institutions.

In respect of primary healthcare, which serves the entire rural population, all political parties swear by the concept of decentralized management. The 73rd and 74th amendments of the Constitution of India enjoin upon all states to delegate authority to local institutions in respect of all local social infrastructure, including education and health. The reasoning is that locally elected bodies, such as Panchayats, are closer in touch with the needs of people than officials of the government. The basic principle of empowerment of local self-government is in tune with the arrangements that have been working successfully in advanced democracies. It appears all the more relevant for developing nations like India, where the teaching and medical professions do not attract private practitioners in villages. Sadly, in our country, these laudable intentions for democratic decentralization are slow in the process of execution.

In respect of secondary healthcare, on the other hand, some state governments are considering experiments in joint ventures between the public sector and the private sector. The models seek to combine the management skills and financial resources of the private sector with the physical infrastructure and technical skills available in government. Certain basic precepts that should guide the structure of the partnership are :

(a) The facilities for the poor sections of society, especially for those below the poverty line, should be available free of cost as made available in the Government hospitals today.
(b) The rates to be charged (user charges) would be mutually decided between the Government and the private sector.
(c) The Board of Directors of the Joint Venture institution would include Government nominees as well as representatives of the private sector.
(d) Management and control would be the responsibility of the private partner.
(e) The Government staff would need to be withdrawn. The partner would be free to make appointment of professionals from the open market or even take doctors and para-medical staff on deputation or otherwise from the Government.
(f) The project would be monitored on a regular basis.
(g) Government must demand the highest quality of healthcare for the public for which agreed standards would be laid down, effective monitoring and periodic review carried out.
(h) The two partners in proportion to their investment would share any profits from the joint venture.
(i) The private sector is expected to bring in state of art equipment and modern management practices, and linkages with reputed institutions.

As an experiment, the partnership can be beneficial to both the parties, provided that the focus on better quality of service to the common man is maintained. The greater potential would unfold in the set-up by the rapid ease with which the project can be brought to fruition. With the increasing population, many states face shortage of trained and qualified technical staff, but they have limited budgetary resources. In a situation where a state has managed to build health infrastructure that it is unable to man immediately, a private partner can be expected to perform, provided that a viable legal partnership is created. A simple and efficient model in position in the U.K. is for buildings belonging to the government and local bodies to be leased to reputed Health Trusts for serving the population under the National Health Service. India could well develop an original model suited to the socio-economic conditions here.

Primary schooling is being decentralized to the Panchayats in the same manner as contemplated for primary health, although at the same tedious pace. Private education is flourishing in the country, as ambitious parents invest in schooling as a perceived good. Those who can afford, put their wards in private schools. Needless to mention reform of schooling in the public sector is the responsibility of the Government. The partnership that the private sector seeks is in the allotment of public land for creating quality infrastructure in identified locations. The facts and figures of current performance of students are a testimonial to the capacity and success of private schooling.

In regard to the tertiary sector in health and education, the various levels of technical education, as also research bodies, the national policy has already opened the gates to private enterprise. There is general freedom for institutions to bring in funds, experience and know-how to meet the emerging needs of a rapidly growing economy. Just last week, the Prime Minister has announced that a Commission would be set-up to make our universities world-class and reorient the priorities of our laboratories. The idea of a Commission, which would include distinguished persons from government as well as the private sector, has stirred some debate. Without joining issue, it is clear that this initiative itself will facilitate private-public partnership, and suggest appropriate linkages.

CONCLUSION

Both the private and the public sector have to stand on

their own feet rather on collaborative plank as they expand to meet the demands of an upwardly mobile society in a globalizing environment. The explosive issue is equitable distribution of the fruits of development, as also of the opportunities that beckon. The potential of India to dominate the world in the 21st century has been recognized within the country and also abroad. Even as we aspire to attain the heights, we must also pay heed to a warning, "There is no greater burden than great potential" (Charles Schulz). If the two partners are wise, they can shoulder their burden of identifying specific of potential and exploiting it—the same together.

Public-Private Partnerships in Economic and Social Infrastructure

JAGBANS SINGH

INTRODUCTION

Infrastructure development is at a crucial juncture in India today. Tentative steps have been taken towards a more pluralistic provisioning, especially by the private sector, and as a result infrastructure as a whole has reached a point of irreversibility. It is no longer possible to go back to the old mode wherein the state, both centre and provincial, actively provided the bulk of physical infrastructure. The reason is not that 'the state has not funds', as many believe, but the enormous waste, including the dead-weight losses of the old mode, that stands exposed. In a broader sense, what has failed is not state ownership *per se*, but the assumption that in a large market economy, many infrastructural sectors could indefinitely be run non-commercially.

Even if change necessarily involves signaling, to both the concerned public and the world at large, that India is moving away from its closed door controlled economy, enough time has already passed. Many more pressing priorities beyond mere communication of the intent of change have emerged. The need for action and for demonstration of an ability to address the problems of change as they come along, through the framework of an overall stated strategy, is acute. Thus the viability of the infrastructure business of domestic financial institutions, encouraged to lend to commercially-oriented infrastructure, is itself at stake. The growth rates of infrastructural development in sectors like power, water and roads have fallen well below the rates achieved in the 1980s.

Outright privatization is no longer being seen as the panacea that it once was thought to be. Privatization in the form of private ownership and management of key utilities may not be the overall solution. The public sector has basic social and economic tasks and liabilities. A fundamental role for the state in safeguarding and providing for the economic and social welfare of the citizens is a condition of democratic government. The fabric that promises a cooperative venture between the state and private business and synergises their respective strengths is what the policy-makers are now looking at. Of course, part of the impetus for the growth of the liberal state was to inhibit these kinds of cooperative ventures by carefully defining and policing the boundaries between the private and public domains. This entailed both an elaborate overlay of administrative policy on public sector activity and a burgeoning regulatory apparatus to protect the public interest from private one. The movement for privatization in the 1980s (in the West) and 1990s (in India) endorsed the existence of a clear boundary separating the two sectors by contesting the division of responsibility between them. The idea of partnership between the public and private sectors represents a different set of conceptual premises altogether.

The United Nations Millennium Declaration articulated a resolution to develop strong partnership between the private sector and the civil society organizations in development and poverty eradication. Public-Private Partnerships (PPPs) reflect this quest for a positive interaction between the public sector and private enterprise that in turn ensures that policies at the local, national and global levels are capable of promoting the common good. While the PPP straddles an entire spectrum of possible relationships and concerns ranging from local to global, the essential ingredient of any PPP is private sector participation in the delivery of traditionally public-domain services.

PUBLIC-PRIVATE PARTNERSHIP (PPP) DEFINED

A Public-Private Partnership is a contractual agreement between a public agency (federal, state or local) and a for-profit corporation. Through this agreement, the skills and assets of each sector (public and private) are shared in delivering a service or facility for the use of the general public. In addition to the sharing resources, each party shares in the risks and rewards potential in the delivery of the service or facility.

PPPs can be attractive to both the government and the private sector. For the government, private funding can support increased infrastructure investment without immediately adding to government borrowing and debt, and can be a source of government revenue. At the same time, better management in the private sector, and its capacity to innovate, can lead to increased efficiency; this in turn should translate into a combination of better quality and lower cost services. For the private sector, PPPs present business opportunities in areas from which it was in many cases previously excluded.

Partnerships require actors from each sector to adopt characteristics and points of view that once defined and stabilized the identities of their counterparts. Government actors would need to think and behave like entrepreneurs, and business actors would need to embrace public interest considerations and expect greater public accountability. The elaborate demarcations that defined roles and set the rules of engagement between business and government earlier are in large part ameliorated, removing the impetus for the adversarial character of their interactions. Thus, PPPs offer alternatives to full privatization (through divestiture of government assets) by combining the social responsibility, environmental awareness and public accountability of the public sector, with the finance, technology, managerial efficiency and entrepreneurial spirit of the private sector.

To say that partnerships are yet another effort at shrinking the state by privatizing its functions is to misconstrue the significance of the partnership idea. Firstly, stretching one sector by shrinking the other no longer applies because the meaning of the sectors in many of the world economies is itself shifting. Secondly, the partnership advocates talk of new roles and innovative tools for the public manager, leveraging private capital for public policy initiatives. Partnerships arise as a derivative reform in areas where full privatization seems less tractable, perhaps due to technical problems attending the assignment of property rights. By the late 1990, privatization had lost much of its earlier momentum yet infrastructure concerns remained in many countries. It was at this time that PPPs began to emerge significantly as a means of obtaining private sector capital and management expertise for infrastructure investment, both to carry on where privatization had left off and as an alternative where there had been obstacles to privatization.

Financing of Partnerships

The private sector can raise financing for PPP investment in a variety of ways. Where services are sold to the public, the private sector can go to the market using the projected income stream from a concession (e.g. toll revenue) as collateral. Where the government is the main purchaser of services, service payments by the government under operating contracts can be used for this purpose. The government may also make a direct contribution to the project costs. This can take the form of equity (where there is profit sharing), a loan, or a subsidy (where social returns exceed private returns).

Where a government has claim on future project revenue, it can contribute to the financing of a PPP by securitizing that claim. With a typical securitization operation, the government would sell off a financial asset—its claim on future project revenue—to a Special Purpose Vehicle (SPV). The SPV would then sell securities backed by this asset to private investors and use the proceeds to pay the government, which in turn would use them to finance the PPP. Interest and amortization would be paid by the SPV to investors from the government's share of project revenue.

Basic Features

A typical PPP takes the form of a design-build-finance-operate (DBFO) scheme.

Under such a scheme, the government specifies the services, it wants the private sector to deliver, and then the private partner designs and builds a dedicated asset for that purpose, finances its construction, and subsequently operates the asset and provides the services deriving from it. This contrasts with traditional public investment where the government contracts with the private sector to build an asset but design and financing is provided by the government. In most cases, the government then operates the asset once it is built. The difference between these two approaches reflects a belief that giving the private sector combined responsibility for designing, building, financing, and operating an asset is a source of increased efficiency in service delivery that justifies PPPs.

The government is in many cases the main purchaser of services provided under a PPP.

These services can be purchased either for the government's own use, as an input to provide another service, or on behalf of final consumers; a prison, a school and a free-access highway would fall into these respective categories. Private operators also sell services directly to the public, as with a toll road. Such an arrangement is often referred to as a concession, and the private operator of the concession (the concessionaire) pays the government a concession fee and/or a share of profits. Typically, the private operator owns the PPP asset while operating it under a DBFO scheme, and the asset is transferred to the government at the end of the operating contract, usually for less than its true residual value (and often at zero or a small nominal cost).

The term PPP is sometimes used to describe a wider range of arrangements.

In particular, some PPPs exclude functions that characterize DBFO schemes. Most common in this respect are schemes which combine traditional public investment and private sector operation of a government-owned asset. This arrangement sometimes takes the form of an operating lease, although in case where the private operator has some responsibility for asset maintenance and improvement, this is also described as a concession. Operating leases and similar arrangements are typically regarded as PPPs. However, private sector involvement in asset building alone—which can take the form of a design-build-finance-transfer (DBFT) scheme—is not strictly speaking a PPP. The box below describes the many variants of Public-Private Partnership Schemes.

PPP Schemes and Modalities

Schemes	*Modalities*
Build-operate-transfer (BTO)	The private sector designs and builds an asset, operates it, and then transfers it to the government when the operating contract ends. The private partner may subsequently rent or lease the asset from the government.
Build-own-operate-transfer (BOOT)	
Build-rent-own-transfer (BROT)	
Build-lease-operate-transfer (BLOT)	
Build-transfer-operate (BTO)	
Build-own-operate (BOO)	The private sector designs, builds, owns, operates and manages an asset with no obligation to transfer ownership to the government.
Build-develop-operate (BDO)	
Design-construct-manage-finance (DCMF)	
Buy-build-operate (BBO)	The private sector designs, builds, owns, operates and manages an asset with no obligation to transfer ownership to the government.
Lease-develop-operate (LDO)	

Theoretical Underpinnings—Five Constructs

There are at least five distinctive uses of the term, P-P partnership. Each use makes a claim about what partnerships are and conveys an understanding of their intended purpose and significance. Each use invokes certain premises about what the relevant problems are and how best to solve them.

P-P Partnership as Management Reform

Partnerships, in this instance, are linked to the privatization movement's quest for efficiency gains. As a management reform, partnerships are promoted as an innovative tool that will change the way government functions, largely by tapping into the discipline of the market. The core presumption is that the skills needed to find new markets, enhance productivity, and stay ahead of the competition can also improve the way government functions. Government managers learn by emulating their partners, as they adapt to the rigours of competition. If successful, they will become more entrepreneurial and flexible, occupied with deal making and attracting capital rather than with administrative procedure. The premises of this construction are prototypically neoliberal. The market stands as the superior source of production and service efficiencies, and its competitive character stimulates innovation and creative problem-solving. Rather than divesting government altogether, however, its culture and operations can be changed with the right kind of intervention. Partnership, as a management reform, is meant to serve this purpose.

P-P Partnership as Problem Conversion

A variation on the management reform, partnerships are viewed from this perspective, not as a tool for changing managerial practices, but rather as a universal fix for most problems attending public service delivery. The task for government managers shifts from getting their own practices in the line with entrepreneurial mores to reframing the problems they face in a way that will attract profit-seeking collaborators. In other words, commercialize problems to bait the market-place. Here, the manager's duty is not to reform himself but to induce others, wise to the ways of the market, to perform government's tasks for less money. The intent of the United Nations Development Programme for the Urban Environment (1996), for example, is to accelerate private sector involvement by creating business opportunities out of gaps in infrastructure. Private firms bring their know-how and capital. Government eases the regulatory and tax burdens and may add funds. The public gets its roads and water treatment. In fact, the United Nations depicts partnerships as the principal means of obtaining sustainable development in urban areas. Sustainability, in this context, appears to coincide with commercial viability; one must attract enough business that is not only willing to stay put, but able to shoulder the costs of infrastructure development largely on its own.

P-P Partnership as Risk Shifting

The usage here portrays partnering as a means of responding to fiscal stringency on the part of the government. From the government's perspective, the partnership arrangements are a means of getting private interests to sign on, and they promise profit potential for doing so. The British Government's Private Finance Initiative (PFI) encourages government managers to refashion property-rights assignments to attract private capital to shoulder start-up costs. Under the PFI, contractors pay for the construction costs and then rent the finished project or facility back to the public sector. Thus, through special lease-purchase arrangements, private investors assume the financial risks of ownership once the projects are complete.

P-P Partnership as Restructuring Public Service

In theory, partnerships can not only relieve projects of some of the weight of administrative procedure, which has restricted public agencies' ability to adapt to changing circumstances, at least on the private partners' side, they can also move from a public to a private workforce, one that is disciplined by the labour market. Partnerships could also be used to control labour standards via formal agreements on wages, as well as non-commercial features, such as gender and social discrimination.

P-P Partnership as Power Sharing

Although privatization has been promoted by some as empowerment because it devolves control vertically downward towards the consumer, partnerships, according to this usage, spread control horizontally, especially in regulatory matters where control has been concentrated in the government. Partnerships as power sharing can alter business-government relations in fundamental ways. First, an ethos of cooperation and trust replaces the adversarial relations endemic to command-and-control regulation. Second, any relationship between partners will involve some mutually beneficial sharing of responsibility, knowledge, or risk. Third, there is an expectation of give-and-take between the partners, negotiating differences that were otherwise litigated.

PPPs—Keys to Success

In order for a PPP to be viable, there are several conditions that ought to prevail before a PPP is structured.

Political Commitment and Good Governance are Prerequisites

A PPP is a major commitment on the part of private sector, which needs to know that politicians are also committed to private involvement. Uncertainty in this regard gives rise to political risk that is not conducive to making long-term business decisions. At the same time, potential private partners need to know that the government is fair in its dealing with the private sector, and will meet the commitments it makes under PPPs. An appropriate legal framework can provide reassurance to the private sector that contracts will be honoured. Most developed countries have such legislation in place. Widespread corruption in government would be a major obstacle to successful PPPs, in the same way that it prevented successful privatization.

A Clear and Sustained Need for the Project

The project must have a strong public need and that need must be extant for a foreseeable future. Future need is essential to be able to justify funding for the project to be derived from the revenue provided by the product or service delivered by the project.

A Solid Project Scope Definition

There must be no question as to the project scope, at least in terms of performance. Agreement on project performance requirements by the partners must be absolute.

The project must produce a product or service that can be measured.

Project financing is almost always derived from the product or service produced by the project. Whether financing is provided by the public partner or the private partner, it is essential that the revenue stream from the project is quantifiable so that an appropriate financing mechanism can be set-up. If private financing is to be an option, the public partner must be willing to enter into a long-term agreement to take the product or service provided by the project and to pay for it—a so-called "take-or-pay" agreement. The partners must be able to agree on how to share the project risk.

The roles and responsibilities of the partners must be clear and complete for both sides and must be reduced to writing.

The project must have a strong political champion willing to confront the interest groups who may be opposed to it.

PPPs are different. There will be opposition from various interest groups who see the PPP as an infringement on their normal rights and responsibilities. There must be a strong political champion willing to work with these groups to mitigate their concerns.

PPPs—The Indian Experience

Though PPPs have been around in India for a while now, it was only in August, 2004 that Government of India formulated 'Guidelines on Support to Public-Private Partnerships in Infrastructure'. Besides setting out its commitment to promoting PPPs in infrastructure development, there guidelines provide for establishing a special facility within the Department of Economic Affairs for extending government support to reduce project costs. This support, generically termed as 'viable gap funding', is available to projects in the sectors of roads, railways, seaports, airports, power, water supply, sewerage and solid waste disposal in urban areas, and international convention centres.

The major thrust in infrastructure development in India through the PPP route has come in the road sector. The National Highway Development Project (NHDP) undertaken by the National Highway Authority of India (NHAI), envisages road construction work of 13,146 kilometers at a total cost of Rs. 58,000 crores. Four modes of financing are being used for funding the NHDP, namely EPC contracts, Special Purpose Vehicle (SPC), Annuity Concessions and BOT Concessions. The last two mentioned typically fall in the category of PPPs. While in BOT projects, the investor base their projections on the toll revenues, in the case of Annuity Concessions, the private investors initially invest in the project and NHAI pays the capital cost under a fixed annuity. Under the annuity scheme, the risk devolves on the NHAI while under BOT concessions, the risk rests with the investors as they invest, operate and maintain the project during the concession period and collect the toll. There are five ongoing BOT projects (287 km.)—another four (179 km.) have already been completed—and eight Annuity-based projects (476 km.) handled by NHAI. The nine completed and ongoing BOT projects cost around Rs. 3355 crores and the annuity-based project Rs. 2354 crores with annual annuity commitment of Rs. 2.88 crores.

Under the BOT scheme, NHAI prepares the detailed project report, undertakes traffic survey, etc. and firms up the cost. It then invites expression of interest from private parties for construction of certain selected stretches. Based on evaluation, the successful concessionaire is awarded the contract, who then finances and constructs the selected stretch within the stipulated time and is eligible to collect toll at prescribed level for each category of vehicles for a specified period (concession period) to cover his capital cost. During this concession period, he operates and maintains the road. For shortfall in collection, the Government/NHAI lends to the concessionaire and may also release grant upto 40 percent of the capital cost to fund the project.

For the Annuity scheme the NHAI prepares the detailed project report, conducts traffic survey, etc. and firms up the cost. It then invites expression of interest from private parties for construction of certain selected stretches. The selected concessionaire, selection being done after due evaluation, finances the entire project, constructs and maintains the stretch of road till the end of the concession period. The concessionaire is assured of a return for his capital cost based on a specified internal rate of return. The annuity is paid at 6 months intervals.

The following table sums up the difference between the toll-based concession (BOT) and annuity based concession.

Toll-based	*Annuity-based*
Toll is the main source of repayment of capital and interest. Shortfall in toll collection will be compensated by Government/NHAI through revenue grants. Therefore, the future liability is unknown.	Annuity is the main source of repayment of capital and interest. The amount paid is fixed and hence the future liability is known.
Fee is levied based on usage and is paid by actual users.	Fee is paid for making the pubic utility (road) available and is paid by the authority responsible for providing the infrastructure (Govt./NHAI).
Up to 40% of the capital cost is given as grant and is paid upfront or in stages according to the agreement.	Amount is repaid in six-monthly instalments based on an agreed rate of return.
The concessionaire collects tolls on agreed rates.	Government/NHAI collects the toll.
The concessionaire comes forward only for stretches which have the potential to earn profits/adequate revenue.	Mainly given where stretches have lesser potential for earning profits/ adequate revenue.

As will be apparent from the above, under the Annuity-based concession, the cost and the internal rate of return is also firmed up and the total investment is paid over a period of fifteen years. Hence, the market risk is taken up by the public authority (NHAI), i.e. in favourable interest rate regime, NHAI ends up incurring higher interest charges. On the other hand, under the BOT concession, even though the cost is firmed up, NHAI gives grant to the extent of 40% of the capital cost and any shortfall in revenue is met by loans granted by NHAI up to Rs. 5 crores to help the concessionaire to repay the loans it hand taken. Thus, the concessionaire bears the market risk in this case.

The Indian Experience—Pitfalls

The number of Public-Private Partnerships continue to grow in India and are being resorted to more and more by public authorities responsible for development of infrastructure. Some of the major projects, other than those commissioned by NHAI, through this rote include the "missing link project" in Maharashtra for connecting Mumbai over the sea, development of ports, construction and operation of an international airport of Cochin, etc. However, the success of these projects will depend to a large extent on the adaptability of the political and government set-up to the requirements imposed upon them for the success of the Partnership process and also the acceptability of the public at large to the idea of having to pay for the services received. The cost recovery of services lies at the very foundation of structure of Partnerships.

The above contention is best illustrated in the context of the road sector itself. Toll roads in India are till now a relative failure in the present context as user mindset still perceives roads as a public good which is to be made available free of any charge. Tolls are recognized as an additional form of taxation in addition to fuel cess and vehicular taxes. It is also true that only small stretches of roads are viable for tolling. If the entire Golden Quadrilateral were to be taxed, it would be too expensive for the transporters. In addition to the above factors, unrealistic traffic projections have also led to failures in many cases.

It would also be interesting to observe how Indian PPP projects measure up on the "key to success" indices discussed earlier in this paper. Consider the case of Cochin International Airport Limited (CIAL). The Cochin International Airport is the first airport in India to be built in the joint sector with public-private participation. The airport users and other benefactors, mainly non-resident Indians, the general public, Government of Kerala and the airport service providers came together to build an airport of international standards. The fund requirement for the new airport was estimated at roughly Rs. 200 crores. An innovative approach to funding this amount by involving the Gulf-based NRIs, who stood most to benefit from the airport, was mooted. Investment was to come in the form of interest free loans and donations from NRIs as well as corporates, other societies and local public. Half of the loan raised this way was to be invested in Kissan Vikas Patras (KVPs), which on maturity after 66 months would be used for repaying the full loan amount. 75% of the balance requirement was to be raised as a soft loan from Government of India under its policy of lending back 75% of the collected amount against KVPs to the states for developmental purposes. The remaining gap in funding would be raised as donations from corporate bodies. Thus, in a nutshell, four lakh investors, constituting 20% of the Gulf-based Keralitites could build the airport by contributing Rs. 5000 each. However, this funding scheme failed to yield results and against the anticipated Rs. 200 crores, only Rs. 4 crores could be raised. In this scenario, it was decided to incorporate a public limited company, as result of which Cochin International Airport Limited (CIAL) came into being on 30th March 1994. The financing of the project was now envisaged through equity share capital of Rs. 70 crores and loan funds of Rs. 130 crores. Fifty-one per cent of the equity capital was to be contributed by the Government of Kerala (GOK), thus becoming a majority share-holder while the balance was to be mobilized from NRIs and general public. Capital from NRIs and other public was 31.1% as of March 2001, GOK held 41.6% of the paid-up capital, and airport service providers 27.3%, thereby giving the flavour of a public-private enterprise to CIAL. In addition, interest-free deposits had also been provided by other parties who had a commercial interest in the airport. After almost one and a half years of operations up to December 2000, CIAL, though making an operating surplus, was running into heavy losses whereas it was expected to have a net profit from the second year onwards.

The reasons for the under-performance of CIAL in its initial years of operation are not difficult to find and make an interesting reading when compared with the essential ingredients required to make a PPP succeed. Political and governance issues are at the fore of this discussion. With GOK hogging the Board of CIAL because of its status as a major share-holder, there was a dearth of professionals on the Board who could advise and guide on key technical issues. This negated the very basis of having private participation in the airport project as professional management was lacking. The state government exercised its leverage over critical decisions and even interfered in daily operational issues. Even the investor confidence was shaken as the state government failed to honour its commitment to subscribe to 51% of the equity capital, eventually leading to the failure of a rights issue floated by the company. Changes in the political climate and the consequent power shifts also proved detrimental as priorities assigned to the project changed mid stream placing the private partners in the project at risk. Local political activism only added to the uncertainty. The need and viability of the Cochin airport was not established. There was competition from Calicut and Thiruvananthapuram airports, both of which were already undertaking upgradation work. That this affected the operations in Cochin is reflected in the lower-than-projected revenues from the aeronautical stream. With lesser passenger load, the non-aeronautical revenue stream was much lower than projected.

CONCLUSION

Irrespective of their teething problems, PPPs are beginning to emerge as an important vehicle for providing social and economic infrastructure in India and other developing countries. There are success stories of projects, may be small ones, in the development of roads, waste treatment plants, sewerage and water supply systems in towns and cities across the country. PPPs have already proved their utility in most developing countries where a legal framework is already in place to ensure that these mutually beneficial partnerships are institutionalized. Ultimately the responsibility for providing basic social and economic services to the populace lies with the government, but PPPs have shown that the private sector is a willing and equal partner in this task.

REFERENCES

Sebastian Morris, 'Issues in Infrastructure Development Today : The Interlinkages.

Public-Private Partnership—UNDP's Experience in India in the Environment Sector.

United Nations Development Programme (UNDP): Public-Private Partnerships for the Urban Environment (PPPUE):

Stephen H. Linder, *University of Texas, Huston:* Coming to Terms with the Public-Private Partnership; A grammar of multiple meanings.

Osmo T. Seppala, *Tampere University of Technology, Finland; Jarmo J. Hukka, University of Pristina, Kosovo; Tapio S. Katko, Tampere University of Technology, Finland:* Public-Private Partnerships in Water and Sewerage Services; Privatization for Profit or Improvement of Service and Performance?

James Smith, *Texas A & M University:* Design-build-finance-own-transfer Approaches.

International Monetary Fund: Public-Private Partnership (Paper prepared by the Fiscal Affairs Department—March 2004).

Government of India; Ministry of Finance, Department of Economic Affairs (Infrastructure Division): Guidelines on Support to Public-Private Partnerships in Infrastructure.

Biju Varkkey and G. Raghuram: Public-Private Partnership in Airport Development—Governance and Risk Management Implications from Cochin International Airport Ltd.

Development of Economic Infrastructure—Public and Private Participation

PERMINDER KHANNA

INTRODUCTION

The Tenth Plan (2002-07) has been implemented in a liberalised economic environment amidst market dominated economic decisions. In this market-oriented system, achieving a target of 8 per cent of Gross Domestic Product (GDP) against a backdrop of the slow growing Agriculture and Infrastructure sectors is highly sceptical. Accordingly, the reforms process is a pre-requisite for attaining the desired targets, stressing the urgent need for a 'change' from—

- inefficiency to efficiency;
- bureaucratic delay to business-like speed;
- structural rigidity to developmental flexibility;

- rules-frame to performance orientation;
- plural layers decision to a delayered decision process;
- inward-looking policy to an outward-looking policy;
- import-substitution to two-way trade maximisation;
- an insulated economy to a competitive economy;
- local resource dependence to accessing global resources;
- government ownership to private ownership;
- high taxation to low taxation; and
- centralisation to decentralisation.

Growth needs commitment to market which in turn implies commitment to creativity and innovation. There is, hence, no option for us but to learn to grow in the fast changing economic environment of liberalisation, globalisation and privatisation and earnestly endeavour to minimise the constraints inherent in our economy.

The paper thus focuses on the "Development of Economic Infrastructure: Public and Private Participation", in terms of commercial energy—coal, oil and electricity, the shortfalls in the supply of energy against demand and the 'crisis' further aggravated by the international oil price hike ever since 1973-74. A critical evaluation of the economic infrastructure comprising of commercial energy has been conducted during the years (1960-2005), and for a comparative analysis further sub-divided into:

PERIOD I	:	(1960-1985)
PERIOD II	:	(1985-2005)

ECONOMIC INFRASTRUCTURE

The importance of energy, a critical infrastructure, to growth and development depends upon structural adjustments and policies designed to change the linkage between the growth in energy demand and economic activity. It is an uncertain area depending upon changing patterns of world economic growth and trade, fuel availability, responses to changing energy prices, economic structural change, technological change, availability of international finance, balance-of-payments constraints, role of market forces and government policies. Stock price increases have a direct impact on the balance-of-payments and an indirect effect on economic activity and terms of trade. A physical cut off of supplies when it cannot be offset by recourse to an alternative source, means a reduction in the amount of energy on which the country's economic machinery depends, disrupting production and entailing lower standards of living.

Persistent energy shortages continue reflecting inadequate investment. It has been estimated that India has the potential to absorb US $ 150 billion[1] of FDI in the next five years (2006-2011) in the infrastructure sector alone. During 2005-06, the overall index of four core industries (energy, steel, cement, transport and communication) having a direct bearing on infrastructure and accounting for 27 per cent weight in the Index of Industrial Production (IIP) registered a growth of 4.5 per cent, which was lower, than 6.4 per cent in the corresponding period previous year. In the first nine months of 2005-06, crude oil production registered a decline, and there was a deceleration in the growth of coal, electricity, refinery and steel sectors throughout. Thus, India today faces an 'energy crisis' with demand exceeding supply and further exacerbated by the ever increasing international oil prices. The Indian economy can adjust to shocks below $ 40 a barrel. Anything above that is a discomfort zone. And thus makes the case for private participation an imperative, in energy exploration and exploitation.

COAL

Coal is India's most predominant and the lowest cost source of energy. But as per experts, the public sector monopoly in mining and evacuation has long stultified output and blocked investments and technology upgradation.

India ranks third in coal production next of China and Russia. Globally coal accounts for 26 per cent of energy consumption. In India, it has a share of 65 per cent. In power generation, the share of coal on a global basis is 36 percent and in the Indian context, it is 60 per cent. At present, barring a few captive mines, all collieries are in the nationalized sector. They were taken over by the government in two stages:

- Coking coal on October 17, 1971 to form Bharat Coking Coal Limited (BCCL).
- Non-coking coal mines on January 30, 1973.

These two have subsequently come under Coal India Limited (CIL), a holding company with about 50 mines spread over ten states. CIL comprises nine companies, of which four are in loss and five in profit.

Resources

As per the Geological Survey of India estimates, the coal reserves are placed at 220 billion tonnes upto a depth of 1200 meters, of which 25 per cent is coking coal.[2] At the present level of consumption, coal can last for more than 250 years. India possesses three per cent of the world's reserves of coal.

But experts have scaled down extractable coal in India to just 40 billion tonnes (bt) against 220 by the GSI. The current estimates suggest that domestic coal would last only 40 to 50 years.

PERIOD I : 1960-85

Production

The production of coal increased from 55.66 million tonnes in 1960-61 to 75.72 million tonnes in 1969-70 and recorded a positive annual average growth rate, thereby culminating into a negative growth rate of 3.7 per cent and 0.7 per cent over the next two consecutive years (1970-72). There was again a dip in the year 1977-78 due to the emergence of active power shortages and transport bottlenecks in the period subsequent to the international oil price hike of 1973 (Table 16.1). A grave shortage of diesel in 1979–80 further added to the existing problem. Together with this, low labour productivity due to the low level of mechanisation in the coal industry and the existence of surplus labour accentuated the constraints. Moreover, coal output per man shift in India is only 0.8 tonnes, which is low by international standards.[3] However, since 1980-81 administrative restructuring has led to the improvement in the working conditions and wages of the coal workers.

Consumption

Coal consumption[4] witnessed a positive trend over the period 1960-85, but for a dip in the year 1973-74, followed by a marginal increase in 1976-77 and then almost a steady increase over the next eight years.

As the period 1980-88 experienced a distinct rise in production on account of the restructuring of the coal industry, there was a spurt in consumption too, recording an average growth rate of 10.6 per cent in 1981-82 but again sliding down to 2.4 per cent in 1984–85.

Demand and Supply Gaps

With regard to the data relating to the production and consumption of coal, it was observed that it is not the constraint of resources to the requirements of the country, but the want of timely availability to the consumer that led to shortages in the supply of coal during the years 1960-85, viz.,

TABLE 16.1
Production and Consumption of Coal

(*Million tonnes*)

Year	*Production*	*Average Annual Rate of Growth (per cent)*	*Consumption*	*Average Annual Rate of Growth (per cent)*
(1)	*(2)*	*(3)*	*(4)*	*(5)*
1960-61	55.66	10	42.20	00
1961-62	55.23	(–)0.8	47.07	11.5
1962-63	63.45	14.9	52.22	11.0
1963-64	65.13	2.6	51.78	0.8
1964-65	62.78	(–)3.6	60.43	16.7

(*Contd.*)

TABLE 16.1 (*Contd.*)

(1)	*(2)*	*(3)*	*(4)*	*(5)*
1965-66	67.79	7.9	55.83	(–)7.6
1966-67	68.56	1.2	55.50	(–)4.2
1967-68	68.52	(–)0.1	55.53	3.8
1968-69	71.41	4.2	57.85	4.2
1969-70	75.72	6.0	59.09	2.1
1970-71	72.95	(–)3.7	52.71	(–)10.8
1971-72	72.42	(–)0.7	55.70	9.5
1972-73	77.22	6.6	63.93	10.8
1973-74	78.17	1.2	61.94	(–)3.1
1974-75	88.49	13.2	77.90	25.8
1975-76	99.68	12.6	80.12	2.9
1976-77	101.04	1.4	80.54	0.5
1977-78	100.97	(–)0.1	87.32	8.4
1978-79	101.95	1.0	81.07	(–)7.2
1979-80	103.95	1.9	85.57	5.6
1980-81	114.00	9.7	87.50	2.3
1981-82	124.30	9.0	96.80	10.6
1982-83	130.60	5.1	100.40	3.7
1983-84	138.40	6.0	107.40	7.0
1984-85	147.44	6.4	110.00	2.4

Note : Columns (3) and (5) have been computed.
Source : *Economic Survey*, various issues. Report of the Working Group on Energy Policy, Government of India, 1979.

- Infrastructural bottlenecks (power, transportation, etc.).
- Accumulating pithead stocks.
- Inferior quality (high ash content).
- Low labour productivity in mines.
- High incidence of transportation.

PERIOD II : 1985-2005

Production

Coal production (coking and non-coking) exhibited a steady growth over the period 1985-2005. It was 154.20 mn tonnes in 1985-86 and 382.61 mn tonnes in 2004-05, recording a positive average annual growth rate, but for the year 1998-99 which witnessed a negative growth rate of 1.25 per cent (Table 16.2).

TABLE 16.2
Production of Coal

(Million tonnes)

Year	*Production*	*Average Annual Rate of Growth (per cent)*
(1)	*(2)*	*(3)*
1985-86	154.20	0.00
1986-87	165.77	7.50
1987-88	179.72	8.42
1988-89	194.60	8.28
1989-90	200.89	3.23
1990-91	211.73	5.40
1991-92	229.28	8.29
1992-93	238.26	3.92
1993-94	246.04	3.27
1994-95	253.80	3.15
1995-96	270.13	6.43
1996-97	285.66	5.75
1997-98	295.93	3.60
1998-99	292.22	(–)1.25
1999-2000	299.97	2.65
2000-01	309.63	3.22
2001-02	327.79	5.87
2002-23	341.29	4.12
2003-04	361.25	5.85
2004-05	382.61	5.91

Note : Column (3) has been computed.
Source : *Economic Survey*, 2005-06, Government of India.

Consumption

The demand estimates for coal conducted by the Chari Committee (May 13, 1996) for the year 2001-02 was placed at 513 million tonnes. According to the Planning Commission, the requirement was to the tune of 460 mn tonnes in 1999-2000. However, the official figure of the demand for coal in 2001-02 was placed at 370.8 million tonnes, leaving a gap of 48.18 million tonnes. Most of the production comes from open cast mines (70 per cent), and raisings from underground mines have stagnated at around 65 million tonnes a year. However, the area for open cast mining is getting fast depleted.

Anticipated Demand and Supply

The demand estimates of coal conducted by the government agencies for the years 2005-07 and the likely shortfalls are exhibited in Table 16.3.

TABLE 16.3
Demand Estimates for Coal

(Million tonnes)

Year	*Demand for Coal*	*Supply of Coal*	*Demand Supply Gap*
(1)	*(2)*	*(3)*	*(4)*
2005-06	338.00	316.66	21.34
2006-07	365.00	334.00	31.00

Source : *Economic Survey*, 2005-06, Government of India, 1979.

The Government feels that it is not possible for the nationalised coal companies and captive coal mining companies to bridge this gap. Import of coal is not sustainable (Table 16.4). It is only in the very recent past that the percentage share of coal imports has gone up significantly from 1.8 to 2.6 over the years 2003-05.

The past experience reveals that shortfalls existed in several important consuming sectors due to mounting pit-head stocks. This was because of a lack of a 'SYSTEMS' approach to

TABLE 16.4
Coal Imports (2000-05)

(Million tonnes)

Year	*Percentage Share*	*Percentage Change*
(1)	*(2)*	*(3)*
2000-01	2.2	3.4
2001-02	2.1	2.3
2002-03	2.0	3.0
2003-04	1.8	13.7
2004-05	2.6	97.5

Source : *Economic Survey,* 2005-06, Government of India, 1979.

production, movement, consumption and stocks. Deficiencies in production planning brought in qualitative imbalances, and adversely affected the consumers whose requirements were quality specific. To add to this, there were shortages in power supply and railway wagons for coal movement.

The Tata Energy Research Institute (TERI) has scaled down the Central Mine Planning and Design Institute's (CMPDI) projections, a subsidiary of Coal India, according to which domestic coal production would be 500 million tones by 2006-07, 600 mt by 2011-12 and would plateau at a level of 770 mt by 2016-17. TERI, on the other hand, estimated that even production from open cast mines will start declining from the year 2030. Thus, at the most, based on proven reserves without considering the inevitable decline, the domestic coal production is likely to level off at 450-460 mt per year.[5]

TERI and CMPDI estimates follow norms framed by the United National Framework Classification to ensure a more practical perception of resources.

The GSI estimates include resources in all the categories—provided, indicated and inferred, which give the wrong indication of mineable reserves.

Thus, the demand and supply gap over the yeas (2020 A.D.) would accentuate due to inferior quality and infrastructural constraints.

The major growth in coal demand is envisaged in the power sector. While the actual off-take in the power sector in 1999-00 was 193.4 million tonnes, it is expected to rise to 261.23 million tones at the end of the Xth Plan and 347.22 million tonnes at the end of the XIth Plan. Here, the demand and supply gaps would be very conspicuous. While the total domestic production of coal, coking and non-coking, was 382.61 million tonnes in 2004-05, imports were 20-22 million tonnes, 50 per cent of which were coking coal. Current import of non-coking coal is less than 3 per cent of the domestic production.

Mineral production from mining and quary sector recorded a negative 12 per cent growth in April 2003 mainly due to less production of coal, lignite and petroleum.

Moreover, increased Natural Gas availability would surely impact the coal industry, since it is regarded as a dirty fuel. In the absence of clean coal technologies and increased availability of a cleaner fuel would further reduce the use of coal.

Imported coal has not been able to make a sizeable dent in the Indian market due to high freight cost. With freight rates as high as 250 per cent of the price of coal being transported, imported coal has only been able to capture market in coastal areas. Indian Railways transport 51 per cent of mined coal, while a further 23 per cent is transported by industry's owned railway net works.

According to the Planning Commission, the industry requires a massive investment of Rs. 220 billion in the Tenth Plan period (2002-07) and this makes the case of Foreign Direct Investment imperative to step up coal production.

The Government has so far allowed Foreign Direct Investment (FDI) in the coal sector on the following lines:

- Private Captive Mining Operator engaged in the production of coal can have foreign equity upto 100 per cent.
- Private Captive Mining Operator engaged in the production of iron and steel can have foreign equity upto 74 per cent.
- Automatic approvals for foreign equity upto 50 per cent in all the aforementioned cases is allowed. FDI over 50 per cent is subject to FIPB approval.

The average price of coal in 1972-73 was Rs. 40 per tonne and by 2002 it went up to Rs. 2500 per tonne for coking coal and Rs. 1300 per tonne for non-coking coal. Despite the rise in price, the three major subsidiaries of Coal India Limited (CIL), ECL,[6] BCCL[7] and CCL[8]—have been perpetually sick and incurring huge losses. Moreover, investments to the tune of Rs. 100 billion and budgetary support of Rs. 100 billion have been made in this sector.

Though CIL's coal is priced the lowest in the world, but the problem is with the quality, a high ash content and low calorific value. Also the cost of washing the coal in order to lower its ash content from the ecologically hazardous level of 40 per cent to the stipulated level of 34 per cent is responsible for the price hike.

The decision by the Government in April 2003, to allow independent marketing and pricing policies for various CIL subsidiaries will open up competition.

For prime non-coking coal—ECL's Raniganj grade A or grade B priced at Rs. 1450 and Rs. 1370 per tonne, the basic differences with MCL,[9] NCL[10] and SECL[11] coal of the same grade was around Rs. 500-600 per tonne, lower in the case of the latter two companies. Besides, ECL mines located in West Bengal pay a higher cess than royalties paid in the other states by the other CIL subsidiaries.

Though companies like ECL and BCCL always have the option to under-cut prices in a free and independent pricing regime, mounting losses in these weaker companies do not leave them with such a choice.

The problem of huge leakage due to coal off-take by spurious consumers in the non-core sectors viz., brick kilns, rubber and glass units, which offload coal in the open market, adds to the existing shortages in supplies to the genuine users.

The freight charges for transporting Indian coal for a distance of 750 kms. amount to nearly 60 per cent of the price of coal, whereas there is a 10 per cent preference given by the Indian Railways for transporting imported coal. An import duty on coal of 50 per cent is permissible under the WTO regime, the present level being only 10 per cent. The profit margins of the

CIL are further affected by the high rate of royalty and taxes. Thus the grey areas that could be looked into are:

- The cumbersome process of project clearance by the government increases cost and time overrun. A royalty of 13 per cent on coal production is one of the highest.
- The non-payment of dues by the users is a grave problem. In 2002, CIL had total outstanding credit of over Rs. 92 billion of which Rs. 45 billion was owned by the state electricity boards.
- The high level of ash content of domestic coal has led to a number of power and steel plants to opt for imported coal from Australia, New Zealand and China.
- Labour laws are not conducive to the growth of the coal industry. Restrictions on the use of contract labour in jobs in the non-core sectors of the industry (hospital, canteen, security, etc.) should be removed. The CIL has 540,000 employees on its payrolls reflecting disguised unemployment.

The Coal Mines Amendment Bill, 2000, would allow the Indian companies to mine coal and lignite without the existing restriction of captive mining. The bill also seeks to attract smooth flow of private investment for the formation of joint venture companies with CIL.

The Coal Ministry has recently declared that chronically loss-making mines will be closed down, fake companies which have managed to get supply linkages will be eliminated, and the nexus between contractors, transporters, and employees of Coal industry will be severely dealt with.

But the existence of infrastructural constraints, the inferior quality of coal, project delays and cost overruns, royalty fixation and labour laws ultimately lead to shortages in the supply of coal and thus the domestic demand cannot be fully met by the public sector industry or the existing captive mines and thus increased dependence on imports (a share of 2.6 per cent in 2004-05) makes private sector participation in coal exploration and exploitation all the more imperative.

OIL

Resources

The prognosticated geological resources of hydrocarbons are estimated at about 17 billion tonnes, of which 63 per cent are expected to be off-shore and 37 per cent on land. Out of this, the geological reserves established are only 4 billion tonnes. Our proved reserves of oil represent only 0.5 percent of the world oil proved reserves.[12]

PERIOD I : 1960-85

Production

Domestic crude oil production, a mere 0.5 million tonnes in 1960-61 went upto 29.0 million tonnes in 1984-85 exhibiting a positive trend (Table 16.5). However, the years 1965-70 and 1970-74 were marked with a conspicuous decline in growth rates. Thereafter, an intensification in crude oil exploration eased the availability of crude oil in the domestic market. The decline in imports also contributed to the shortages due to the international oil price hike of 1973-74, 1978-79 and 1980-81. Because of the drastic shift in the supply policies of the oil exporting countries ever since 1973-74, there is a considerable uncertainty in the international oil market.

Consumption

The consumption of oil increasing from 8.3 mn tonnes in 1960-61 to 26.7 mn tonnes in 1984-85 showed a discernible rising trend. There was a dip in the average annual growth rates during the years 1972-76, 1978-79, and 1980-82 because of the multiple increase in the international price of oil initiated by OPEC (Oil Producing and Exporting Countries).

Demand and Supply Gaps

The period 1960-84 is characterized with a positive demand and supply gap in the context of oil but for the year

TABLE 16.5
Production and Consumption of Crude Oil (1960-85)

(Million tonnes)

Year	*Production*	*Average Annual Rate of Growth (per cent)*	*Consumption*	*Average Annual Rate of Growth (per cent)*
(1)	*(2)*	*(3)*	*(4)*	*(5)*
1960-61	0.5	—	8.3	—
1961-62	0.5	0.0	8.9	6.6
1962-63	1.1	120.0	9.9	11.9
1963-64	1.7	54.5	10.9	10.4
1964-65	2.2	29.4	11.8	8.0
1965-66	3.5	59.1	12.7	7.2
1966-67	4.9	40.0	14.5	14.4
1967-68	5.8	18.4	15.4	6.4
1968-69	6.0	3.2	17.5	13.3
1969-70	6.8	13.3	18.5	5.3
1970-71	6.8	0.0	19.3	4.2
1971-72	7.3	7.4	22.3	15.7
1972-73	7.3	0.0	22.4	1.9
1973-74	7.2	1.4	24.4	7.5
1974-75	7.7	7.0	24.6	1.1
1975-76	8.4	9.1	23.9	(–)3.1
1976-77	8.9	6.0	26.3	5.3
1977-78	10.8	21.4	27.9	10.2
1978-79	11.6	7.4	29.3	4.1
1979-80	11.8	1.3	39.2	10.2
1980-81	10.5	(–)10.7	333.6	4.2
1981-82	21.1	30.3	37.4	6.4
1982-83	21.1	30.3	37.4	6.4
1983-84	24.6	23.2	39.3	5.1
1984-85	29.0	11.5	26.7	7.2

Note : Columns (3) and (5) have been computed.

Source : *Economic Survey*, various issues, Government of India.

1984-85. Since 1980-81, with sizeable augmentation and implementation of oil production capacity in the country, these quantitative shortfalls have diminished to some extent. But reduction in gaps does not directly imply the dilution of 'oil crisis' impact as the latter is attributable to a number of factors viz.,

- The shortfalls between the demand and supply of energy are still prevailing and are likely to persist till such time that supply exceeds demand.
- The continuous dependence on oil and petroleum product imports to meet the deficit in domestic requirements, leading to mounting import bills, despite a quantitative decline in oil imports since 1980-81.
- Infrastructural bottlenecks due to financial constraints in stepping up the production of oil add to the increasing dimension of the existing energy crisis.

Hence, the case of private participation in oil exploration and improving/increasing the installed capacity is inevitable.

TABLE 16.6
Demand and Supply Gaps

(Million tonnes)

Year	*Demand and Supply Gaps*
(1)	*(2)*
1960-61	7.8
1961-62	8.4
1962-63	8.8
1963-64	9.2
1964-65	9.6
1965-66	9.2
1966-67	9.6
1967-68	9.6
1968-69	11.5

(Contd.)

TABLE 16.6 (*Contd.*)

(1)	*(2)*
1969-70	11.7
1970-71	12.5
1971-72	15.0
1972-73	15.1
1973-74	17.2
1974-75	16.9
1975-76	15.5
1976-77	16.4
1977-78	17.1
1978-79	17.7
1979-80	20.4
1980-81	23.1
1981-82	18.8
1982-83	16.3
1983-84	14.1
1984-85	(–)2.3

Note : Columns (2) has been computed.

PERIOD II : 1985-2005

Production

The production of crude oil went up from 30.2 million tonnes in 1985-86 to 34.0 mn tonnes in 2004-05, registering negative average annual growth rates during the years 1990-93, 1996-97, 1998-2000 and 2001-02. Regarding the total availability of crude oil, there has been a consistent surge in imports over the years dominated by the price impact (Table 16.7).

International crude oil prices, trending upwards since 2002, on an average rose from US $ 27.6 in 2002-03 to US $ 28.9 in 2003-04, US $ 42.1 in 2004-05, and further to US $ 56.64 per barrel in April-November 2005.

The stiffening of global crude oil prices was contributed by a combination of heightened demand, limited spare capacity

TABLE 16.7

Crude Oil Production and Consumption

(*Million tonnes*)

Year	*Production*	*Average Annual Rate of Growth (per cent)*	*Consumption*	*Average Annual Rate of Growth (per cent)*
(1)	*(2)*	*(3)*	*(4)*	*(5)*
1985-86	30.2	—	12.5	—
1986-87	30.5	0.99	45.7	6.53
1987-88	30.4	(–)0.33	47.8	4.60
1989-90	34.1	6.56	51.6	26.84
1990-91	33.0	(–)3.23	51.8	6.35
1991-92	30.0	(–)7.88	51.4	(–)0.77
1992-93	27.0	(–)11.18	53.5	4.09
1993-94	27.0	0.00	54.3	1.50
1994-95	32.2	19.26	56.5	4.05
1995-96	35.2	9.32	58.7	3.89
1996-97	32.9	(–)6.53	62.9	7.16
1997-98	33.9	3.04	65.1	3.50
1998-99	32.7	(–)3.54	68.5	5.22
1999-2000	31.9	(–)2.45	86.0	25.54
2000-01	32.4	1.57	103.4	20.23
2001-02	32.0	(–)2.45	86.0	25.54
2002-03	33.0	3.13	112.6	4.94
2003-04	33.4	1.21	121.8	7.98
2004-05	34.0	1.80	127.1	4.35

Note : Columns (3) and (5) have been computed.
Source : *Economic Survey*, 2005-06, Government of India.

and geopolitical threats to the existing capacity. Given India's relatively high oil intensity and increasing dependence on imported crude oil, strategic oil reserves are being developed equivalent of about 15 days requirement, to minimize the impact of crude price volatility in the short-term. POL imports now account for 30 per cent in India's import basket (Table 16.8).

TABLE 16.8
Crude Oil Petroleum Products Imports

(*Million tonnes*)

Year	*Crude Oil*	*Petroleum Products*
(1)	*(2)*	*(3)*
1960-61	6.0	2.5
1970-71	11.7	1.1
1980-81	16.2	7.3
1990-91	20.7	8.7
2000-01	74.1	9.3
2001-02	78.1	7.0
2002-03	82.1	6.7
2003-04	90.4	7.9
2004-05	95.9	8.8

Source : *Economic Survey*, 2005-06, Government of India, Ministry of Finance.

Consumption

The consumption of crude oil exhibits a consistently rising trend recording specifically a high growth rate of 25.54 per cent in 1999-2000 as against a negative growth rate of production (2.45 per cent) in the same year.

Demand and Supply Gaps

The demand and supply gaps particularly in the case of oil are very significant (Table 16.9).

There has been a quantum increase in gaps since 1999-2000 and energy crisis has come to exist because of the increasing oil and petroleum product import bill, consequent upon the frequent hike in the price of oil since the mid-seventies.

Thus intensification of exploration, management of demand, increasing the productive efficiency of capacities already created and of equipment used are of prime importance in view of the dependence on imports to meet the domestic oil requirements. And this calls for privatization to create a

TABLE 16.9
Demand and Supply Gaps of Crude Oil

(Million tonnes)

Year	*Demand and Supply Gaps*
(1)	*(2)*
1985-86	15.2
1986-87	12.7
1987-88	17.4
1988-89	16.4
1989-90	17.8
1990-91	18.8
1991-92	21.0
1992-93	26.5
1993-94	27.3
1994-95	24.3
1995-96	23.5
1996-97	30.0
1997-98	31.2
1998-99	35.8
1999-2000	54.1
2000-01	71.0
2001-02	75.3
2002-03	79.6
2003-04	88.4
2004-05	93.1

Note : Column (2) has been computed.

competitive industry structure as the international oil market will continue to play an important role in our energy planning strategies.

ELECTRICITY

Electricity is a critical infrastructure for economic development. The demand for electricity in India is substantially in excess of the available supply. So the country has adopted a blend of thermal, hydel and nuclear sources with a view to increase the supply of electricity.

PERIOD I : 1960-85

Production

Energy generated gross (utilities and non-utilities) accounted for 20.1 Billion KWH in 1960-61 and in 1984-85, it was 169.1 Bn. KWH (Table 16.10).

The share of Hydel, Thermal and Nuclear energy in the total electricity generated was to the extent of 31.87 per cent, 58.4 per cent and 2.42 per cent, respectively, in the year 1984-85.

There were dips in the production of hydroelectricity as the acute power drought of 1979 and inadequate rainfall in 1980 had left most of the reservoirs severely depleted. In the context of Thermal energy, an increase in electricity generation was observed in absolute terms. But it was far less than the operational efficiency of the thermal plants due to problems relating to organization and management, equipment supplies, labour discipline and skill, quality and availability of coal. Hence, the significant dip in the average annual rate of growth (1.47 per cent) in 1981-82. The potential thus lies in developing the nuclear energy resources.

Demand and Supply Gaps

As far as electricity is concerned, the plan-wise targets and achievements in the creation of the installed generation capacity were such that shortfalls came to exist to the extent of:

Plan after plan, the gap between the target for enhancing the generation capacity and the actual addition was widening due to:

- Inadequate planning techniques.
- Cost escalation because of inordinate delays in project formulation and implementation.
- Unremunerative functioning of the State Electricity Boards.
- Under-utilization of the installed capacity.

TABLE 16.10
Energy Generated (Gross)

(Billion KWH)

Year	Utilities				Non-Utilities	Total (5+6)	Average Annual Rate of Growth (per cent)
	Hydro	Thermal	Nuclear	Total			
(1)	(2)	(3)	(4)	(5)	(6)	(7)	(8)
1960-61	7.8	9.1	—	16.9	3.2	20.1	—
1970-71	25.2	28.2	2.4	55.8	5.4	61.2	204.5
1975-76	33.3	43.3	2.6	79.2	6.7	85.9	40.4
1979-80	45.5	56.3	2.9	104.7	8.2	112.9	31.4
1980-81	56.5	61.3	3.0	120.8	8.4	129.2	14.4
1981-82	49.6	69.5	3.0	122.1	9.0	131.1	1.47
1982-83	48.4	79.9	2.0	130.32	10.0	140.3	7.0
1983-84	50.0	86.7	3.5	140.2	10.8	151.0	7.6
1984-85	53.9	98.8	4.1	156.8	12.3	169.1	12.6

Source : *Economic Survey*, various issues, Government of India.

(Per cent)

Plan	*Shortfalls*
Third Plan (1960-66)	33.0
Three Annual Plans (1966-69)	19.30
Fourth Plan (1969-74)	50.20
Fifth Plan (1974-79)	18.40
Sixth Plan (1979-85)	25.90

- High transmission and distribution losses, over 20 per cent as against 8 to 9 per cent in many developed countries.

PERIOD II : 1985-2005

Production

The generation of electricity in totality for the period 1985-2005 is presented in Table 16.11.

The average annual growth of power generation (utilities and non-utilities) varied between 3.00 per cent to 4.45 per cent over the period 1996-2003. While nuclear generation showed a sharp turn-around for the better, thermal generation dipped during this period.

The Plant Load Factor (PLF), an important measure of the operational efficiency of the thermal power plants, of the Central Power Plants was higher than that of the State Electricity Boards (SEBs), while PLF of private plants exceeded that of the public sector (Table 16.12). The drop in PLF in southern and western States during 2003-04 was due to a good monsoon boosting hydro-generation and reducing the demand from thermal plants. The PLF for the eastern and north-eastern states was relatively lower.

Targets and Achievements

While there is a shortfall *vis-a-vis* the targets, the shortfalls are limited compared to the earlier plans. In the Eighth and Ninth Plans, achievements were less than 50 per cent of the

TABLE 16.11
Energy Generated (Gross)

(Billion KWH)

Year	Utilities				Non-Utilities	Total (5+6)	Average Annual Rate of Growth (per cent)
	Hydro	Thermal	Nuclear	Total			
(1)	(2)	(3)	(4)	(5)	(6)	(7)	(8)
1985-86	51.0	114.4	5.0	170.4	13.0	183.4	—
1986-87	53.8	128.9	5.0	187.7	13.6	201.3	9.76
1987-88	47.5	149.6	5.0	202.1	16.9	219.0	8.79
1988-89	57.9	157.7	5.8	221.4	19.9	241.3	10.18
1989-90	62.1	178.7	4.6	254.4	23.0	268.4	11.18
1990-91	71.1	186.5	6.1	264.3	25.1	289.4	7.82
1991-92	72.8	208.7	5.5	287.0	28.6	315.6	9.05
1992-93	69.9	224.8	6.7	301.4	31.3	332.7	5.42
1993-94	70.4	248.2	5.4	324.0	32.3	356.3	7.09
1994-95	82.7	262.1	5.6	350.4	35.1	385.5	8.20
1995-96	72.6	299.3	8.0	379.9	38.2	418.1	7.46
1996-97	68.9	317.9	9.1	395.9	40.8	436.7	4.45

1997-98	74.6	337.0	10.1	421.7	44.1	465.8	6.66
1998-99	82.9	353.9	11.9	448.5	48.4	496.9	6.68
1999-2000	80.6	286.8	13.3	480.7	51.5	532.2	7.10
2000-01	74.5	408.1	16.9	499.5	55.0	554.5	4.19
2001-02	73.5	424.4	19.5	517.4	61.7	579.1	4.44
2002-03	64.0	493.4	19.4	532.7	63.8	596.5	3.00
2003-04	75.2	472.1	17.8	565.1	68.2	633.3	6.17
2004-25	101.2	490.4	17.0	608.6	71.4	680.0	7.37

Note : Column (8) has been computed.
Source : *Economic Survey*, various issues.

TABLE 16.12

Thermal Plant Load Factor

(*Per cent*)

	2000-01	*2001-02*	*2002-03*	*2003-04*	*2004-05*
SEBs	65.6	67.0	68.7	68.4	69.6
Central Sector	74.3	74.3	77.1	78.7	81.7
Private Sector	73.1	74.7	78.9	80.5	85.1
Regions					
• Northern	73.1	75.1	75.4	76.3	77.1
• Western	73.4	74.1	75.8	75.1	78.6
• Southern	82.0	82.4	86.4	83.4	84.1
• Eastern	47.9	48.7	52.1	56.9	60.4
• N. Eastern	18.5	16.7	14.8	14.0	150
All India	69.0	69.9	72.2	72.7	74.8

Source : *Economic Survey*, 2005-06, Government of India, Ministry of Finance.

target. By the type of ownership, the anticipated shortfall (13 per cent) is the highest in the Central Sector, while by the type of plants, it is the highest (9 per cent) in thermal plants (Tables 16.13 and 16.14).

Out of the total power generated in the country, about 66 per cent comes from the coal-fired power stations. Domestic coal production is not keeping pace with the growing demand for coal in the power sector resulting in a generation loss of 1512 Million Units during 2004-05 hampering the growth of thermal generation. The crisis is further aggravated by the inefficient functioning of SEBs.

- Annual losses of SEBs at the end of the Ninth Plan (2001-02) were estimated at around Rs. 24,000 crore.
- Low operational efficiency.
- Political interference.
- Overstaffing and corruption.
- High transmission and distribution losses (nearly one-fourth of the total power).

TABLE 16.13

Tenth Plan Targets/Achievements in the Power Sector (by ownership)

(MW)

	Target		*Additional Capacity: Status*		
	Original	*Mid-Term Appraisal*	*Commissi-oned*	*Under Execution*	*Overall Anticipated*
(1)	*(2)*	*(3)*	*(4)*	*(5)*	*(6)*
Central	22832	1987	8325	8900	17225
State	11157	12240	3946	7955	11901
Private	7121	4899	1145	3753	4898
Total	41110	39956	13416	20608	34024

Source : *Economic Survey,* 2005-06, Government of India, Ministry of Finance.

TABLE 16.14

Tenth Plan Targets/Achievements in the Power Sector (by type)

(MW)

	Target		*Additional Capacity: Status*		
	Original	*Mid-Term Appraisal*	*Commissi-oned*	*Under Execution*	*Overall Anticipated*
(1)	*(2)*	*(3)*	*(4)*	*(5)*	*(6)*
Thermal	25417	23261	7446	13784	21230
Hydro	14393	11125	5380	4794	10174
Nuclear	1300	2570	590	2030	2620
Total	41110	36956	13416	20608	34024

Source : *Economic Survey,* 2005-06, Government of India, Ministry of Finance.

The rate of return of SEBs was (–) 12.70 per cent in 1991-92 and (–) 31.94 per cent in 2004-05. The resources foregone through such poor returns continue to be very large.

In 2005-06, while the direct transfers from the State Governments to SEBs was Rs. 11,562 crore, an uncovered subsidy of Rs. 15,987 crore remained, indicating the large potential that reforms have in improving not only the electricity sector itself but also the fiscal position of the states.

Capacity shortages and lack of adequate investments are among the most important challenges faced by the energy sector in the developing countries. And hence, privatization is advocated to facilitate the necessary investments in the coal, oil and electricity sectors. There is an urgent need for an integrated approach involving all the state-holders i.e., government, industry, agriculture, academic institutions and end users for the success of the national energy policy.

POLICY MEASURES

As per energy demand forecasts, the per capita commercial energy consumption would go up by 2.5 times during 1985-2020. The strain on the balance of payments is imminent by way of the escalating oil import bill. Energy—GDP elasticity coefficient of 1.50 indicates high intensity of energy use to GDP. An increase in crude and petroleum product prices directly contributes to the increase in domestic prices of administered commodities—coal, oil, electricity, fertilizers, mineral oils and prices of goods using petroleum products as inputs.

An indepth analysis of this problem implies that the two areas of vital importance in rendering the infrastructural constraints to the minimal, are the management of the supply of energy and that of its demand, and this could be diffused in different ways:

- Reduction of energy intensity by way of optimizing fuel utilization in various sectors.
- Interfuel substitution in the wake of external dependence, rising prices and supply uncertainties.
- Phasing out the faster development of coal and electricity on cost benefit analysis.
- Pragmatic planning for hydro thermal plants depending on the availability of capital, local inputs, based on existing state of knowledge and socio-economic framework.
- Supply activities of all forms of energy-extraction to conversion and transportation stages and prices are

managed by the government and its agencies. Herein, private participation has to be encouraged to step up efficiency to achieve the desired results.

- India cannot afford to switch over to the new developments in the interest of efficiency alone till the end of the useful life of the existing infrastructure.
- Power system (hydro, thermal and nuclear) has to be viewed as an integrated whole and the policy of adhocism must go.
- Distribution of physical resources needed for power development is unevenly spread over the country as most of the coal reserves are in Eastern and Central India while many of the major load centers are far away. North East India has unexploited hydro potential while the load centres are located in Southern and Western India.
- Development of power, mainly the responsibility of the states, is characterised with a mismatch between the availability of physical and financial resources resulting in sub-optimal investment decisions. Disputes over the sharing of power and irrigation benefits lead to inordinate delays towards project completion, cost overruns burdening the capital resources of the country. Institutional constraints may be removed with continuous state/central level monitoring by way of constitutional and legal changes for timely completion of power projects.
- Readjustments of the economy in response to the growing energy scarcities in terms of energy conservation are required. In industry, the energy conservation potential ranges from 5 to 15 per cent in the short-run and 15 to 30 per cent in the long-run. As per TERI estimates, energy savings from six industries viz., steel, cement, aluminum, pulp, paper, fertilizers and textiles amount to Rs. 300 crores which is equivalent to a saving of 20 mn tonnes of coal.
- Demand management of energy takes a backseat in the domestic, agriculture, manufacturing, commercial and transport sectors. Thus, the whole proposed mechanism entailing management of energy supply

vis-a-vis its demand through a country-wide network under the government nodal agency as also with the co-operation of the private sector, can go a long way to help India to become self-reliant in energy in the years to come, if not in the immediate future.

Notes and References

1. *Economic Survey*, 2005-06, Government of India, Ministry of Finance.
2. Geological Survey of India, *The Economic Times*, December 2002.
3. *Economic Survey*, various issues, Government of India.
4. Coal is consumed essentially for providing heat/steam to industry and railways.
5. Dr. S.K. Chand, Advisor, Tata Energy Research Institute, December 2002.
6. ECL—Eastern Coalfields Limited.
7. BCCL—Bharat Coking Coal Limited.
8. CCL—Central Coalfields Limited.
9. MCL—Mahanadi Coalfields Limited.
10. NCL—Northern Coalfields Limited.
11. SECL—South Eastern Coalfields Limited.
12. Seventh Five Year Plan, Vol. II, Government of India, p. 126.

References

Fischer, J.C. and Pry, H.J., "Technological Forecast", Social Change, 3, 1972.

Floyd, A., "Trend Forecasting: A Methodology for Figure of Merit", in Proceeding of the First Annual Technology and Management Conference, New Jersey, 1968.

Khanna, P., "Energy Scenario in India (1960-85)", National Energy, Policy, Crisis and Growth; National Seminar on Energy Policy, Centre for Indian Development Studies, Chandigarh, 30th/31st January, 1990, Edt. V.S. Mahajan, "Investment Management: Planning and Forecasting", Research Methodology in Management, Theory and Caste Studies, SAP Seminar (UGC), Edt. P.P. Arya and Yash Pal.

Sterman, John D., "Expectation Formation in Behavioural Simulation Models", *Behavioural Science*, Journal of the Society of General System Research, Vol. 32, No. 3 July 1987.

Economic Survey, 2002-06.

Report of the Working Group on Energy Policy (WGEP), India, 1979.

Part IV

Sources of Revenue and their Management : Union and State Governments

Pricing of Public Services and Return on Investment

Janak Raj Gupta

In a Welfare State, the pricing of public goods and services has always occupied a central stage. The typical questions often asked are : Should public services be provided on "no profit no loss" basis? Or being monopolist, the government should charge on the principle, what the traffic should bear, and earn at least a minimum rate of return both on fixed and operational cost? Or in a welfare state, it is the duty of the government to provide subsidised services to maximize social welfare and so on.

Then the question is what costs should be considered? Should we consider only the operational cost (as the investment has been made in the past) or the total cost including fixed cost? It is just possible that building of economic and social infrastructure like roads, railway lines, canals, etc., may be necessary on the part of the government because of the lack of private initiative. But its maintenance and operational cost may be recovered from the users. Or being faced with scarcity of resources, the infrastructure facilities are provided on BOT (build, operate and transfer) principle.

Another thing to remember is that answers to the above questions cannot be given in a static sense. Answers would vary with changes in the socio-economic and even political frameworks. Whatever was true in the fifties when we started on the path of economic development, is not true today when we have opened up our economy and are dreaming to enter the developed world club very soon, offshoot of which is our claim for a permanent seat in the U.N.O. To put it differently, the same pricing criterion for the same service cannot hold true for all times to come, nor can the uniform pricing criteria hold good for all types of services. The pricing criteria will vary with the nature of the product, i.e., whether it is pure public goods, merit goods or nearer to private goods.

The most important thing to take note of here is that in this paper, the words 'public services' have been used in a wider economic sense, i.e., in the sense of 'public goods and services', because in economic literature till recently, we used to talk about 'public goods' *vs*. 'private goods'. And this distinction would help us to examine the question of pricing public goods or public services in a proper perspective.

PRIVATE *VS*. PUBLIC GOODS AND MERIT GOODS

The distinction between the public and private goods can be well understood on the basis of the following characteristics of goods:

(a) Product Divisibility
(b) Externalities

(a) Product Divisibility

There are goods and services which are priced in the market and their use is exclusively restricted for those who are willing to pay the stipulated price. The use of such commodities is governed by the principle of exclusion. All those who are not inclined to pay its market price or those who cannot afford to pay that price are excluded from its consumption. Thus the commodity becomes divisible in so far as its use is concerned. Such goods are termed as private goods. On the opposite, there are certain other goods called as public goods for the use of which no discrimination is made amongst the users and all the members of the society, whether they are capable of paying for them or not, indiscriminately make use of them. For instance, law and order services, the defence services, etc. are equally utilized by all the inhabitants of a country. No section of the society can be excluded from their use. It means that these services are indivisible. They cannot be priced in the market and their use is not governed by the principle of exclusion.

In case of divisible products, since the supply can be made available only to those who can pay for them, the consumers of such goods, voluntarily pay for maintaining a requisite level of their supply. In case of these goods the demand preferences and the price which the consumers are willing to pay provide good indication of the type of commodity which should be produced. Thus all decisions about the divisible goods, such as the type of commodity and its quantity to be produced are dictated by the market prices. But in case of the indivisible goods, the market mechanism fails to make such vital decisions and all these decisions are made by the society or the government. As mentioned above, the divisible goods are paid for by the individuals who use them. But the indivisible goods, like defence services and police services will pose the problem of financing them. In case of these services, everyone knows that even if he does not pay for them, these will still be available to him. This creates a tendency to avoid payment towards them. As a result, most of the people will not pay voluntarily on the assumption that the supply of these services will continue owing to the payments made by others. Bunchanan has referred to this as the problem of free riders.[1] It means that everybody is inclined to enjoy the benefit of such services without having to contribute voluntarily towards the cost of supplying these services. In such a situation, their financing becomes problem. To overcome this difficulty, a provision for compulsory contribution by the members of the society through taxation is made. Thus, it is clear that in case of indivisible goods or services not only the decisions concerning their production are left to the government or to its agencies but also the financing of the production is carried through taxation.

Such goods as are indivisible and the benefits of which are not governed by the principle of exclusion are called as the pure public goods. On the opposite, the pure private goods are those which are completely divisible and in case of which the principle of exclusion applies in full measure.

(b) Externalities

A pure public good can be distinguished from a pure private good on the basis of the existence or otherwise of externalities. The term "externalities" refers to the economic effects that arise due to the production or use of the goods to other parties or economic units. These are in the form of an economic gain or an economic loss and are responsible for creating a certain divergence between their private and social marginal costs and benefits. The process of production may create certain bad effects on the society, although this may be completely disregarded by the individual producing units.

When there are such bad or negative externalities, the people have to bear some social costs that may be somewhat reduced by the government through taxation.

Just as there are bad social effects of certain goods and services, similarly there are externalities in the form of economic gain or benefits to the society. The construction of a railway line linking a steel plant benefits not only the steel plant but also the people of the entire area through which that line passes. Benard P. Harber has put such externalities into two categories market and non-market external effects.

(i) Market External Effects

When the external effects, both social costs and social benefits, can be priced in the market with reference to the supply and demand behaviour, they are known as the market external effects. For instance, if an irrigation project is started in an area, the net increase in the production of agricultural crops and the area rendered unavailable for cultivation due to the construction of dam or erosion of land by the canal tributaries and a consequent fall in production determine the market external effects of the project.

(ii) Non-Market External Effects

When the external effects of goods and services produced cannot be priced with reference to the demand and supply behaviour, these are termed as the non-market external effects. For instance, a new road is constructed but it is difficult to determine the extent to which different economic entities derive benefit from it. Certain categories of beneficiaries can, of course, be identified. But if the benefits of such categories of road users, called primary beneficiaries, alone are taken into account, that will exclude either secondary and tertiary beneficiaries. Thus, the pricing principle cannot strictly be applied in case of such projects or goods and services.

Such goods and services as have non-market external effects should be preferably produced and distributed through public authorities because they can take economic decisions irrespective of profit considerations. Thus we arrive at the conclusion that such pure public goods as have non-market external effects should be included in the public sector and those having market external effects may be left to the private sector. This rule, of course, cannot be applied rigidly. Even such goods and services that are left to the private sector may in certain cases be reallocated to the public sector provided the government is convinced that such course of action is likely to promote social welfare. Alternatively, the government may subsidise their production in the private sector if their consumption is necessary for health and efficiency and will thus promote social welfare.

Merit Goods

There are certain goods which, on the basis of the above mentioned criteria, may be regarded as private goods. The state may, however, in the larger interest of society, include them in the public sector. Such goods are termed as the merit goods as their use is considered desirable for certain members of the society. Normally, in case of private goods, all the basic economic decisions concerning their production and distribution are guided by individual preferences. But the meritorious characteristic of the merit goods makes it obligatory for the public authorities to deliberately interfere in individual choices and modify the choice pattern of society. For instance, the government may subsidise low cost housing, provide free education to the people or provide mid-day meals to the students. Undoubtedly, the state interference in supplying these goods and services will be viewed as an encroachment upon the freedom of choice. But the broader objectives of public policy will justify such a course of action on the part of the state. If education is left to the private sector, many brilliant children belonging to the poor families will be forced to seek work rather than schooling for want of funds. Education, particularly primary education, therefore, is the merit good. The want for education is the merit want which almost every member of the society must be able to satisfy. Similarly, if basic health services in a country are left to private agencies, only those members of the society can avail of them who are better-off while the poor may have to go without them. The public authority, in case of this merit good, also will supplement its availability in cooperation with the private agencies. In all such cases of merit goods, the considerations of maximum social benefit override ideological or any other considerations against state interference in economic choices. In fact, this interference is most desirable for it attempts to correct distortion in the exercise of consumer choices. Thus, merit goods are those goods which are provided publicly like social goods but whereas the latter are meant for all sections of the community, the former are considered desirable for certain sections of the society.

Now return on public investment and pricing of impure public services which are nearer to private goods is the most crucial issue. There cannot be a simple answer to the whole issue. We will have to go to the very objectives of making public investment, which can be manifold, e.g., to keep private sector at bay by holding monopoly power, to promote economic development by providing necessary infrastructure, to promote and maximize social welfare, etc. Then pricing of public services and return on public investment or for that matter pricing and return of any investment involves the consideration of costs also. But in case of public services, it would mean commercial cost and social cost. Similarly, returns would mean commercial returns or commercial benefits and social returns or social benefits. We will have to adopt a holistic approach so far as public services are concerned.

Suppose a public service involves high commercial cost but if social benefits are equally higher, i.e., even if such services involve huge commercial losses, we should not hesitate to make investment in such enterprises.

Coming back to the pricing of public services while commercial costs and commercial benefits are easy to estimate, social cost and social returns or social benefits may be difficult to quantify. But we can easily tell whether the public investment is set to achieve any social and economic goals like removal of poverty and hunger, reducing inequalities in the distribution of income, generation of employment opportunities, and so on. Then public investment or provision of public services may be in terms of depleting or exhausting nature resources, polluting the environment and disturbing the ecological balance, or even in terms of opportunity costs, i.e., withdrawing the resources which could otherwise have been used for some other purposes. Recently, it has been reported that Professor Amartya Sen, Nobel Laureate, 1998, while advocating huge additional investment in social sector, viz., education and medical services, cautioned that this should not mean that resources are diverted from other sectors.[2] In other words, we should have a holistic view of the entire issue of public pricing considering all aspects of the problem, i.e., social and economic.

Further, as already mentioned in the beginning, the whole issue of pricing public services and returns thereon can not be tackled in a static sense. For example, when India was facing famine like conditions in the early sixties, food grain production had to be promoted at all costs. In the mid-sixties, agricultural inputs including power were highly subsidised in the promising areas to achieve self-sufficiency in food grain production. But that involved social costs also. Water level was depleted. Ecology was disturbed. And even inter-regional disparities widened. But the overall social consideration to achieve self-sufficiency in the basic food requirements overrode all other negative externalities.

But in the present scenario what social benefits we are now drawing by subsidizing agriculture. There is no increase in agricultural production, no reduction in poverty or inequalities, i.e., while there are no social and even economic gains, there are huge social costs. Last year, and even during the current rabi session, power had to be diverted from other sectors to sustain the production of wheat and rice.[3] Now if the objective is to sustain the income of the farmers, which it should be because of their falling income which is already substantially lower than the non-agriculture sector, then the same objective can be achieved by spending the same amount of resources through other means, (say by recharging the ground water or by promoting eco-friendly cropping system) where social costs are less or social benefits more. That is we should de-subsidise the electric power to farm sector and fix the price accordingly.

Now coming to some individual cases of public services before I sum up.

Power-Sector

Power sector, notably the State Electricity Boards (SERs), has shown the most dismal performance. Although, when the idea of state-owned electricity boards was conceived, these were expected to earn about 3 per cent rate of return on their investment. However, because of some extraneous considerations, the average tariff in most of the cases does not even cover the cost of generation and supply and this gap has progressively widened over the years." This in financial terms is reflected by gross subsidy for the power sector which accounted for 11 per cent of state government budgets . . . the gross subsidy enjoyed by the power sector increased from Rs. 27,804 crore in 1998-99 to Rs. 31,941 crore in 2003-04. Accordingly, commercial losses also mounted upward, resulting in a negative Rate of Return (RoR) from 12.7 per cent in 1991-92 to 21.2 per cent in 1998-99, to 30.86 per cent in 2003-04."[4] Since these losses are not sustainable, an appropriate price policy has to be evolved for electric power. As already stated that subsidised power supply to agriculture is not serving any useful social or economic objectives, further dynamism in the price of power is also revealed by the fact that whereas electricity charges earlier were inversely related with the consumptions, i.e. as you consumed more of electricity, the per unit price charged declined. Now, these charges are positively and progressively related with the consumption of electricity i.e., as you consume more of electricity, per unit price will also increase. However, while pricing the public goods, it should be kept in mind that the cost of inefficiency in the public sector should not be transferred to the consumers. This is possible, if private sector is allowed to operate side by side with public sector, as is the case for banking services, telecommunication services, etc.

Passenger Road Transport

In 1997-98, there were 71 State Road Transport Undertakings (SRTUs), having a fleet of nearly 1.1 lakh buses and these carried nearly 6.4 crore passengers per day. Most of the SRTUs were incurring losses, estimated at Rs. 1108 crores for the year 1997-98.[5] The main reasons for the poor financial health of the SRTUs were low fare fixed more or less on political grounds, absence of regular fare revision due to procedural delays, concessions in fare to students and other weaker sections of the society, operation on the uneconomical routes, etc. According to the Tenth Finance Commission, the SRTUs which had an investment of Rs. 3084 crores at the end of 1994-95 had a dismal physical and financial working. The Tenth Finance Commission further observed that "it is a matter of serious concern that investment in irrigation, power and road transport, which constitute the bulk of State Government investments do not yield enough returns. A shortsighted perception of political necessity, perhaps, has persuaded state after state to fix user charges at levels which do not cover even the operation and maintenance (O&M) expenditure in irrigation and generate meagre surpluses, if at all, in power Several State Electricity Boards (SEBs) are over staffed and run at substantial losses. The artificially depressed user charges result in criminal waste of water and electricity—both very scarce resources.[6] The National Institute of Urban Affairs, in one of its studies observed that the under-recovery of charges led to deterioration in the services. Therefore, the important issue is to identify the chargeable costs and general rule for efficient pricing of public services is to set price equal to marginal cost.[7]

As compared to road transport, railway transport is operated on more professional lines. Consequently, Indian Railways perform better. The latest example of construction and operation of Metro Railway in New Delhi bears testimony to the fact that given professional freedom and political non-interference, public service can be provided at affordable prices but covering both the operational and the fixed costs.

Education

Education is one of the social service activities representing around 60 percent of the total expenses on all social service activities. The budgetary allocation to education, both by the Centre and states has increased from Rs. 17,000 crore in 1990-91 to Rs. 81,000 crore in 2003-04. However, total expenditure on education in relation to GDP was 3 per cent in early 1990s, the ratio was lower at 2.7 per cent during mid-90s and this is against the goal of 6 per cent set by the National Education Policy, 1986. The structure of expenditure on education reveals that although the share of higher education in education expenditure has fallen sharply in India during 1990s, the adverse consequences of heavy emphasis on higher education earlier are still being felt, with high illiteracy of 34-35 per cent and more than half of the world's children being out of school. The greatest pinch has been felt by the poor, with adverse consequence on equity.

Therefore, education services can be divided into two categories: merit services and non-merit services. While primary education is a merit service, higher education can be considered as non-merit service and dealt with accordingly. Higher education may be further sub-divided into general education and technical education. Wherever possible, some self-financing schemes for the students like earn while you learn should be introduced.

Social and Public Health

The expenditure on medical and public health by the Centre and states as proportion to GDP is 0.9 percent only, whereas the National Health policy 2002 has the objective to raise it to 2 percent of GDP. The health care delivery system has imbalances in terms of under-utilisation at some levels and over-utilisation at others. Without going into the details what ails our health care delivery system, for pricing purpose we can divide medical and public health services again into two categories—merit services and non-merit services, though, by and large, all medical services must fall into the merit category, In any case, all preventive health care, viz., vaccination, sanitation, etc., must be termed as merit services and dealt with accordingly. Whereas the curative health measures may be merit goods for the underprivileged, who must be identified on some objective fool proof basis. For others, who could afford to buy these services from the market, some price may be charged. But care should be taken that prices charged by the government agencies are reasonably less than those prevailing in the open market because of some concealed costs (in terms of inefficiency and more time consuming) involved in purchasing health services from the government agencies. Then as for as possible revenue earned this way must be retained and reinvested in the same institutions to improve the health services.

Summing Up

There should be no ambiguity that, so far as merit services are concerned, these must be provided by the State at less than the commercial cost since here social benefits should override all other considerations. So far as pure public goods are concerned, these can not be priced and have to be financed by appropriate tax policies. In case of other public services, those be operated on professional lines. The tragedy of our system is that we have never given any freedom to the managers of these enterprises to operate on commercial principles. There had been political interference to use these PSUs to serve the political ends. Then lastly, no single pricing principle can be applied for all types of public services nor the same pricing principle can hold good for all times to come, i.e., no static answer can be given so far as pricing of public goods is concerned. It must also be borne in mind that non-recovery of O&M costs leads ultimately to the deterioration of public services.

Finally, what ails our public services and how to get out of it, Samuel Paul, a noted authority on public services, points out that it is the external pressure which works. In case of private sector, it is competition. Similarly, wherever the external pressure through privatization has been introduced, public services have improved, e.g. banking, telecommunication, etc. Where such external pressure through privatization is not possible, there the pressure of civic society can work. But the tragedy is that our indifferent attitude and vested interest do not allow us to move forward. It should also be borne in mind that along with efficiency of operating public services, equity should also be the concern of the government services. Last but not the least, whenever the need is felt to raise the prices of public services, it should be in marginal doses so as to ensure a smooth transition.

Notes and References

1. Buchanan, J.M., The Demand and Supply of Public Goods, R and Mc Nally and Co., Chicago, 1969.
2. Based on the Press Reports.
3. In the kharif season of 2004, the Punjab Government had to buy power @ about Rs. 6.0 per unit in order to sustain the paddy crop and thereby incurred huge losses.
4. Nand, Dhameja, "State Government's Finances—Public Services Finances", *Indian Journal of Public Administration*, Vol. L, July-September 2004, pp. 619-38.
5. *Ibid*.
6. GOI, Ministry of Finance, *Report of the Tenth Finance Commission*, for 1995-2000.
7. As quoted in *Indian Journal of Public Administrative, op. cit.*

Major Sources of Revenue of the Central Government : The Indian Experience

B.S. GHUMAN

The classical economists prescribed *laissez faire* policy by limiting the role of the state to areas such as internal and external security, revenue collection and provision of select public utilities. Limited liability of state was accompanied by limited sources of revenue of the state and thus fiscal policy and its administration were low profile activities of the state.

The collapse of classical economists policy prescription during the Great Depression (1929-34) led to the acceptance of the Keynesian policy prescription of active role of the state in economic affairs. The most important policy prescribed by Keynes for Great Depression ridden economies was the fiscal policy, particularly deficit financing component of it. The effectiveness of fiscal policy as instrument to get rid of Great Depression established its superiority over monetary policy. The

Second World War and reconstruction of the war affected economies followed by adoption of planning in most of the developing countries as mechanism for resource allocation and development provided further fillip to the increasing role of the state in the economy.

The theoretical strength for the provision of goods and services by the state was derived from 'Theory of Market Failure'. The "Theory of Market Failure" postulates that private sector is likely to fail towards the provision of certain goods and services particularly 'public goods' and mixed goods like education and health and hence active role of the state is advocated. Empirical evidence provided by the New Right School of Thought particularly Public Choice Theorists led by Niskanen (1971) suggests that state has entered in the areas where there is no fear of market failure. Three actors, namely, politicians, bureaucrats and interest groups, motivated the entry of state in almost all the areas of the economy. According to public choice theory, these three actors used government for the maximization of their private interests at the cost of state exchequer.

According to New Right School of Thought, state involvement leads to increasing monopoly, increasing budget and suppressing of entrepreneurial behaviour, limiting choice, over-production of unwanted services, encouragement to waste and inefficiency (Gray and Jenkins, 1995; Walsh, 1997). In view of this, the New Right has forcefully argued for lower taxation; imposing of constitutional limit on public expenditure as proportion of the gross national product; reduction of inflation; deregulation; privatization and reducing the influence of interest groups and corporatist institutions in budgeting (Ashford, 1993).

The phenomenal growth of governmental activities and mounting inefficiencies in government sector led to fiscal crises all over the globe, which is loosely described as 'State Failure'. The universal character of financial distress renewed interest in both financial and expenditure patterns of government the world over. The governments, irrespective of the economic system adopted, the policy analysts are engaged in the exercises to mobilize additional resources and apply principles of economy measures for curbing expenditure. In this backdrop, the present paper aims to identify the major sources of finance of Central Government and their management in India.

METHODOLOGY

In this study, secondary data have been used. The major sources of data include publications of Reserve Bank of India, Economic Surveys, Union Budgets and publications of Centre for Monitoring Indian Economy. With a view to examine the effectiveness of tax reforms (1991), the study period has been divided into two sub-periods, (I) Pre-reform period (i.e. from 1980-81 to 1990-91) and (II) post-reform period (i.e. from 1992-93 to 2002-03). Two methods, namely, the percentage, and tax buoyancy have been employed to analyse the data. Tax buoyancy refers to impact of changes in tax rates and expansion in tax base of tax revenue in relation to change in national Income.

FINDINGS

The major sources of finance of the Union and State Governments are clearly documented in the Indian Constitution. The major sources of finances of the Central Government are of two types, namely, the revenue receipts/ funds, and capital receipts/funds. Further, major sources of revenue of the Government are of two kinds: tax revenue, and non-tax revenue. The major sources of capital receipts are many, out of which net market borrowing, external borrowing, and small savings are worth mentioning.

The relative strength of revenues receipt and capital receipts during pre- and post-reform periods is shown in Table 18.1. Table 18.1 reveals that revenue receipts during both pre-reform period and post reform period contributed maximum share towards the finances of the central government. The share of revenue receipts in total receipts was 61 percent in 1980-81, which declined to 56.21 percent in 2002-03.

REVENUE RECEIPTS

Revenue receipts consist of two sources : (i) Tax Revenue; and (ii) Non-tax revenue.

Tax Revenue

Taxation is one of the oldest sources of revenue of government. In India, since independence, tax revenue has remained amongst the chief sources of finances of the federal government. The government, from time to time, appointed committees/commissions to mobilize more and more resources through taxes by introducing new taxes and restructuring the existing ones. During pre-reform period, the commissions/committees include Taxation Enquiry Commission of 1953-54 (chaired by Dr. John Mathai); Nicholas Kaldor Committee (1956); Bhuthalingam Committee (1967); Direct Taxes Enquiry Committee (Chaired by Dr. Wanchoo, 1971); Committee on Taxation of Agricultural Wealth and Income (1972) chaired by Dr. K.N. Raj; Indirect Taxation Enquiry Committee (1978), under the chairmanship of Dr. L.K. Jha. The Committee on Tax Reform (1991) under the chairmanship of Raja J. Chelliah; Advisory Group on Tax Policy and Tax Administration for the Tenth Plan constituted by the Planning Commission in 2000; Task Forces on Direct and Indirect Taxes (2002) under the chairmanship of Vijay L. Kelkar, are important committees constituted by the Central government for reforming tax administration during post-reform period.

A quick perusal of government policies on taxation suggests that during the pre-reform period, the tax regime was characterized as suspicion ridden, procedure centric, cumbersome, harassment generating and coercive (Government of India 2004), resulting in a very complex, secretive, and discretion based tax administration. Economic reforms postulated paradigm shift in tax administration patterned on the recommendations of Raja J. Chelliah Committee and other Committees. The tax reforms are guided by the philosophy of voluntary compliance, simplification of tax returns, limited number of rates, incentive for housing, infrastructure and education and also for special categories of tax payers like senior citizens and physically handicapped, tax holidays for limited period for investment in hilly states. These reforms paved the way for simple, transparent, objective and taxpayer-friendly management.

A comparison of net tax revenue during pre and post-reform periods does not show consistently positive impact of recent tax reforms on tax revenue. For example, the share of net tax revenue in total receipts was 47.79 percent during 1980-81. It came down to 45.75 percent during the last year of the pre-reforms period (i.e. 1990-91). The share of net tax revenue in total receipt suddenly increased to 49 percent in the beginning of economic reforms (i.e. during the year 1992-93) and reached the peak level (i.e. 50 percent) during 1996-97. It fluctuated later on and settled around 40 percent during 2002-03. The buoyancy estimates of tax revenue (i.e. tax revenue as percent of GDP), for the pre and post-reform period clearly exhibits ineffectiveness of tax reforms for overall tax revenue. For example, the buoyancy of the overall tax revenue works out to be 9.15 during 1980-81. It increased to 10.12 percent in 1990-91. In the beginning of economic reforms (1992-93) it came down to 9.97 percent. It furthers came down to 8.76 percent in 2002-03. (CMIE, November 2004, p. 182). Rates of growth of tax revenue before and after economic reforms also show the ineffectiveness of tax reforms. Overall tax revenue grew at 16.51 percent per annum during pre-reform period (i.e. from 1980-81 to 1990-91). Tax revenue experienced a lower rate of growth per annum (i.e. 11.69 percent) during post-reform period, i.e. from 1992-93 to 2002-03 (also see Sreekantaradhya, 2000; D' Souza, 1995; Bagchi, 1994).

Analysis of impact of tax reforms on each tax undermines the facile generalization about the ineffectiveness of tax reforms. It has been found that in certain cases, the tax reforms are very effective while in others, these seem ineffective particularly due to the interplay of exogenous factors.

(i) Corporation Tax

In case of corporation tax the, positive impact of tax reforms is explicitly clear. For example, corporation tax was 10.47 percent of total gross tax revenue in 1980-81. The share of

TABLE 18.1
Financing of Central Government; Revenue and Capital Receipts

(*Rs. Crores*)

Year	*Revenue Receipts*	*Capital Receipts*	*Buoyancy of Revenue Receipts (i.e. revenue receipts as % of GDP)*	*Buoyancy of Capital Receipts (i.e. capital receipts as % of GDP)*
Pre-Reform Period				
1980-81	11937 (60.97)	7643 (39.03)	2.97	1.90
1990-91	54954 (58.49)	38997 (41.51)	7.93	5.62
Post-Reform Period				
1992-93	74129 (67.20)	36179 (32.80)	10.05	4.91
2002-03	231748 (56.21)	180531 (43.79)	17.58	13.69

Note : Figures in parentheses are percentages of total receipts.

Sources: 1. Centre for Monitoring Indian Economy (2004), *Public Finance*, Mumbai, p. 81.

2. Government of India (2004), *Economic Survey*, 2003-04, New Delhi.

corporation tax in total tax revenue increased two-fold (i.e. 21.35 percent) in 2002-03. The share of corporation tax to total receipts also confirms the increasing proceeds from corporation tax during post-economic reform period. For example, corporation tax contributed 7.03 percent to total receipts in 1980-81. The share of corporation tax in total receipts reached 11.59 percent in 2002-03. On account of buoyancy, also the corporation tax validates the effectiveness of tax reforms. The buoyancy of corporation tax during pre-reform period was 0.96 and 0.94, respectively, during 1980-81 and 1990-91. The buoyancy of corporation tax experienced almost consistent improvement during post-reform period. For example, it was 1.19 in 1992-93 and reached 1.87 in 2002-03.

(ii) Income Tax

In case of income tax also, the tax reforms have succeeded in mobilization of more resources. For example, the share of gross tax on income in gross tax revenue was 10.95 percent and 9.33 percent, respectively, during 1980-81 and 1990-91 (pre-reform period). The share of income tax in total tax revenue reached as high as 17.04 percent during 2002-03. Similarly, in case of total receipts, the share of income tax has witnessed improvement after the introduction of tax reforms. In the pre-tax reform period (i.e. 1980-81), the share of income tax in total receipts was 7.35 percent, which increased to 9.24 percent during the post-reform period (i.e. 2002-03). Buoyancy of income tax is also in tune with the above-mentioned findings. For example, income tax buoyancy was 1.00 in 1980-81 and 0.94 in 1990-91 (pre-reform period). It increased to 1.05 in 1992-93 and to 1.49 in 2002-03.

(iii) Custom Duty

Custom duty is another important source of revenue of the Union Government. In the 1950s and the 1960s, the share of custom duty in total tax revenue used to be the highest. However, since the early 1970s the custom duty lost its first position. It is relevant to mention here that since the inception of Second Five Year Plan (1956-61), the heavy industry strategy and deficit food grain situation necessitated import of heavy machinery, capital equipment, raw material, petroleum products, chemical fertilizers, food grains, etc. The implementation of 'import substitution' strategy helped in widening the industrial base and reduced the reliance upon the imports of machinery and plants. The introduction of New Agricultural Technology resulting in Green Revolution also helped in reduction in importing of food grains. With a view to protect the emerging industrial economy, the government imposed heavy custom duties which acted as deterrents for imports. These factors pushed the custom duties to second position in tax revenue. The recent tax reforms are extra-friendly to custom duty. Custom duties have been slashed considerably.

The peak custom duty was high as 300 percent during pre-reform period. Now peak custom duty is in the vicinity of 25 percent. The drastic reduction in import duty has helped in importing of more and more consumer and capital goods but the custom duty is losing its importance as source of tax revenue. The share of custom duty was 25.93 percent in gross tax revenue in 1980-81. It increased to 35.86 percent in 1990-91 (end year of pre-reform periods). Since then, the share of custom duty in gross tax revenue barring few years is declining. The share of custom duty was 31.86 in the beginning of economic reforms (i.e. 1992-93) and it reached as low as 20.74 percent in 2002-03. Custom duty's share in total receipts also confirms declining importance of custom duty as source of resource mobilization. For example, custom duty contributed 17.41 percent towards total receipts in 1980-81. The share came down to 11.25 percent in 2002-03. Declining trend in custom duty as percentage of imports is also noticeable. For example, custom duty was 27.17 percent of total imports in 1980-81, which declined to 15.07 percent in 2002-03.

The foregoing analysis regarding custom duty suggests that government of India, under international commitment and pressure, has been reducing custom duty in an attempt to integrate the Indian economy with economies of the rest of globe but in the process losing a significant source of revenue.

(iv) Union Excise Duty

Union excise duty is another important source of tax revenue of the Union Government. Union excise duty continued to contribute maximum share in gross tax revenue of the Union Government during both pre and post-reform periods. The share of union excise duties has, however, witnessed a declining trend during post-reform period. The share of the union excise duties was around 50 percent in 1980-81. It come down to 42.58 percent in 1990-91. During post-reform period, the share of union excise duties witnessed further decline. The share of the union excise duties was 41.31 percent in 1992-93 and it came down to 38.06 percent in 2002-03.

The buoyancy of union excise duties has experienced improvement during post-reform period. For example, the buoyancy of the Union excise duties was 1.62 and 3.53, respectively, during 1980-81 and 1990-91. During post-reform period it increased from 4.18 in 1992-93 to 6.24 in 2002-03.

The management of excise duties was very complex specially during pre-reform period mainly due to the levying of

excise duties by the government in a number of forms. Another weakness of union excise duties was taxation of inputs, including raw material, components and other intermediate inputs which distorted the production structure and resulting in 'cascading' of taxes. Based on the Chelliah Committee's and other committee's recommendations, the government introduced drastic changes in the excise duties like extension of modified value-added taxation (MODVAT) to capital goods and petroleum products, shift in the bulk of excise taxation from specific to *ad valorem* tax rates; application of uniform rates for similar commodities where ever possible; reduction of the number of special exemption notifications; and finally rationalization of excise duties with the introduction of a three-tier duty structure of 8 percent, 16 percent and 24 percent (except for petroleum products, pan masala, textiles and specific rated products).

(v) Service Tax

The Indian economy has moved from agrarian economy stage to service economy stage. At present, share of service sector in gross domestic product is in the vicinity of 50 percent. Keeping in view the growing importance of service sector, the government has recently decided to impose new tax on service sector. A humble beginning of imposing service tax was made in 1994-95, and since then service tax has been gaining momentum as a source of resource mobilization. The share of service tax in total tax revenue was negligible (0.44 percent), in 1994-95 but the share improved consistently and reached 2 percent in 2002-03. The share of service tax in total receipts also increased from 0.25 percent in 1994-95 to 1.03 percent in 2002-03. The buoyancy of service tax was very low (0.05) in the beginning (i.e. 1994-95). It gradually improved and reached 0.31 in 2002-03.

(vi) Other Taxes

The remaining taxes and duties of the union government include estate duty, interest tax, wealth tax, gift tax, other taxes and duties and taxes on Union Territories.

DIRECT AND INDIRECT TAXES

Another approach of analyzing tax revenue is in the form of the relative strength of direct and indirect taxes. According to theory of taxation (Hidrichs, 1966; and Musgrave, 1969), in the early stages of development, direct taxses contribute relatively more towards tax revenue. As economy moves from agrarian stage to industrial stage, indirect taxes establish their predominance. Further maturing of the economy, particularly reaching the stage of service economy, motivates the governments to rely more and more on direct taxes.

The Indian experience relating to direct and indirect taxes is partly in consonance with above mentioned theoretical model. The share of indirect taxes has remained more than that of direct taxation since independent. For example, the share of indirect taxes in total tax revenue was 57 percent in 1950-51, which increased to 79 percent in 1990-91. The experience of post-reform period lends some support to taxation theory. For example, the share of direct taxes in total tax revenue started increasing during post-reform period and it reached 41.4 percent during 2003-04.

Non-tax Revenue

As referred earlier, non-tax revenues mainly include interest receipts, including interest paid by the Railways and Telecommunications; dividends and profits (i.e. internal resources of departmental and non-departmental undertakings); external grants and other non-tax revenue. Out of these two, namely, interest receipts and dividends and profits have been analysed in this paper.

(i) Interest Receipts

Interest receipts are the major constituents of non-tax revenue. However, their contribution particularly during post-reform period has declined. For example, in 1980-81 interest receipts contributed around 70 percent in overall non-tax revenue. The share declined to 49.13 percent in 2002-03.

(ii) Dividends and Profits

The internal resource mobilization by the departmental and non-departmental undertakings in the form of dividends and profits has gained importance over time. In 1980-81, the share of dividends and profits in overall non-tax revenue was 9.48 percent which experienced phenomenal growth during post-reform period and contributed 29.35 percent in 2002-03. This increasing trend of internal resource mobilization within departmental and non-departmental undertakings is partly due to restructuring of the undertakings and the introduction of market disciplines within these undertakings.

Capital Receipts

Capital receipts comprise many sources such as net market borrowing; recovery of loans; disinvestments; small savings; state provident funds; special deposits; special borrowing from R.B.I.; short-term, medium and long-terms loans; and net miscellaneous capital receipts. However, net market borrowings, small savings, and external borrowings are the major constituents of capital receipts.

(i) Net Market Borrowing

Tax and non-tax revenues are not sufficient to meet growing expenditure, particularly developmental expenditure of the Union Government. The government resorts to market borrowing to raise resources specially for financing developmental projects. Net market borrowing emerged the most favourable method for mobilizing resources by the Union Government particularly during post-reform period. For example, in 1980-81, net market borrowing contributed 35.05 percent towards capital receipts. Its share came down to 20.52 percent during the last year (i.e. 1990-91) of the pre-reform era. In the beginning of economic reforms, the share reached all time low, i.e. 10.16 percent in 1992-93. Since then, the share of net market borrowing in total capital receipts has been experiencing phenomenal growth. It reached as high as 54.06 percent in 2002-03. The share of net market borrowing in total receipts has also increased during post-reform period. The share of net market borrowing in total receipts was 13.68 percent in 1980-81. It increased to almost two-fold (i.e. 25 percent), in 2002-03. The increasing reliance of Union Government on net market borrowing is partly due to inability of the union government to meet revenue expenditure from revenue receipts. In other words, government partly utilizes proceeds of market borrowing for meeting revenue expenditure which is the most dangerous tendency in the field of public finance and financial administration. Increasing reliance on market borrowing also results in increasing interest liabilities of the Union Government. Interest payment liability of the government is as high as 30 percent of total expenditure and 35 percent of revenue expenditure. Further, interest payments, according to one estimate, pre-empt nearly 50 percent of revenue receipts (*Economic Survey,* 2003-04, p. 27). The high interest liabilities necessitate more market borrowing. More and more market borrowings by the government result in what is known as 'crowding out effect', i.e. depriving the private sector the required resources. According to *Economic Survey,* (2003-04). "The indirect cost of debt is the incremental growth foregone by the economy as a result of the diversion of resources from the private to government sector" (p. 28).

(ii) Small Savings

Small savings are another important source of capital receipts. No visible trend, however, is noticeable so far as the share of small savings in total receipts during pre and post-reform period is concerned. The share of small saving in total receipts was 5.35 percent in 1980-81. Later on, it reached its highest level, i.e. 24.32 percent during 1989-90. In the post-reform period the highest share of small savings in total capital receipts was 25.40 percent in 1998-99. Later on, it declined considerably. It was as low as 5.39 percent in 2001-02.

(iii) External Borrowings

External borrowings are also amongst the major sources of capital receipts. Prior to economic reforms, strict regulations were in place for external borrowing. Since the inception of economic reforms, liberalized regime was set in motion to promote external borrowing. The empirical evidence, however, suggests that the share of external borrowing in total capital receipts came down during post-reform period. This phenomenon may be due to the fact that other countries like China mere also aiming to attract foreign recourses during the same period. The share of net external borrowing in total capital receipts was 22.47 percent in 1980-81. It came down to 8.16 percent in 1990-91. The share of net external borrowing towards net capital receipts increased to 14.2 percent in 1992-93. However, the heavy external repayment liabilities (Rs. 24286 crores) exceeded gross external borrowings (Rs. 12352 crores) in 2002-03 resulting in negative share (-6.61 percent) of net external borrowing in capital receipts. Thus heavy dependence on external borrowing results in financial distress in the economy when the repayment of external borrowing starts.

CONCLUSIONS

From the foregoing analysis, the following inferences can be drawn:

1. Tax revenue since independence is the most important and trusted source of revenue of the Central Government in India.
2. Within tax revenue during the 1950s and the 1960s, custom duties contributed maximum to the total tax revenue of the Central Government. Later on, union excise duties took the lead in the form of contributing maximum to tax revenue.
3. Service tax, introduced recently, has been gaining importance as a source of revenue of the Central Government.
4. Since independence, indirect taxes have been contributing maximum to the tax revenue. However, during the post-reform period, the share of direct taxes has started increasing.
5. The Government of India has set-up various

Committees and Commissions for improving the share of taxation further in overall revenues of the economy.

6. The administration and management of taxes, prior to economic reforms, was characterized as suspicion ridden, procedure centric and complex, even harassment generating and coercive.
7. Tax administration and management during post-economic reforms is guided by the philosophy of trust, voluntary compliance, simplification of tax returns, limited number of rates, more transparency, etc.
8. The impact of tax reforms on the overall tax revenue is not positive. The share of overall tax revenue in total receipts has rather declined during post-reforms period.
9. Tax-wise breakup reveals that income tax, corporation tax and union excise duties responded positively to tax reforms.
10. Custom duties have suffered considerably during post-reform period.
11. In case of non-tax revenue, interest receipts were major contributors during pre-reform period. However, during post-reform period the share of dividends and profits earned by departmental and non-departmental undertakings in total non-tax revenue increased considerably.
12. Net market borrowing is the most favourable method for raising capital receipts. Increasing reliance on market borrowing, however, has dangerous implications particularly when a part of market borrowing is utilized for meeting revenue expenditure. More and more market borrowing results in increased interest liability of the government. Heavy market borrowing also restricts private sector's access to funds.
13. External borrowing, in spite of consistent efforts of government, could not emerge as significant source of financing of the Central Government. Increasing external repayment liabilities in the recent past has resulted in negative net external borrowing.

References

Ashford, Nigel (1993), "The Ideas of the New Right", in Jordan, Grant and Nigel Ashford (ed.)

Bagchi, Amresh (1994), "India's Tax Reform: A Progress Report", *Economic and Political Weekly,* October 22.

Centre for Monitoring Indian Economy (2004), *Public Finance,* Mumbai.

D' souza, Errol (1995), "The Budget, Tax Reforms and Public Policy", *Economic and Political Weekly,* May 6-13.

Government of India (1954), *Report of the Taxation Enquiry Commission,* 1953-54, New Delhi.

Government of India, (1967), *Final Report on Rationalization and Simplification of the Tax Structure,* New Delhi.

Government of India (1971), *Report of the Direct Taxes Enquiry Committee,* New Delhi.

Government of India (1972), *Report of the Committee on Taxation of Agricultural Wealth and Income,* New Delhi.

Government of India (1978), *Report of the Indirect Taxation Enquiry Committee,* New Delhi.

Government of India (1991), *Tax Reforms Committee, Interim Report,* New Delhi.

Government of India (1992), *Tax Reforms Committee, Final Report,* New Delhi.

Government of India (2002), *Report of the Task Force on Direct Taxes,* Ministry of Finance, New Delhi.

Government of India (2002), *Report of the Task Force on Direct Taxes,* Ministry of Finance, New Delhi.

Government of India (2004), *Economic Survey,* 2003-04, New Delhi, Gray, Andrew and Bill Jenkins (1995), "From Public Administration to Public Management: Reassessing a Revolution?", *Public Administrative,* Spring, Vol. 73.

Hinrich, H.H. (1966), *A General Theory of Tax Structure Development,* Harvard Law School International Tax Programme.

Jordan, Grant and Nigel Ashford (1993, edited), *Public Policy and the Impact of the New Right,* Pinter Publishers, London.

Kaldor, Micholas (1956), *Indian Tax Reform; Report of Survey,* New Delhi.

Musgrave, R.A. (1969), *Fiscal Systems,* Yale University Press, London, Niskanen, W. (1971), *Bureaucracy and Representative Government,* Aldine Press, Chicago.

Reserve of Bank of India, *Reports on Currency and Finance,* Mumbai.

Sreekantaradhya, B.S. (2000), *Structure and Reform of Taxation in India,* Deep and Deep Publications Pvt. Ltd., New Delhi.

Walsh, Keiren (1997), *Public Services and Market Mechanism: Competition, Contracting and the New Management,* Macmillan, Hampshire.

Capital Account Convertibility in India

P.K. Vasudeva and Monika Aggarwal

INTRODUCTION

The question of rupee convertibility comes up time and again with the improvement of balance of payment situation since 1992 onwards. This is a very serious question for India because the decision-making on the convertibility cannot be taken hastily. There was a rather widespread belief that free international capital movements were as much a part of a liberal economy as free product markets, a liberalised domestic financial system, or free trade during the 1990s. So strongly was this belief held that in 1997, the IMF was on the verge of extending its limit to include supervision and controls on international capital flows, with an objective of helping its member countries to move progressively to a situation where they had no such controls? The IMF's Interim Committee (now renamed the International Monetary and Financial Committee)

affirmed its intention of having the IMF amend its articles to that effect during the annual meeting in Hong Kong in September 1997, after the Asian crisis had already swept through South-East Asia but before it had engulfed Hong Kong and Korea.

Since then, the main pressure for liberalising capital flows has come from the US treasury. When countries wanted to negotiate bilateral free trade agreements with the US, they found that the US treasury insisted US negotiators, therefore, demanded the partner country to commit itself to never reimposing effective capital controls for any length of time. Several of the partner countries that had made effective use of such controls in the past, like Chile and Singapore, found them with the object of avoiding or at least attenuating crises. Given that governments, like markets, typically take a rather short-term view of costs and benefits, and that the countries could not see the prospect of a crisis on the horizon at the time the negotiations were taking place, the US treasury got its way.

But elsewhere, the pressure to move to capital account liberalisation seemed to have disappeared. In particular, IMF research—which one may assume was inclined to find support for capital account liberalisation if a serious case could be made—concluded that there was at best mixed evidence of net benefits from free capital flows (Prasad *et. al.*, 2003).

This did not mean that there were no benefits from certain types of capital flows. There is overwhelming reason (and abundant empirical evidence) to think that foreign direct investment is highly beneficial, because it provides an efficient mechanism for spreading the fruits of technological innovation and intellectual property around the world. There is also solid empirical evidence to believe that liberalising the flow of portfolio investment is beneficial, because it reduces the cost of capital to enterprise and it enables investors to gain the benefits of diversification (Henry, 2000a, b). Hence it is not at all surprising that in some empirical studies (such as Quinn, 1997), where the question asked was whether liberalisation of the capital account was beneficial, a positive result should have been obtained, since many of the liberalising moves that provided the independent variable in such studies referred to liberalisation of FDI or portfolio investment.

But the studies in Prasad *et. al.* (2003) are not of this type. They ask whether countries without capital controls do better than countries with them, and they failed to find evidence to support the conjecture that a complete absence of controls brings faster growth or other economic benefits. What this surely suggests is that what is usually the last step in liberalising the capital account, namely, the liberalisation of short-term loans, may bring costs that outweigh the benefits. It is not difficult to believe this. All the evidence is that bank flows—which are the part of the capital account that is separately recorded and that falls most clearly in the short-term loan category—are highly volatile. As soon as a developing country hits a difficult patch, whether because of low prices of the commodities it exports or political uncertainties or contagion from neighbours, bank loans are liquidated—and (unlike equity investments, where the investor at least tends to pay through the nose for surrendering to panic) they can be liquidated without cost to the lender.

RISK OF SHORT-TERM LOANS

The charge of critics is that short-term loans contribute nothing to welfare. They cannot safely be used to expand investment, since they may be withdrawn before the investment project matures. They tend to disappear just when they could play a useful role in helping to smoothen consumption. (Remember the old adage that a banker lends only to those who do not need the money). And inherently, they do not provide an instrument for portfolio diversification. Yet it is primarily variations in the flow of short-term capital, like bank loans, that give rise to the pro-cyclicality of the capital account, which provides the main mechanism by which free capital flows create problems. Some people would add tax evasion as another channel for creating problems. In view of this anomaly, capital convertibility at this stage is not advisable.

Why was there so much pressure in India for liberalisation of the capital account in 1997, when the first Tarapore Committee (1997) proposed "gradual" (over three years) liberalization of the capital account? The main reasons were: First, that was the spirit of the age, (before the Asian crisis), as manifest in the pressures from the IMF as stated earlier. Second, and doubtless more important, because of the desire for cheaper credit on the part of Indian business, which looked with envy at the relatively low dollar interest rates prevailing in the outside world and contrasted them with the high rupee interest rates then prevalent in India. Indian business wanted to be able to access cheap external credit without having to ask permission of the Reserve Bank of India.

The desire was understandable, but the cost of giving in to it would have been to expose India to the danger of contagion similar to that which laid the whole of East Asia low when Thailand had a balance of payments problem. For there is no serious doubt that the countries that suffered crises in 1997 were those that had accepted a large volume of short-term capital and number of those that were particularly corrupt. Like China, India was not among them, not because there is no corruption in China or India, but because they did not have an open capital account and, therefore, had not imported a lot of capital that could flee when investors panicked.

Tarapore Committee's Conditions

Should India now change its policy and allow free flows of capital, including short-term loans, by all and sundry? The first Tarapore Committee specified three preconditions that needed to be satisfied before it would be sensible to move to capital account convertibility. First, the country needed to have established fiscal discipline to make sure that capital inflows did not provide an easy way of perpetuating what is ultimately unsustainable. A failure to do this would eventually lead to a crisis when the market finally decided to cease financing the deficit. Second, the country needed to reduce the rate of inflation to the range of 3 to 5 per cent per year, and to make the pursuit of an inflation target the central mandate of the Reserve Bank of India. Third, India needed to have cleaned up its banking system, so that one could be confident that capital inflows would be efficiently intermediated to where they would be profitably invested, rather than used by banks to borrow more with the object of postponing bankruptcy. These conditions come squarely out of the economic literature on capital account liberalization, and all three are completely reasonable. In addition, the literature suggests that countries need to have liberalized their trade regime before accepting large capital inflows, so that one could expect the profitability of investment to be closely correlated with the social returns to the investment, rather than having investment flow into profitable but socially inefficient import substituting industries.

Progress in two Areas

In the last ten years since it last considered capital account liberalization, India has made important progress in two of the three areas specified by the first Tarapore Committee as preconditions, and in liberalizing trade. Inflation has fallen from over 7 per cent in 1997 to under 4 per cent in 2005, and the RBI has been told to pursue an inflation target of further reducing it. The percentage of advances classified as non-performing—which is the best single measure of the health of the banking system—has fallen from 14.7 per cent in March 1997 to 5.2 per cent in March 2005. And while Indian trade is still far from completely free, it is now far less restricted than it then was: in particular, the quotas on imports of consumer goods have now been phased out. Unfortunately that still leaves one important area in which India has not made progress, which concerns fiscal discipline: the total size of the public sector deficit has actually risen from 7.3 per cent of GDP in 1997-98 to an estimated 7.7 per cent of GDP in 2005-06 (with even higher figures in between), while the ratio of public debt to GDP has increased from under 65 per cent to over 83 per cent. So, even on the conditions suggested by the first Tarapore Committee, a quick move to capital account convertibility would be premature.

It is worth-noting also that the first Tarapore Committee rightly argued that acceptance of capital account convertibility presupposed a pretty flexible exchange rate policy, so that a change in capital flows could be absorbed by a change in the exchange rate rather than a surfeit of reserves or their possible exhaustion. But this in turn is something that is easier for an advanced industrial country to fully accept than it is for an emerging market, in which growth has to be largely exported. It is a mistake, especially critical for an emerging market, to allow its exchange rate to be pushed up to an uncompetitive level. This consideration suggests that current Indian exchange rate policy is sensibly balanced, whereas any rapid move to liberalise capital flows could create problems for maintaining that balance.

The conditions suggested by the first Tarapore Committee omitted one important consideration. Specifically, the committee did not acknowledge the fundamental importance of having become completely trusted in international markets. When a mature industrial country gets into trouble and wishes to borrow more in order to tide over bad times, it can always do so, because lenders do not doubt that it will be able and willing to continue servicing its debts. Markets may charge more, or exchange rates may depreciate, but ultimately industrial countries can continue to borrow if they need to and are willing to pay the price. Unfortunately, this is not true for emerging markets, even if they have an exemplary past record of debt service. And the fact that some of them don't (think of Argentina as the most recent example), does not make it easier for the others. Situations, in which markets simply will not lend, on any terms, have continued to recur in recent years, until the cyclical upswing started in 2003 and avoided further crises for the moment. Think of Latin American countries, like Brazil in 2002 or Chile in 1998. Or think of the Asian crisis (a particularly vivid example). Or, to go slightly further back in history, think of India itself in 1991.

This is not to argue that India and other emerging markets never should or will have capital account convertibility. As they grow and as per capita income increases, it is to be expected both that market trust will increase and the efficacy of capital controls will fall. If a country becomes a net creditor to the rest of the world, it can expect greater returns if it allows most of its investments to be made by private investors than if they are all invested by the authorities in US treasury bills or similar low-yielding instruments they like to hold (so as to avoid the charge of losing public money, which they do not expect to be levelled against them as long as the securities do not depreciate in terms of the US dollar). A time will, therefore, come when it will be entirely appropriate for the state to allow free capital flows. Judging by the European experience after the Second World War, it takes about 30 years from when a country starts the process of liberalisation and financial integration before it makes sense to move to capital account convertibility.

Foreign Exchange Reserves

Countries do not suffer capital flight when their central banks are sitting on reserves of $150 billion odd (approaching 23 percent of GDP) and a world boom is in progress. But the case for restraint in moving to capital account convertibility does not rest upon a conviction that any short-run danger lurks through such a move. The question is whether when circumstances turn difficult, the country will be in an equally solid position to maintain its growth if in the interim it has taken on a load of short-term debt and given investment banks the right to play games with its money. For example, if as some of us fear is quite likely, the US one day confronts a crisis caused by a collapse of the dollar, the consequence for the rest of the world is likely to be even more traumatic. Recession in the US will be tempered in the medium run by the shift in expenditure toward American-made goods caused by the dollar depreciation, but in other countries expenditure switching and expenditure-reduction will reinforce each other in making for recession. Countries whose exchange rates float uncontrollably upwards will suffer the most. India should not be willing to play a role as a responsible member of the international community in accepting its fair share of the dollar depreciation, but simply that it would be advantageous to avoid the greater burden that might be thrust upon it by a market in which the free flow of capital dictates how far exchange rates move. And if India sought to maintain spending during a world of recession through expansionary macroeconomic policies, it might well find that its reserves got run down even without a strong initial effective appreciation. At that point, the danger would be the more traditional one of a run out of the rupee.

India should, therefore, adopt go-slow approach in moving to liberalise the capital account. That it would be wise to liberalise after a few more years when the Indian economy gets more stabilised. That there is some liberalising measures that should be made early—of FDI, of portfolio investment, of small private transactions—which may be under compelling circumstances. But there are many other liberalising reforms—from electricity pricing to making the courts work expeditiously to pruning the fiscal deficit—that deserve to be priorities over complete capital account liberalisation for the next 10 years. At this stage, full capital account liberalisation promises no large benefits, while it increases the risk of things going bad to worse.

Free Float of the Rupee

Nine years earlier, in 1997, another expert group, also headed by Mr. S.S. Tarapore, had prescribed a road map for the introduction of full convertibility, also known as capital account convertibility. Then, as now, the launch of capital account convertibility was made conditional on the attainment of specific macroeconomic goals.

The details vary but both reports lay stress on fiscal consolidation and financial sector reforms as crucial preliminaries to full convertibility of the rupee. The time-tables drawn up by the expert groups—just three years beginning 1997 (by the first committee) and now five years—are meant to underline the importance of economic consolidation and provide a sequence for the proposed liberalisation.

Capital account convertibility has always been a much-hyped subject, often without much understanding of what it entails. Specifically, the benefits it is supposed to confer on the economy are exaggerated while its pitfalls are blithely ignored.

In fact, there may be a fundamental misconception of what it denotes. In India, most current account transactions have been freed from controls over the years. Resident individuals now have the freedom to remit as well as receive foreign exchange on a variety of transactions. Thus, unlike a decade ago, anyone can finance his overseas education with practically no limit. Foreign exchange is freely available for travel abroad as well as for medical expenses.

No Precise Definition

Neither current account convertibility nor capital account convertibility admits of a concise definition. While there are internationally understood norms for indicating a country's "convertibility" status, these are not precise. All they connote is that the authorities will stipulate fewer controls on money transfers into and out of a country. However, whether on current or capital account, even developed countries have some kind of negative lists. Incidentally, these lists have expanded with tough anti-money laundering laws and the all-pervasive need to fight terrorism.

It follows that there is not such thing as full convertibility of the domestic currency in absolute terms. Capital account convertibility in the sense of residents freely investing in property or financial assets abroad and foreigners in India still remains a distant, impractical dream. In any case, even if the monetary authorities in India allow residents to invest anywhere in the world, it does not automatically make such investments possible. This is because many countries restrain investments in specific sectors of their economies. That is easily understood in the light of the debate on sectoral caps for foreign direct investments in India. It is often forgotten that even developed countries have such restrictions.

The title of the Tarapore Committee report is "Towards fuller convertibility" and not "Full convertibility". The distinction is crucial to an understanding of convertibility, its status as also the various safeguards suggested.

Hence the clamour for capital account convertibility is really for relaxations on capital transactions rather than for a withdrawal of all types of control. Critics of the report say its time-table is too long. They ignore the fact that substantial liberalisation has already occurred in India even on capital account transfers. It is difficult to see what other benefits will accrue to the economy from liberalisation, especially when it is carried out quickly ignoring the commonsense safeguards.

On the other hand, many developing countries, from South-East Asia to Latin America, that have had a more liberal exchange control regime including "fuller capital account convertibility" have suffered grievously. At the first sign of a loss of confidence in the economy, non-residents and domestic investors alike in those countries shifted their capital abroad.

In fact, since 1998, following the debacle in many East Asian and Southeast Asian countries, capital account convertibility has ceased to be fashionable among policy-makers.

Exhaustive studies conducted by international rating agencies prove the point that a full convertibility status does not by itself make a country a more attractive investment destination. More important are traits such as fiscal rectitude and a strong financial sector. These are exactly the signposts the Tarapore Committee has advocated. The fact that these are difficult to reach in the current Indian context is an entirely different matter.

For instance, in the area of banking sector reform, while everyone agrees that greater autonomy is good for the public sector banks and that there should be equal treatment for banks irrespective of ownership, it is difficult to visualize a reduction in government stake in PSBs to 33.33 per cent as suggested by the committee. Even fiscal consolidation as enshrined in the FRBM legislation is now being called into question insofar as it is seen a hindering resource mobilisation for the Eleventh Plan.

Participatory Notes

The recommendations to phase out participatory notes (PNs)—instruments issued by foreign financial institutions that are backed by shares in India—through which unidentified overseas investors can access Indian markets—is unlikely to be accepted by the Government. However, the course suggested is a prudent one, as PNs are widely believed to be conduits for unaccounted money in India flowing back.

With many signposts that are difficult to reach, it is hardly likely that India will move towards fuller convertibility by adhering to the path set out. In that sense, the value of the Tarapore Committee's report might well lie in its focus on crucial macro-economic and procedural issues of the day.

A Capital Market Perspective

Looking for easy solutions by abandoning the path of opening up the economy and not getting out of the 'control mindset' is unlikely to be acceptable to a modernizing India.

The recent report on fuller capital account convertibility of rupee has received mixed reactions from market participants. While most of the recommendations are supported by sound arguments in support of the changes, in some cases, the articulation of the intellectual basis is somewhat weak. The issues covered by the convertibility report that are of immediate concern to the capital market are the recommendations involving the banning of participatory notes, abolition of discriminatory tax treaties, continuance of the policy of discouraging NRIs from investing directly in the Indian capital market and the issue raised in one of the dissenting notes making the case against further liberalisation of outflows from resident Indians.

The arguments in support of the ban on PNs are about the anonymity of the beneficial ownership of the holders, that PNs are freely transferable and that it is also not possible to prevent trading in PNs as the entitles subscribing to the PNs cannot be restrained from issuing securities on the strength of the PNs held by them. To address these very concerns, the capital market regulator has, since February 2004, put in place regulations that allow FIIs/sub-accounts to issue PNs only to regulated entities and further downstream issuance of such derivative instruments cannot be made to unregulated entities.

Issuers of PNs are responsible for exercising due diligence on their clients based on 'know your client' (KYC) principles. This is on the same lines as the FCAC committee's recommendation to allow, subject to KYC and financial action task force (FATF) norms, investment by non-resident corporate through Sebi registered entities and allowing FNR(B) deposit facility to non-NRI non-residents. Given the same level of due diligence on the regulated entity, there is no sound justification offered by the committee to discriminate against a particular instrument.

There is no effort to deal with the fundamental reasons behind the popularity of PNs among even those investors who are eligible to get a FII or FII sub-account registration—the reasons being the procedural issues relating to registration, establishing broker and custodian relationships, undertaking forex transactions and more importantly, dealing with tax certifications, filling of I-T returns and getting tax assessments completed. In addition, there is the added uncertainty about the tax status of foreign investors with the revenue authorities interpreting the provisions of tax treaties differently on different occasions with issues like permanent establishment, classifying investment income as business income, etc., being subject matters of frequent disputes.

For a foreign investor, PNs offer an elegant solution to procedural hassles and tax uncertainties, by transferring these risks to the FII, thus enabling the investor to focus attention on stock picking. The regulator has been insisting that the PN issuer should be able to disclose the identity of the ultimate beneficiary whenever asked, thus reducing the possibility of anonymous holding. Anecdotal evidence does not seem to suggest that the PN holders are any more short-term oriented than the general class of investors. The bit about PN holders being able to issue securities on the strength of the PNs is untenable because this could be the case with any security.

The committee also suggests doing away with discriminatory tax treaties. This needs to be put in context because despite the professed commitment to free trade, most developed countries have special free trade agreements and discriminatory tax treaties in their national interests. Such treaties find favour with investors only because of the complexities of the taxation regime and procedural hurdles in the host country. The best way out, therefore, is to streamline procedures and reduce the level of arbitrariness and subjectivity in the taxation regime.

As a reaction to the last stock scam, we have effectively prevented NRIs from directly participating in the Indian market. While most developing economies try hard to harness the economic strength of their non-resident citizens, there can be nothing more perverse than preventing these investors from participating in the growth of the Indian market. Even when an NRI has the necessary knowledge to invest in the Indian market, the system discourages this other than through pooled funds, thus imposing a significant transaction cost on our non-resident citizens.

The dissenting note arguing against liberalising outflows from Indian residents also appears to be on somewhat weak grounds. If the argument about a significant portion of the population seeking to remit their savings out of the country in concert during times of crises were strong concert during times of crises were strong enough, it is unlikely that any country in the world would lift forex controls and the world would be poorer for this. An extrapolation of this argument would strike at the root of commercial banking as we know it. It can be nobody's argument that extreme emergencies require the use of State power, like the recommendation about imposing an unremunerated reserve requirement on fresh FII inflows when the economy is inundated with excess liquidity arising out of FII inflows. While one needs to have contingencies for the outlying phenomenon in place, a system that is designed for anything other than the handling of the overwhelming number of near normal transactions is unlikely to be efficient. Central banks conduct effective currency and monetary policies despite the type of worries highlighted in the dissent note.

It is rather ironic that the retirement and pension funds of the advanced economies are benefiting from the high returns of the Indian equity market but this is denied to the organised working class of the country. As the committee observes, there is an undeniable role for foreign capital inflows in supplementing the domestic savings to accelerate the economic growth of the country. A well functioning capital market serves as the wealth-creating engine for the economy for which it is essential to have a diversity of investors with differing investment philosophies and horizons. Looking for easy solutions by abandoning the path of opening up the economy and not getting out of the 'control mindset' is unlikely to be acceptable to a modernizing India.

References

Bhatt, U.R. (2006), 'FCAC: A Capital Market Perspective', *The Economic Times*, September 11, p. 10

Henry, Peter (2000a), 'Stock Market Liberalisation, Economic Reform, and Emerging Market Equity Prices', *Journal of Finance*, 50(2), pp. 529-64.

Ila Patnaik (2006), 'The Inevitability of Capital Convertibility' *The Sunday Express*, September 17, p. 8.

Narasimhan, C.R.L. (2006), 'Capital Account Convertibility, a Mirage?', *Business Review, The Hindu*, September 11, 2006, p. 15.

Prasad, Eswar, Kenneth Rogoff, Shang-Jin Wei and M. Ayhan Kose (2003), 'Effects of Financial Globalisation on Developing Countries: Some Empirical Evidence', IMF, Washington.

Quinn, Dennis (1997), 'The Correlates of Changes in International Financial Regulation', *American Political Science Review*, 91(3), pp. 531-51.

Tarapore Committee (1997), *Report of the Committee on Capital Account Convertibility*, Reserve Bank of India, Mumbai.

Williamson, John (2006), 'Why Capital Account Convertibility in India is Premature', *Economic and Political Weekly*, May 13-19, Vol. XLI, No. 19, pp. 1848-50.

———, (2000b), 'Do Stock Market Liberalizations Cause Investment Booms?' *Journal of Financial Economics*, 58(1-2), pp. 301-34.

Corporate Governance and Policy Framework in Indian Banking Sector—A Bird's Eyeview

D.P.S. RATHORE

Corporate governance has become a subject of significance for both public policy and markets recently. It is useful to recognise that it is a dynamic concept, in terms of scope, thrust and relevance. For example, the issue is approached very differently today compared to original view of the Cadbury Committee on the subject. Corporate governance got an altogether new dimension in the context of financial stability after East-Asian crisis.

The OECD set out its corporate governance principles in 1999 but revised them in 2004. Under the aegis of Bank for International Settlement (BIS), Basle Committee on Banking Supervision published guidelines on corporate governance in 1999. Subsequently, the Basle Committee issued a Consultative Document on enhancing corporate governance for banking organisations in 2005. Finally, the New Basle Capital Accord (Basle II) contains the first detailed framework of rules and standards that supervisors can apply to the practices of senior management and the board for banking groups.

There is also considerable divergence in the understanding and practice of corporate governance in general, and in respect of banks, in particular across the world. However, an increasing tendency towards convergence on corporate governance has been noticed off late on account of various reasons. The Corporates are getting listed in multiple stock exchanges in different countries and carry out corporate operations in several jurisdictions while the cross-border financial flows seek an assurance of some commonly understood standards of governance, which have a mutually reinforcing tendency (Y.V. Reddy, 2005). Banking sector, in particular, have been getting a special attention for corporate governance, especially in view of its fiduciary role. The cross-border operations of banking sector provide an added impetus for convergence in such standards.

Multiple agencies are involved in public policy framework in regard to corporate governance across the countries. For example, in case of India, these agencies are Department of Company Affairs, Securities and Exchange Board of India for listed entities besides Reserve Bank of India in respect of banks. Harmonising their policies in a dynamic setting is a daunting task for policy-makers and adds to the complexities of the Corporates or banks concerned to ensure compliance (Y.V. Reddy, 2005).

In view of cross-border transactions and multiple activities, role of corporate governance becomes pivotal in the banking sector in India. Against this background, an attempt has been made to explain the existing policy framework of corporate governance in the banking sector in India. Section I presents the definitional aspects of corporate governance, while the New Basle Capital Accord (Basle II) and corporate governance has been explained in Section II. Policy framework/response in respect of corporate governance in the banking sector in India have been covered in the Section III. Section IV contains conclusion.

Section I

CORPORATE GOVERNANCE : DEFINITIONAL ASPECTS

Corporate governance is the set of processes, customs, policies, laws and institutions affecting the way a corporation / entity is directed, administered or controlled. Corporate governance also includes the relationships among the many players involved (the stakeholder) and the goals for which the corporation is governed.

The principal players are the shareholders, management and the board of directors. Other stakeholders include employees, suppliers, depositors, customers, banks and other lenders, regulators, the environment and the community at large

Some commentators take too narrow a view and say it (corporate governance) is the fancy term for the way in which directors and auditors handle their responsibilities towards shareholders. Others use the expression as if it were synonymous with shareholders democracy.

Alan Greenspan, former President of the US Federal Reserve commented upon Corporate Governance saying that "Corporate governance has evolved over the past century to more effectively promote the allocation of the nation's savings to its most productive uses."

Corporate Governance has become buzzword in the context of India economy in general and banking sector in particular off late. Generally, it is seen that people have higher expectations from governance of banks as compared to other firms. It is so may be because banks have to act in a way that promotes "confidence" in the public and the markets in general and more specifically to their primary stakeholders. Banks play a crucial role in the flow of capital within an economy and are charged with a special public trust to safeguard customers' wealth. A stable and healthy banking system is essential for having sustainable long-term growth in the economy.

Banking supervisors also have long recognized the importance of good governance and it is often said that supervision can not function properly if sound corporate governance is not in lace. Good corporate governance and

measures to strengthen the corporate governance in the banking sector in India.

In this context, recognizing the fact that corporate governance is crucial for promoting effective risk management and financial stability, a detailed guidelines on corporate governance for implementation by banks, both public sector and private sector, were issued in June 2002.

Most banks now explicitly state their governance philosophy in their Annual Reports as part of 'Notes on Accounts' to their balance sheets and also provide information on the number of Board meetings, the functions and workings of the sub-committees of the Board, price performance of bank shares (if listed) along with auditors' certification on the procedures and implementation for ensuring compliance.

Furthermore, as a follow-up of the Ganguly Committee report, the concept of "fit and proper" criteria for directors of banks was formally enunciated in the Mid-Term Review of the Monetary and Credit Policy in November 2003. This also included the process of collecting information, exercising due diligence and constitution of a Nomination Committee of the board to scrutinise the declarations made by directors. However, there is no legal provision as of now for the Reserve Bank of India to insist on the "fit and proper" status of the directors nominated by the government or elected by the shareholders to the Boards of public sector banks. The appointment of the CEOs in the public sector banks, as well as their removal, is also within the domain of Government of India.

Further strengthening the corporate governance, the Reserve Bank of India has withdrawn its nominee directors from almost all the private sector banks. Observers have been appointed as transitional measures mostly in respect of those banks which are yet to fully comply with the Reserve Bank's guidelines of ownership of governance. The Government of India has also been requested to keep in view the policy framework for governance in private sector banks while deciding on appointment of the directors on the Boards' of public sector banks and constitution of various committees of the Board (Y.V. Reddy, 2005).

Some of the other measures indirectly relating to corporate governance in the banking sector in India have also been undertaken. A Master Circular on risk management and inter-bank dealings was released on July 1, 2004 whereby banks were advised to put in place necessary risk management systems. The analysis of market risks reflects the interest rate risk, foreign exchange risk and the risk arising from the exposure of banks and financial institutions to the commodities and the capital market.

To take into account the risks faced by banks out of foreign exchange exposure of their clients, foreign currency loans above US $ 10 million (or such lower limits as may be deemed appropriate *vis-a-vis* the banks' portfolios of such exposures), can be extended only on the basis of a well laid out policy with regard to hedging of such foreign currency loans. The draft Guidance Note on management of operational risk was placed on the website (www.rbi.org.in) on March 11, 2005 for wider access and feedback.

An efficient credit information system enhances the quality of credit decisions and improves the asset quality of banks, apart from facilitating faster credit delivery. The compilation and dissemination of credit information covering data on defaults to the financial system was undertaken by Credit Information Bureau of India Ltd. (CIBIL) set-up in 2001. The Credit Information Companies Act, 2005 is expected to contain informational asymmetries and curb the incidence of NPAs.

With the operationalisation of Prevention of Money Laundering Act, 2002 on July 1, 2005, establishment of Financial Intelligence Unit (FIU-IND) and issuance of comprehensive 'Know Your Customer' (KYC) norms for banks by the Reserve Bank on November 29, 2004, the Government and the Reserve Bank have taken necessary steps towards the establishment of anti-money laundering regime in India.

Banks were advised to ensure that a proper policy framework on KYC and anti-money laundering measures were formulated and put in place with the approval of their respective Boards within three months. They were also advised to ensure that the provisions of the revised guidelines were fully complied with before December 31, 2005. Banks were advised to treat the information collected from the customer for the purpose of opening of account as confidential. Banks were also advised to ensure that any remittance of funds by way of demand draft, mail/telegraphic transfer or any other mode and issue of travellers' cheques for value of rupees fifty thousand and above is effected by debit to the customer's account or against cheques and not against cash payment. These measures aid and support the policies and rules of taxation authorities.

Policy framework on corporate governance by other regulatory agencies is also evolving slowly. The Clause 49 of the listing agreement of Securities and Exchange Board of India (SEBI) ensures corporate governance through its requirement of Independent Directors mandatory from 1st January, 2006. Insurance Regulatory and Development Authority (IRDA) is still formulating the guidelines—major impediment being is that most of the companies/major players were unlisted as of now.

SECTION IV

CONCLUSION

Policy framework/response related to corporate governance in India banking sector has been evolved based on recommendations by various groups/committees and cross-country experiences. However, banks in India need to continuously improve/upgrade themselves to comply with international standards and best practices of corporate governance. In this regard, Reserve Bank of India as a regulator is also continuously updating its policy framework in conformity with evolving best practices of corporate governance internationally. Increasing regulatory comfort in regard to standards of governance in banks gives great confidence to shift from external regulation to internal systems of controls and risk-management. More importantly, good corporate governance practices in the entities, if exercised, give great level of confidence and comfort to the all stakeholders.

However, one of the stakeholders, i.e. clientele and depositors of banks, have to be really kept in view for benchmarking the actual effects of all these measures related to corporate governance. The common feeling still remains that banks have to further improve their performance and general functioning to reach a level where common man feels comfortable in dealing with the banks at all levels. No doubts there are gaps and to take care of the same, RBI has been consciously using the tool of monetary policy to bring in focus the need of consumers of banking services in the country. Towards that end, number of measures have been progressively included, e.g. Fair Practices Code, Banking Codes and Standards Board of India, Financial Inclusion and Financial literacy, etc. Fair Practices Code has been introduced for enabling the delivery of customer services transparently, efficiently and cost effectively. Banking Codes and Standards Board of India has been set-up in February 2006 as a society promoted by banks and management of the Board has been entrusted to a Governing Council. Financial exclusion of masses has been a major concern of RBI and in this regard all banks have been asked to introduce "no-frill" account with basic banking facility to under-privileged as well as to identify all those who can be financially included to use banking services. For further augmenting the process of financial inclusion RBI has recently started emphasising on financial education/ literacy, also. All these can be achieved only if, there is commensurate implementation of concept and guidelines related to corporate governance in the banking.

References

Reddy, Y.V. (2005), *"Corporate Governance in Banks in India"*, Address at the Seminar on Corporate Governance for Bank Directors organised by the Indian Institute of Management, Bangalore, International Institute of Finance, Washington and Indian Banks' Association at Mumbai on December 16, 2005.

Leeladhar, V. (2006), *"Indian Banks and the Global Challenges"*, Address at the Seminar organised jointly by the Indian Merchants' Chamber and the Indian Banks' Association in Mumbai on January 31, 2006.

Gopinath, Shyamala (2006), *"Approach to Basle II"*, Address at the IBA briefing session on "Emerging Paradigms in Risk Management" at Bangalore on May 12, 2006.

Mohan, Rakesh (2006), *"Financial Sector Reforms and Monetary Policy: The Indian Experience"*, Address at the Conference on Economic Policy in Asia at Stanford, organised by Stanford Center for International Development and Stanford Institute for Economic Policy Research, on June 2, 2006.

Bibliography

Allen Schick, The Federal Budget (Brookings Institute, Washington, 2000), pp. 258-61.

As Quoted in *Indian Journal of Public Administrative, op. cit.*

Ashford, Nigel (1993), "The Ideas of the New Right" in Jordan, Grant and Nigel Ashford (ed.)

Bagchi, Amresh (1994), "India's Tax Reform: A Progress Report", *Economic and Political Weekly*, October 22.

Banerjee, Nirmala, Krishnaraj Maithrey (2004), "Sieving Budgets for Gender", *Economic and Political Weekly*, October 30, 2004.

Bernia, Lourdes and Amy Lind (1995), "Engendering International Trade: Concepts, Policy and Action", *GSD Working Paper Series*, No. 5, Cornell University Gender, Science and Development Programme and UNIFEM.

Bhatt, U.R. (2006), 'FCAC: A Capital Market Perspective', *The Economic Times*, September 11, p. 10.

Biju Varkkey and G. Raghuram; Public-Private Partnership in Airport Development—Governance and Risk Management Implications from Cochin International Airport Ltd.

Buchanan, J.M., The Demand and Supply of Public Goods, R. and Mc Nally and Co., Chicago, 1969.

Centre for Monitoring Indian Economy (2004), Public Finance, Mumbai.

Chakraborty, S. Lekha (2006), *Financial Express Special*, www.financialexpress.com.

Chowdhary Harnita (2006), "Outcome Budgeting—Moving Beyond Rehtoric", *Economic and Political Weekly*, Vol. XLI No. 25, pp 2515-18.

D'Souza, Errol (1995), "The Budget, Tax Reforms and Public Policy", *Economic and Political Weekly*, May 6-13.

David Osborne and Ted Gaebler: Reinventing Government (Addison Wesley, London, 1992).

E.T. Mathew (1999), "Agricultural Taxation and Economic Development", Deep and Deep Publication Pvt. Ltd., New Delhi, pp. 26-29.

Economic Survey, 2002-06.

Economic Times, Johnson and Mathew Adams.

Elson Diane (2005), "Monitoring Government Budgets for Compliance with CEDA", Report Highlights and Key Conclusions, UNIFEM.

Era Seshiyan: Appropriation and Misappropriation of Excess Expenditure; *Maintream*, July 19, 2003, *op. cit.*, p. 117.

Eswaran Committee, *op. cit.*

Fischer, J.C. and Prey, H.J., "Technological Forecast", Soc Change 3/1972.

Floyed, A ., "Trend Forecasting : A Methodology for figure of Merit", in Proceeding of the First Annual Technology and Management Conference, New Jersey, 1968.

Gandhi, Ved P. (2002), "Tax Burden on Indian Agriculture", Kedar Nath Ram and Co. Publisher, Meerut, p. 2 and Chapters 3-5.

GOI, Ministry of Finance, Report of the Tenth Finance Commission for 1995-2000.

Government of India (1954), Report of the Taxation Enquiry Commission, 1953-54, New Delhi.

———, (1967), Final Report on Rationalization and Simplification of the Tax Structure, New Delhi.

———, (1971), Report of the Direct Taxes Enquiry Committee, New Delhi.

———, (1972), Report of the Committee on Taxation of Agricultural Wealth and Income, New Delhi.

———, (1978), Report of the Indirect Taxation Enquiry Committee, New Delhi.

———, (1991), Tax Reforms Committee, Interim Report, New Delhi.

———, (1992), Tax Reforms Committee, Final Report, New Delhi.

Government of India (2002), Report of the Task Force on Direct Taxes, Ministry of Finance, New Delhi.

———, (2003), Report of the Task Force on Direct Taxes Ministry of Finance, New Delhi.

———, (2004), Economic Survey, 2003-04, New Delhi, Gray, Andrew and Bill Jenkins (1995), "From Public Administration to Public Management: Reassessing a Revolution?" *Public Administrative*, Spring, Vol. 73.

———, "Annual Budget 2001, 2002, 2003, 2004 and 2005".

———, Ministry of Finance, Department of Economic Affairs (Infrastructure Division); Guidelines on Support to Public-Private Partnerships in Infrastructure.

Henry, Peter (2000a), 'Stock Market Liberalisation, Economic Reform, and Emerging Market Equity Prices; *Journal of Finance*, 50(2), pp. 529-64.

Hinrich, H.H. (1966), A General Theory of Tax Structure Development, Harvard Law School International Tax Programme.

http://fecolumnists.expressindia.com/full column

http://www.financialexpress.com/about/feedback.html

In the Kharif season of 2004 the Punjab Government had to buy power @ about Rs. 6.0 per unit in order to sustain the paddy crop and thereby incurred huge losses.

Indira, Rajaraman (2002), "Adding Punch to Panchayats", *The Economic Times*, October 10, 2002, p. 5.

International Monetary Fund: Public-Private Partnership (Paper prepared by the Fiscal Affairs Department—March 2004).

James Smith, Texas A and M University; Design-build-finance-own-transfer approaches.

Jordan, Grant and Nigel Ashford (1993, edited), Public Policy and the Impact of the New Right, Pinter Publishers, London.

Kaldor, Micholas (1956), Indian Tax Reform; Report of Survey, New Delhi.

Khanna, P., "Energy Scenario in India (1960–85)", National Energy, Policy, Crisis and Growth; National Seminar on Energy Policy, Centre of Indian Development Studies, Chandigarh, 30th/31st January, 1990, Edt. V.S. Mahajan; "Investment Management : Planning and Forecasting",

Research Methodology in Management, Theory and Caste Studies, SAP Seminar (UGC), Edt. P.P. Arya and Yash Pal.

Madhav Godbole (2002), "Commentary on Task Force Reports on Direct and Indirect Taxes", *Economic and Political Weekly*, December 7, 2002, pp. 4884-90.

Madhav Godbole, "Commentary on Task Force Reports on Direct and Indirect Taxes", *Economic and Political Weekly*, December 14, 2002, pp. 4975-82.

Ministry of Finance: Report of the Fifth Pay Commission, Vol. 1, January 1997, p. 155.

Ministry of Finances, Department of Economic Affairs: Report of the Committee of Fiscal Responsibility Act, 2003 (July 2004).

Musgrave, R.A. (1969), Fiscol Systems, Yale University Press, London, Niskanen, W. (1971), Bureaucracy and Representative Government, Aldine Press, Chicago.

N.M. Ranka, "Tax Reforms in India"

Nand Dhameja, "State Government Finances—Public Services Finances", *Indian Journal of the Public Administration*, Vol.L, July-September 2004, pp. 619-38.

Nand Dhameja, "State Government Finances—Public Services Finances", *Indian Journal of Public Administration*.

Narasimhan, C.R.L. (2006), 'Capital Account Convertibility, a Mirage ?', *Business Review, The Hindu*, September 11, 2006.

Osmo T. Seppala, Tampere University of Technology, Finland; Jarmo J. Hukka, University of Pristina, Kosvo; Tapio S. Katko, Tampere University of Technology, Finland; Public-Private Partnerships in water and sewerage services; Privatization for Profit or Improvement of Service and Performance ?

Patnaik (2006), 'The Inevitability of Capital Convertibility', *The Sunday Express*, September 17, p. 8.

Paul Posner and Byron Gordon; Can Nations save, in Lawrence R. Jones *et. al.*, Learning from International Public Management Reform (JAI, Amsterdam, 2001), pp. 393-423.

Prasad, Eswar, Kenneth Rogoff, Shang-Jin Wei and M. Ayhan Kose (2003), 'Effects of Financial Globalisation on Developing Countries: Some Empirical Evidence; IMF, Washington.

Public-Private Partnership—UNDP's experience in India in the Environment Sector.

Quinn, Dennis (1997), 'The Correlates of Changes in International Financial Regulation', *American Political Science Review*, 91(3), pp. 531-51.

R.P. Malhotra (2003), "Budget-2003, Making it Less Taxing", *The Tribune*, February 10, 2003, p. 13.

Rao, Madhusudan (1994), "Taxation of Agricultural Income", *Agricultural Banker*, April-June, 1994, pp. 1-3.

Report of Kelkar Task Force on Direct and Indirect Taxes 2002.

Report of the Working Group on Energy Policy (WGEP), India, 1979.

Reserve Bank of India, Reports on Currency and Finance, Mumbai.

Ruddar Datt and Sundhram, K.P.M. (2004), Indian Economy, S. Chand and Company Ltd. Publication, New Delhi Chapter 31, 33-36.

S.D. Naik, "Tinkering with tax reforms".

Salvatore Schiavo—Camp and Daniel Tommasi: Managing Government Expenditure (ADE, 1999) and a Premchand: Control of Public Money (Oxford University Press, New Delhi, 2000).

Samual Paul, "What Ails our Public Services", An Abstract from his book, Holding the State to Account, Books for Change, Bangalore, 2002.

Sebastian Moorris: Issues in Infrastructure Development Today: The Interlinkages.

Sreekantaradhya, B.S. (2000), Structure and Reform of Taxation in India, Deep and Deep Publications, New Delhi.

Stephen Linder, University of Texas, Huston: Coming to terms with the Public-Private Partnership; A Grammar of Multiple Meanings.

Sterman, Jhon D., "Expectation Formation in Behavioural Simulation Models", *Behavioural Science*, Journal of the Society of General System Research, Vol. 32, No. 3, July 1987.

Tanweer Akram, "India's Economic Reforms".

Tarapore Committee (1997), Report of the Committee on Capital Account Convertibility, Reserve Bank of India, Mumbai.

Udayan Ray, "The Radical Path to Tax Reforms".

United Nations Development Programme (UNDP); Public-Private Partnerships for the Urban Environment (PPPUE).

V.B. Eswaran, *et. al.*, Report of the Committee to Review Integrated Financial Adviser Scheme; Ministry of Finance, Government of India, November 1996.

Waishm Keiren (1997), Public Services and Market Mechanism: Competition, Contracting and the New Management, Macmillan, Hampshire.

Williamson, John (2000b), 'Do Stock Market Liberalization Cause Investment Blooms ?' *Journal of Financial Economics*, 58 (1-2), pp. 301-34.

———, (2006), 'Why Capital Account Convertibility in India is Premature; *Economic and Political Weekly*, May 13-19, Col. XLI, No. 19, pp. 1848-50

Index